D1478609

Contribution to the
Correction of the Public's Judgments
on the French Revolution

SUNY series in Contemporary Continental Philosophy

Dennis J. Schmidt, editor

Contribution to the Correction of the Public's Judgments on the French Revolution

J. G. FICHTE

Edited, Translated, and with an Introduction by
Jeffrey Church *and* Anna Marisa Schön

Published by State University of New York Press, Albany

© 2021 State University of New York

All rights reserved

Printed in the United States of America

No part of this book may be used or reproduced in any manner whatsoever
without written permission. No part of this book may be stored in a retrieval
system or transmitted in any form or by any means including electronic,
electrostatic, magnetic tape, mechanical, photocopying, recording, or otherwise
without the prior permission in writing of the publisher.

For information, contact State University of New York Press, Albany, NY
www.sunypress.edu

Library of Congress Cataloging-in-Publication Data

Names: Fichte, Johann Gottlieb, 1762–1814, author. | Church, Jeffrey, 1978–
editor, translator, writer of introduction. | Schön, Anna Marisa, editor,
translator, writer of introduction.
Title: Contribution to the correction of the public's judgments on the French
revolution / J.G. Fichte ; translated by Jeffrey Church and Anna Marisa Schön.
Other titles: Beitrag zur Berichtigung der Urteile des Publicums über die
französische Revolution. English
Description: Albany : State University of New York Press, [2021] | Series:
SUNY series in contemporary continental philosophy | Includes bibliographical
references and index.
Identifiers: LCCN 2020024803 | ISBN 9781438482170 (hardcover : alk. paper) |
ISBN 9781438482163 (pbk. : alk. paper) | ISBN 9781438482187 (ebook)
Subjects: LCSH: France—History—Revolution, 1789–1799—Foreign public
opinion, German. | France—History—Revolution, 1789–1799—Philosophy. |
France—History—Revolution, 1789–1799—Historiography. | France—History—
Revolution, 1789–1799—Influence. | Political science—Germany—Philosophy—
History. | Legitimacy of governments.
Classification: LCC DC158.8 .F52513 2021 | DDC 944.04—dc23
LC record available at https://lccn.loc.gov/2020024803

10 9 8 7 6 5 4 3 2 1

Contents

Introduction

The *Beitrag zur Berichtigung der Urteile des Publikums über die französische Revolution* (hereafter *Contribution*), published in 1793, is the second major published work of the young, up-and-coming philosopher Johann Gottlieb Fichte. Fichte made a splash in the academic community already in 1792 with his *Attempt at a Critique of All Revelation*, an analysis of the justification and limits of claims to religious revelation that drew heavily on Kant's critical philosophy (and, indeed, it was mistakenly thought to be authored by Kant at first). However, the French Revolution and the debate surrounding it in the German states quickly drew Fichte's attention, leading him to write in a more popular vein in an attempt to rekindle public support for the Revolution. The *Contribution* was written in winter 1792–93 (the first part or booklet, comprising the preface, introduction, and chapters 1–3) and summer 1793 (the second part, comprising chapters 4–6), during some of the bloodiest periods of the Revolution.[1] The work represents Fichte's first sustained popular writing, characterized by his distinctive blend of abstract philosophical language and concrete, passionate calls for reform. After completing the second part of the first book Fichte accepted an offer for a prestigious professorship in Jena in critical philosophy and so abandoned this project, leaving the entire second volume unfinished.[2] He then proceeded in Jena

---

1. See the editor's introduction to the *Contribution* in Johann Gottlieb Fichte, *Gesamtausgabe der Bayerischen Akademie der Wissenschaften*, Reihe 1, Band 1, *Werke 1791–1794*, ed. Hans Jacob and Reinhard Lauth (Stuttgart-Bad Cannstatt: Fromann-Holzboog, 1964), 196–97.

2. Fichte abandoned the project before writing the second book because of the considerable expectations of his academic position in Jena, as well as a desire to avoid further controversy as a radical when Fichte was revealed to be the author of the *Contribution*. See especially his letter to Goethe, translated in the first appendix, requesting political protection from the prince, in exchange for not writing any more pamphlets.

to develop his philosophical system in a series of works—above all the *Wissenschaftslehre* of 1794—which made him one of the most profound and influential philosophical minds of post-Kantian idealism.

The *Contribution* is an important text for several reasons. First, it sheds light on the German debate about the French Revolution, much less widely known than the contemporaneous debates in France, England, and the United States. Second, it is an innovative work in the history of political theory, as it synthesizes Locke's and Rousseau's social contract theory and Kant's moral philosophy, yet applies contractualist principles in a much more individualistic, even anarchist, direction. Finally, the work provides insight into the development of Fichte's thought, not only in his political philosophy, but also in his foundational theoretical work, the *Wissenschaftslehre*. In what follows, we will take up each of these topics, placing the work in the context of the German debate over the French Revolution (section 1), in the context of modern social contract theory (section 2), and in the context of Fichte's philosophical development in the 1790s (section 3).

1. The French Revolution in Germany

The early response of the German public to the Revolution was celebratory. The year 1789 seemed to mark a new stage in humanity's history for many thinkers, providing hope for the creation of a regime founded on reason, merit, and the "rights of man" rather than superstition, corruption, and privilege. Indeed, even moderate to conservative thinkers weighed in with their support. Friedrich Gentz, for example, who would go on to be one of the most vehement critics of the Revolution after translating Edmund Burke's *Reflections on the Revolution in France* into German in 1793, wrote in 1790:

> The Revolution constitutes the first practical triumph of philosophy, the first example in the history of the world of the construction of government upon the principles of an orderly, rationally-constructed system. It constitutes the hope of mankind and provides consolation to men elsewhere who continue to groan under the weight of age-old evils.[3]

---

3. Quoted in Klaus Epstein, *The Genesis of German Conservatism* (Princeton, NJ: Princeton University Press, 1966), 436.

As the Revolution proceeded, however, many authors found the increasing radicalism and violence of the revolutionaries abhorrent. The French revolutionary army occupied Mainz in 1792–93, and peasant revolts broke out in Saxony in the wake of revolutionary enthusiasm, further damp-ening support. Conservative governments of many of the German states promulgated repressive policies against political subversion. Nevertheless, in journal publications throughout this period, the debate between Burke and Thomas Paine became well-known and well-rehearsed.[4]

One of the most important and influential critics of the French Revolution in Germany—and a target of Fichte's polemic in the *Contri-bution*—was August Wilhelm Rehberg. Rehberg hailed from the elector-ate of Hanover in Northwest Germany, which had a close relationship dynastically and hence politically with Great Britain. Like many fellow Hanoverians, Rehberg studied and was influenced by Britain's moderate constitutional monarchy and its empiricist philosophy, embodied above all in the skepticism of David Hume. Rehberg's friend and fellow writer Ernst Brandes travelled to England, struck up a friendship with Edmund Burke, and attempted to shape Hanoverian politics according to the model of British constitutional monarchy. Rehberg himself was commissioned by the *Allgemeine Literatur Zeitung* to review the latest French and English pamphlets about the Revolution. These reviews became the basis for Rehberg's influential work, *Untersuchungen über die Französische Revolution* (hereafter, *Untersuchungen*), published in January 1793.[5]

Rehberg's *Untersuchungen* consists of two parts: the first volume takes aim at the underlying principles and the deleterious consequences of the Revolution, while the second examines the history of the Revolution, its causes and missteps. Rehberg's main critique of the Revolution's fundamen-tal principles concerns its overreliance on abstract reason. For Rehberg, reason can discern formal, abstract legal principles such as the rights of man or the general will, but, because of its abstractness, it cannot provide any determinate political guidance: "The laws of reason," according to Rehberg, "are not sufficient as a basis to derive the laws of civil society"

---

4. On the Revolution and its reception in Germany, see Epstein, *German Conser-vatism*, ch. 9.

5. August Wilhelm Rehberg, *Untersuchungen über die Französische Revolution*, 2 vols. (Hannover: Ritscher, 1793). On Rehberg's thought and life, see Frederick Beiser, *Enlightenment, Revolution, and Romanticism: The Genesis of Modern German Political Thought, 1790–1800* (Cambridge, MA: Harvard University Press, 1992), 302–9; Epstein, *German Conservatism*, ch. 11.

(*Untersuchungen* 1:12). Rehberg uses Rousseau's distinction between the general will and the will of all as an example. It is a crucial distinction in Rousseau's view, but Rehberg claims that Rousseau gives us no tools for identifying the general will as over and above the aggregation of the interests of each. Reason's impotence in practice, however, paradoxically has a dangerous effect. Since it cannot be constructive in practice, it ends up being destructive, tearing down all institutions that fail to live up to its unattainable standard (1:21). Rehberg's skepticism is at work here in his critique of the Revolution's excessive faith in reason. Reason thus must be supplemented by a deference to inherited tradition, to "arbitrary determinations and orders" that have stood the test of time (1:16). Instead of exclusively relying on universal reason, Rehberg argues, we should attend empirically to the distinct traditions and histories of each country. Our governing principles should be informed by the institutions, mores, language, and religion that animate each regime's history.

Whereas Rehberg's background inclined him to be critical of the Revolution, Fichte's background moved him in the opposite direction. Fichte was born in 1762 in crushing poverty, son of a poor ribbon weaver in a tiny village in Saxony. His remarkable intellectual abilities landed him a spot at the prestigious Pforta boarding school, but, after graduating, he had to scrape by as a private tutor to aristocratic families who treated him with contempt. Fichte was headstrong, ambitious, with a keen sense of self-respect, which meant he did not stay employed with one lord for too long.[6] His personal hatred of inequality was given a philosophical grounding through his reading of Rousseau and Kant in 1790. His reading of Kant, as often noted, was transformative, and Fichte became a convert to Kantianism and its rational defense of the equality and freedom of all humanity.

As such, when Rehberg's *Untersuchungen* appeared in 1792, as public opinion turned against the Revolution, Fichte was moved to respond to it. Fichte's plan for the *Contribution* was that he would establish the Revolution's legitimacy in the first volume and discuss its "wisdom" in the second volume (14),[7] thereby taking on Rehberg's critique of

---

6. For more on Fichte's biography, see Allen W. Wood, *Fichte's Ethical Thought* (Oxford: Oxford University Press, 2016), ch. 1; Anthony J. La Vopa, *Fichte: The Self and the Calling of Philosophy, 1762–1799* (Cambridge: Cambridge University Press, 2001).

7. Page numbers in parentheses are from this volume's translation.

the Revolution's principles and consequences. Fichte never wrote the second book, and so the *Contribution*'s main focus is on the underlying principles and their application. This focus partially explains a strange feature of the work, which is that it references the Revolution itself exceedingly rarely. Fichte scrupulously maintains a distance from the details on the ground in France, in part because of censorship worries in the German states (Fichte published the work anonymously, though he was outed as the author rather quickly after its publication—see the letter to Reinhold, translated in the first appendix), and in part because his aim in the work is to defend universal principles applicable beyond this particular time and place.

Fichte's response to Rehberg in the *Contribution* is frequently ad hominem, yet he does set out to provide a substantive reply to Rehberg's skepticism of rationalism in politics. In the introduction, Fichte challenges Rehberg's empiricist approach to political principles. For Fichte, the appeal to history and tradition does not settle the question of how one's country ought to be governed. It only describes how it has been governed. To settle the question of justice, we can never appeal to the changing content of experience, but only to the universal, formal nature of our subjectivity. Chapters 1–2 of the *Contribution* defend the universal principles underlying the Revolution, thereby justifying the French people's claim to have a right to change their constitution. In these chapters, Fichte develops his distinctive synthesis of Lockean and Rousseauian social contract theory with Kantian moral teleology, which we will discuss in the next section. Finally, chapters 3–6 of the work are explicitly an "application" of his principles (67), and so aim to meet Rehberg's challenge that rational principles are inapplicable to politics. Fichte applies his social contract theory to private property, the family, and civil society (chapter 3), the estates (chapters 4–5), and religion (chapter 6). In each case, he argues that the freedom and equality of all human beings mean that our places in society are not fixed by nature or social authority, but we are free to enter, exit, and form associations as we see fit, ones that redound to the benefit of all, not simply the few.[8]

The *Contribution* saddled Fichte with a reputation as a political radical, even a Jacobin, which did not sit well with government authorities

---

8. For more on Fichte's response to Rehberg, see La Vopa, *Fichte*, ch. 4.

when he took up his university post.[9] Indeed, Fichte's reputation caught up to him in 1799, when he was dismissed from the university on charges of atheism.[10] There is some merit to the claim of Fichte's radicalism in the *Contribution*. The work was published in 1793, after the execution of Louis XVI (January 1793), the establishment of the dictatorial Committee on Public Safety (April 1793), and its purges during the summer of 1793. These events were well-known to the German public, and nevertheless Fichte defended the Revolution. In contrast, consider Kant's critique of the Revolution in his "Theory and Practice" essay, published in September 1793: Kant categorically condemns all revolution as the "highest and most punishable crime within a commonwealth," and states that once a people violates their constitution, then a "condition of anarchy arises with all the horrors that are at least possible."[11] Personally, Fichte also flirted with Jacobinism. For example, when he arrived in Jena, he helped found the Association of the Free Men, which sought to advance the ideals of the revolution and whose "prominent members" included "the Jacobin spy Johann Franz Brechtel."[12]

At the same time, these charges could be overblown. Fichte did not write the second volume of his *Contribution* in which he promised to discuss the "wisdom" of the Revolution's means. It is, of course, quite possible that Fichte could have defended the ends of the Revolution while critiquing its means (Kant in a different way takes this view in the 1798 *Conflict of the Faculties*). Indeed, in a letter to Kant after the first volume of the *Contribution*, Fichte admits he is searching for "proposals concerning the means for remedying these injustices [of the ancien régime] without disorder, since I have not yet advanced to that

---

9. See the letter to Stephani, mid-December 1793, where Fichte related that "it is said in public that we held meetings of a Jacobin Club at Ott's country house." Johann Gottlieb Fichte, *Early Philosophical Writings*, ed. Daniel Breazeale (Ithaca, NY: Cornell University Press, 1992), 370. In the letters from Hufeland and to Goethe, translated in the first appendix, the controversies surrounding the *Contribution* are prominent.

10. See Yolanda Estes and Curtis Bowman, eds., *J. G. Fichte and the Atheism Dispute (1798–1800)* (London: Routledge, 2010).

11. Immanuel Kant, "On the Common Saying: That May Be Correct in Theory, but It Is of No Use in Practice," in *Practical Philosophy*, trans. Mary J. Gregor (Cambridge: Cambridge University Press, 1996), 299–302.

12. Frederick Beiser, "Fichte and the French Revolution," in *Cambridge Companion to Fichte*, ed. David James and Günter Zöller (Cambridge: Cambridge University Press, 2016), 38–64.

point."[13] Moreover, in his "Reclamation of the Freedom of Thought" essay, written just before the composition of the *Contribution*, Fichte adopts a much more gradualist as opposed to radical or revolutionary approach to politics. The essay critiques government censorship, especially Wöll-ner's Religious Edict of 1788, and argues that freedom of thought helps a country make "gradual steps forward," a "more certain path to greater enlightenment" (121). Censorship dams up the public passions, while freedom of thought alleviates them in a constructive way, "so that the waters do not forcefully break through and horribly ravage the fields," in the way we see in the "dreadful spectacle" of the French Revolution (122).[14] In other words, Fichte in this essay adopts the moderate, liberal view that freedom of thought, rather than revolutionary violence or conservative repression, is the best means to achieve the ends of the people and the princes.[15] Since Fichte never wrote the second volume of the *Contribution*, however, we may never know his views about the prudence of revolutionary action.

2. The *Contribution* and Social Contract Theory

The *Contribution* makes very little mention of the French Revolution itself, its personalities, events, and institutions. Instead, the work's ambition is more universal—to develop and defend a novel approach to social contract theory that could justify revolution.[16] It is novel in two ways: first, in its resolute argument for individualism as the basis of revolution, as opposed to popular sovereignty, and, second, in its account of the benefits of freedom for moral and spiritual culture.

---

13. Fichte, *Early Philosophical Writings*, 364–65. Cf. *Contribution*, 9: "Worthiness for freedom must grow from the bottom up; [while] the liberation without disorder may only come from above."

14. Johann Gottlieb Fichte, "Reclamation of the Freedom of Thought from the Princes of Europe, Who Have Oppressed It until Now," in *What Is Enlightenment? Eighteenth-Century Answers and Twentieth-Century Questions*, ed. James Schmidt (Berkeley: University of California Press), 119–42.

15. For more on the debate over Fichte's Jacobinism, see Beiser, "Fichte and the French Revolution"; La Vopa, *Fichte*, 83.

16. This universality of the text was admired by reviewers—see, for instance, the introduction to the review by the conservative Friedrich Gentz, translated in the second appendix.

Political authority in the ancien régime was justified by an appeal to the natural inequality of human beings. Some individuals or groups deserved to rule in virtue of being graced by nature or God with certain attributes. The social contract theory of Hobbes, Locke, and Rousseau challenged this account of natural inequality, holding instead that all human beings were equal, that no individual had a rightful claim to rule over any other. The only basis for political authority, then, lies in the free consent of individuals. Government's legitimacy derives not from nature or God, but from the consent of the governed. It is clear how revolutionary these principles were to the ancien régime, and, indeed, these principles become embodied in the central revolutionary documents—the Declaration of Independence and Declaration of the Rights of Man and Citizen. Indeed, Jefferson expresses this revolutionary character well when in the Declaration of Independence he writes, "when a long train of abuses and usurpations . . . evinces a design to reduce [the people] under absolute Despotism, it is their right, it is their duty, to throw off such Government, and to provide new Guards for their future security."

However, social contract theorists differ as to whether their principles can indeed justify revolution. On the one hand, John Locke famously argues that the people contract with one another to entrust some of their rights to a limited government. If this government manifestly fails to achieve or contravenes its purpose, the people can forcibly replace that government. On the other hand, Immanuel Kant—whose view of revolution appeared, as we saw above, a few months after Fichte's—vehemently denies that the people have the right to revolution. Revolution is based on a judgment of the people. Yet the people never gather together in one place to make such a judgment. Rather, it is an idea claimed by one group or another, that this or that group speaks for the people. On Kant's view, the only group that has a legitimate claim to speaking for the people is the government itself, which would not license a revolution against itself.

Fichte's approach is different. Unlike Locke and Rousseau, Fichte seldom appeals to popular sovereignty or the general will.[17] He does not develop principles to identify the judgments of the people. Instead,

---

17. Schottky notes that Fichte uses the term only once in the entire work. See his introduction to Johann Gottlieb Fichte, *Beitrag zur Berichtigung der Urteile des Publikums über die französische Revolution*, ed. Richard Schottky (Leipzig: Felix Meiner Verlag, 1973), viii–ix.

in chapter 3, Fichte justifies revolution at a point prior to the people's creation of government, namely, the point at which individuals contract with one another to form a people. At that point, individuals stand toward one another in the state of nature. In the state of nature, they are governed only by the moral law and must follow their rational "will" (*Wille*) when that law commands them. Where the moral law is silent, however, individuals possess the freedom to act as they wish, according to their "arbitrary will" (*Willkür*) (109).[18] They can enter into any contract they wish—familial, business, political, religious—and thereby alienate certain rights to enjoy the benefits of that contractual relationship. Fichte's innovation here is to argue that individuals can exit contracts at any time. If an individual exits a contract before either party has fulfilled its duties, then each can freely go its separate ways (74). If an individual exits a contract after the other party has fulfilled its duties and before he or she has, then the individual owes compensation to the other party (75). Much of Fichte's discussion consists in a careful analysis of when such compensation is owed, and when it is not. In contrast to conservatives such as Rehberg Fichte argues that individuals owe very little to the state, for its role either in protecting or educating them.

Fichte applies this right to unilateral exit broadly, and it becomes the basis of the right to revolution. What we refer to as revolution is in fact separate individuals exiting a contract that they find unsuitable to them (101). Moreover, he argues in chapters 4–5 that some contracts, such as the contracts the privileged have made with the less privileged, were so thoroughly unequal and exploitative that no rational being could be assumed to consent to such contracts. Indeed, Fichte argues, the less privileged cannot be assumed to have consented to these contracts at all, as they involve the inheritance of debt and outright servitude. In this case, these contracts violate the inalienable rights of individuals and so cannot be consented to at all. Fichte touches on inequality in a contractual society, arguing that individuals could consent to inequality so long as their basic needs are met (130). If any one peasant goes hungry, the "luxury" of the privileged "must be limited with no mercy" (131). In this way, Fichte justifies forcible redistribution of the Revolution as in accordance with the moral law.

---

18. Fichte's distinction between Wille and Willkür derives from Kant. See Henry E. Allison, *Kant's Theory of Freedom* (Cambridge: Cambridge University Press, 1990), ch. 7.

Fichte's novel approach to social contract theory has been described as a form of anarchism, as it circumvents any sort of collective authority or self-determination in its resolute emphasis on individual freedom. In this way, Fichte stands much closer to Locke than Rousseau or Kant, and could be appealing to those theories of liberalism that uphold individual freedom of contract and denigrate communitarian or collectivist views, and that defend inalienable rights and reciprocity in contractual exchange. At the same time, the anarchism involved in the unilateral right to exit contracts may exact a cost for collective action. If any individual at any time has the right to exit from an association, then who would sign up for such associations in the first place? In his review of the *Contribution* (translated in the second appendix), Friedrich Gentz makes such an argument, which might have caused Fichte to change his view in his mature Jena political philosophy, the 1796–97 *Foundations of Natural Right*.

Finally, it must be said that Fichte adopts an eccentric Lockean approach to property rights, discussed in chapter 3 (76ff.).[19] Like Locke, he justifies private property based on self-ownership and the labor of the first occupant, that this individual impressed upon mere matter her form, which thereby stamped this part of the earth with her freedom. Unlike Locke, however, Fichte argues that once all the land on earth has been claimed, then subsequent individuals have no rightful claim to that land—it is unlucky for them (80, 83). In other words, Fichte does not conceive of all of humanity as sharing in the original, common ownership of the earth, as Locke and later Kant would (instead, for Fichte, no one owns the earth; 78). Furthermore, also unlike Locke, Fichte holds that children can be claimed by any adult who arrives first after the child is born and takes responsibility for their rights and duties (95–96). Fichte severs the natural relationship of parent and child, again underscoring his individualism and his radicalization of the social contract tradition, which seeks to challenge the claims to authority resting on nature or the divine.

Let us shift to the second novelty of Fichte's social contract theory, which is that he defends his account in part through the benefits of freedom for the development of a moral culture. In this way, Fichte synthesizes a deontological justification of rights with a teleological

---

19. For more on Fichte's account of property, see David James, *Fichte's Social and Political Philosophy: Property and Virtue* (Cambridge: Cambridge University Press), chs. 1–2.

account of the purpose of the free community. Such a synthesis was unusual, even though Kant himself would develop a version of it in his political philosophy later in the 1790s. Since Fichte's writings preceded Kant's, however, he set out to combine the social contract tradition with the teleological account of culture he found in Kant's *Critique of Judgment*. In the appendix to the second half of that text, the "Critique of Teleological Judgment," Kant seeks to understand the "purposiveness" (*Zweckmässigkeit*) of the natural world, and argues that the "final end" (*Endzweck*) of nature is the cultivation of all our capacities and skills, which he calls "culture" (*Kultur*). Nature's "ultimate end" (*letztes Zweck*), however, is the perfection of humanity's moral freedom. Kant conceives of political conflict and even war as providentially ordered such that these evils can nonetheless be turned to the good.

Fichte appropriates and expands Kant's understanding of culture. Culture is the community responsible for the general "exercise of all forces to the end of complete freedom" (49), which for Fichte is the purpose or end of our I, or subjectivity, and the only basis of "value" for all things (49). Culture must not only discipline our sensible or embodied nature, but also put it to use in the achievement of humanity's freedom. In addition, Fichte employs the notion of culture not strictly in the context of a theodicy in his philosophy of history, but rather as a moral ideal, a normative standard by which to judge the goodness of a regime and the purpose that regime sets for itself. In other words, in the *Contribution*, Fichte is concerned with evaluating not only the justice of political regimes but also the effect of those regimes on the good life of its members. This dual concern is most evident in the first chapter, in which Fichte first discusses the right of individuals to freedom of their "arbitrary will" (43–48) and then, second, the cultural consequences of a regime that favors or oppresses such freedom (48–60). According to Fichte, the cultural track record of the ancien régime is not good. Culture may have been slightly advanced, but only despite the tendency of the regime. The absolute monarchy's constant desire for power exploited culture for its end, rather than the end of humanity, and the Church's religious repression constrained the mind, hampering artistic, scientific, and moral progress. For Fichte, a government that respects the freedom of individuals would, by contrast, indirectly contribute to the progress of humanity. While the state, Fichte argues, cannot force individuals to believe anything in particular, it can remove the obstacles to their moral progress, eliminating those temptations to self-seeking activity that corrupt culture.[20] By doing so, it can set out to "advance the highest final end of each individual, if the entire union [of the state] shall not be completely useless" (26).

Fichte's treatment of the aristocracy in two chapters (chapters 4 and 5) may be understood in light of these two tasks. Chapter 4 is devoted to an accounting of the injustice of the social contract with the aristocracy. However, he also is concerned with the effects of the aristocracy on culture, which is why he needs another chapter, the longest of the book, on this topic. In chapter 5, his seemingly irrelevant foray into the historical origin and development of aristocracy and the distinction between the aristocracy of opinion and the aristocracy of right can be understood in this context. On Fichte's view, the ancient aristocracy emerged from the noble deeds of individuals, whose noble reputation passed from father to son and down through the generations. This aristocracy of opinion contributed to the development of culture, as individuals respect and are inspired by the exemplary deeds of others. By contrast, the aristocracy of right emerges when noble families seek to consolidate what they have accumulated under law, to preserve what is theirs rather than contribute to the common good by demonstrating their excellence. The aristocracy of right—and here Fichte is thinking about early modern forms of aristocratic privilege—is rife with corrupt, small-souled, self-seeking individuals. These aristocrats arrest the development of culture because they arouse hatred rather than respect.

His discussion of religion in chapter 6 also has this dual character. In the second half of the chapter, Fichte analyzes the rightful basis and scope of church authority, and its relationship to the state. Fichte's view on this matter is liberal—the state's purview is the protection of material rights and it has oversight only of human action, not belief. By contrast, religion's purview is the protection of our soul and so it has oversight of belief. The state's kingdom is that of the visible world, the church's, the invisible world, and so the two do not overlap. Indeed, if the church does attempt to coerce belief by employing the state, it violates the rights of individuals, subjecting them to an association without their consent.

In the first half of the chapter, however, Fichte develops a psychological account of the basis and development of religion. For Fichte, religions

---

20. See David James, *Fichte's Republic: Idealism, History and Nationalism* (Cambridge: Cambridge University Press, 2015), ch. 3, for more on Fichte's view of culture and its teleological aims.

have their origin in the noble drive of human beings to unify around the truth. Different religions profess different truths. However, religions face the challenge that they can never be sure whether their members are fully honest in their profession of faith. As a result, each religion has an incentive to compel its members to profess ever "more fantastical, absurd, and contrary to sound reason . . . teachings," because then a church can be "more firmly convinced . . . of the devotion of such members" (184). As a religion becomes more fantastical, Fichte holds, it requires a system of belief that can defeat the doubts of reason, and it does so by piling absurd doctrines on top of absurd doctrines until our reason tires itself out in analysis. In this way, Fichte's account of positive religion is much more skeptical than Kant's in his *Religion within the Bounds of Reason Alone*, published contemporaneously in 1793. Whereas Kant holds that many positive religions can help advance the aims of natural, rational religion, Fichte holds that positive religion tends to run at cross purposes with religion. Fichte's anti-Semitic screed against Judaism can be read as well in this context (102–103). In sum, rather than furthering the moral aims of humanity, religion seems to arrest our progress.

Fichte's incorporation of culture into social contract theory addresses a powerful conservative worry about contractualism present in Edmund Burke and A. W. Rehberg. A common anxiety of conservative critics of social contract theory is that the development of human reason and contractual exchange leads to the destruction of traditional institutions and practices that would provide some purpose and guidance for our spiritual longings, an unleashing of our self-interested, materialistic drives, and an isolation of one generation from those before and after it. Once the ancien régime fades away, as religion declines, what will fill the void in the human heart? What will keep us from a spiritual barbarism that will then lead to a political barbarism? Many German thinkers, including Lessing, Goethe, Herder, Schiller, Kant, and others, sought to conceive of new, distinctively modern forms of association, as well as a new type of "education of the human race" (as Lessing puts it) to shape and advance human culture. The French Revolution poses this problem in a particularly acute way, with its vivid displays of the destruction of the old and the installation of reason as the new divinity. In the preface to the *Contribution*, Fichte reveals that his aim is not simply to defend the Revolution and its "political consequences" (5). Rather, he is interested in how the Revolution serves as an "instructional portrayal, which the great educator of humanity sets up so that humanity may learn what it is in need of knowing" (5). Far from representing a decline into atomism or anarchy, the Revolution points toward a new form of community, the moral culture of humanity. This culture connects humanity with "links" that "tie into eternity" in an intergenerational pursuit of moral perfection (100). The truth, in other words, is the opposite of what Burke and Rehberg claim: the ancien régime corrupts human character and destroys the sources of moral and spiritual satisfaction, while modern culture promises to improve us artistically and scientifically, morally and spiritually.

3. The *Contribution* and Fichte's Development

The *Contribution* represents a crucial point in Fichte's philosophical development. Before the *Contribution*, Fichte adhered more or less scrupulously to the letter of Kant's critical philosophy. This work, however, effected a fundamental change in his thought, as Fichte himself attests in a famous 1795 draft letter to Jens Baggesen:

> My system is the first system of freedom. Just as France has freed man from external shackles, so my system frees him from the fetters of things in themselves, which is to say, from those external influences with which all previous systems—including the Kantian—have more or less fettered man. Indeed, the first principle of my system presents man as an independent being. During the very years when France was using external force to win its political freedom I was engaged in an inner struggle with myself and with all deeply rooted prejudices, and this is the struggle which gave birth to my system. . . . Indeed, it was while I was writing about the French Revolution that I was rewarded by the first hints and intimations of this system.[21]

While writing the *Contribution*, Fichte conceived what would become his mature Jena system of knowledge, or *Wissenschaftslehre*. Let us examine a few ways in which this work anticipates the *Wissenschaftslehre*, before turning to its influence on Fichte's subsequent views of culture, rights, and the nation.

---

21. Quoted in Fichte, *Early Philosophical Writings*, 385–86.

The story of Fichte's development in the first half of the 1790s is well-known in the literature.[22] In short, Kant's critical philosophy was transformative of the German philosophical scene in the 1780s. However, skeptics nonetheless took issue with many of Kant's claims. One of Kant's defenders and popularizers, Karl Reinhold, sought to reconstruct Kant's philosophy on the basis of a single indubitable principle of consciousness or "representation" (*Vorstellung*), such that it became immune to skepticism. In response, a reviewer under the pseudonym Aenesidemus (G. E. Schulze) argued that Reinhold's reconstruction was subject to skeptical doubt, as Reinhold could not provide a way to bridge the gulf between our representation of being and being itself. Aenesidemus's arguments unsettled Fichte, and led him to abandon the letter of Kant's philosophy, while still defending its spirit. Fichte published his response to Aenesidemus in February 1794, a review he began while writing the *Contribution*. Fichte sought to ground critical philosophy on the I, on the nature of subjectivity. He bridged thought and being by denying the "mischief" of the thing-in-itself. For Fichte, it is "downright impossible" for us to "think of a thing independent of *any* faculty of representation *at all*."[23] As recent scholars have argued, Fichte does not deny the reality of being, but its conceivability independent of an observing subject.[24]

What role does the French Revolution play in this rather abstract philosophical debate? Fichte notes in his letter to Baggesen that the Revolution taught him to liberate human beings from all "external shackles," and these shackles include not only those visible to us, but also those ideas that we invest with an independent authority over us, especially "things-in-themselves." The Revolution pointed toward a form of authority no longer based on nature or God, but on the autonomous will of individuals. In the wake of his *Contribution*, Fichte realized that he must apply this basic insight to philosophy itself, since philosophy has assumed that the authority of nature or God is supreme, and the philosopher's task is to discern what nature or God has to say on this or

---

22. For helpful discussions, see Daniel Breazeale, *Thinking Through the Wissenschaftslehre* (Oxford: Oxford University Press, 2013), ch. 2; Frederick Neuhouser, *Fichte's Theory of Subjectivity* (Cambridge: Cambridge University Press, 1990), ch. 2; Günter Zöller, *Fichte's Transcendental Philosophy: The Original Duplicity of Intelligence and Will* (Cambridge: Cambridge University Press, 1998).

23. Quoted in Fichte, *Early Philosophical Writings*, 72–73.

24. See, e.g., Wood, *Fichte's Ethical Thought*.

that matter. For Fichte, human beings can only be truly free when we liberate ourselves not just from the visible shackles of political author-ity, but the invisible shackles of our own ideas. For this reason, Fichte radicalizes Kant's claim as to the primacy of practical reason—that is, philosophy is first and foremost not a theoretical discipline, which pas-sively seeks to understand what is independent of it, but rather it is a practical discipline, which aims to grasp the purpose or aim of human subjectivity, and how it can best achieve this end. In this way, Fichte's *Wissenschaftslehre*, often understood to be an extravagant exercise in a precritical metaphysics of some superhuman ego governing the world, is instead an account of the practical ideal of humanity, that the world should be governed by the purpose or aim of human subjectivity.[25]

An example of the influence of the *Contribution* on the *Wissen-schaftlehre* project appears in the preface, in which Fichte argues that his aim is not to coerce readers into belief, but rather to the "awakening of independent thinking" (9). One of Fichte's signature approaches in the *Wissenschaftslehre* is to proceed in his argument by asking the reader to perform the same intellectual exercise that Fichte himself undertakes to make his point. In the first introduction to the *Wissenschaftslehre*, Fichte states, "Attend to yourself; turn your gaze from everything surrounding you and look within yourself: this is the first demand philosophy makes upon anyone who studies it."[26] Already in the *Contribution*, Fichte "ask[s] him [the reader]—if he wants—to practice the application [of Fichte's principles] through his own attempts" (9).

The *Contribution*, then, shaped Fichte's view of the nature and aims of philosophy itself. In addition, the work also anticipates several developments in Fichte's practical philosophy. As we saw above, Fichte expanded Kant's notion of culture, which in Fichte's hands becomes the modern community responsible for the cultivation of the "purpose" or "vocation of humanity" (48), the perfection of our cognitive powers and moral nature. The ultimate aim of culture is the overcoming of the differences among human beings that are the causes of our conflicts, and the creation of the "highest unanimity of dispositions" under the moral law (61). Similarly, in 1794, Fichte set out in his second set of lectures

---

25. See Beiser, "Fichte and the French Revolution," for more on the relationship between the French Revolution and the *Wissenschaftslehre*.

26. Johann Gottlieb Fichte, *Introductions to the Wissenschaftslehre and Other Writings, 1797–1800*, trans. Daniel Breazeale (Indianapolis: Hackett), 7.

in Jena—delivered in much more public, accessible language than his first set of lectures on the *Wissenschaftslehre*—to describe the "vocation of man as such" and in particular the "vocation of the scholar."[27] The vocation of humanity is to realize the purpose or aim of human subjectivity, a moral perfection of our freedom. The "ultimate and highest means to [our] final goal" of "complete harmony with [ourselves]" is "culture," that form of community in which each can contribute her own distinctive excellence for the advancement of humanity.[28] By contributing to this community, we connect our labor to the eternal. The lectures on the "Vocation of the Scholar," then, further develop the notion of a unifying, intergenerational moral culture mentioned first in the *Contribution*.

Fichte did, however, reconsider some of his views, particularly on the nature and basis of right. In the *Contribution*, Fichte grounds right on the Kantian moral law. According to the moral law, each human being ought to be treated as an end in himself, which grounds certain inalienable rights, as well as the respect for the arbitrary will of each. By the time Fichte writes the *Foundations of Natural Right* in 1796–97, he developed a justification of right independent of morality. Instead of grounding right on the moral law, Fichte grounded right on the conditions for the possibility of individual self-consciousness. In that work, Fichte also revisited the extreme individualism of the *Contribution*, arguing instead that revolution is justified based on the judgment of the people as a sovereign whole, assembled at regular intervals according to the constitution, not on the judgment of each individual. Indeed, those individuals who put their "private wills" before the "common will" represent "a rebellion and must immediately be punished as such."[29]

Finally, Fichte scholars often see a break between his Jena period work of the 1790s, and the post-1800 writings. This assessment is often motivated by an inability to understand how a philosophical radical of the 1790s could morph into an originating figure of German nationalism in the *Addresses to the German Nation* of 1808.[30] Already in chapter 5 of

---

27. Fichte, *Early Philosophical Writings*, 146.

28. Fichte, *Early Philosophical Writings*, 150.

29. Johann Gottlieb Fichte, *Foundations of Natural Right*, ed. Frederick Neuhouser (Cambridge: Cambridge University Press), 149

30. See James, *Fichte's Republic*, for a recent effort to find commonalities between the *Addresses* and Fichte's Jena period writings.

the *Contribution*, however, Fichte intimated a theory that would become more fully developed in the *Addresses*. In chapter 5, Fichte envisions a historical development from a simple, honorable aristocratic epoch of the ancient world, to the corrupted aristocracy of feudal Europe, to, finally, the emerging era of the self-interested bourgeois. Fichte would systematize this historical narrative in his *Characteristics of the Present Age* and the *Addresses*. However, in the *Contribution*, he also adumbrates a "higher" aim he hopes for from future citizens, which is embraced by neither bourgeois nor aristocrat, namely, the "mightier incentives of altruistic virtue and love of the fatherland" (173). This nationalistic love can serve the end of justice by reconciling the different classes to equality under the law, and it can also unify an otherwise divided civil society toward their common moral aims. In this way, Fichte was already thinking quite early in his career about the role of national spirit in fostering humanity's moral end.

There are several editions of the *Contribution* in German, and the work has been translated twice into French, once in the nineteenth century, and again in the 1970s. It has never been translated into English. This translation makes Fichte's important work accessible to an English audience, where interest in Fichte has grown considerably over the past twenty years.

Translators' Note

This translation is based on the version of the text included in the *Gesamtausgabe der Bayerischen Akademie der Wissenschaften*, which has become the standard critical edition of Fichte's works. In the translation, we include running pagination of the *Gesamtausgabe* for readers who wish to reference the German. In preparing the footnotes, we have consulted the *Gesamtausgabe* notes prepared by Hans Jacob and Reinhard Lauth, as well as Richard Schottky's notes in the edition of the *Beitrag* published by Felix Meiner.

We approached this translation with the twofold aim of literalness and readability. Not knowing with what interests and questions the reader may come to the text, we considered it a priority to render Fichte's original diction as literally as possible. To that end, we sought to translate German words consistently throughout the work, even where the English sounded unusual in a given context. (See the distinction between *Besitz* and *Eigentum* below.) Where the English language permits, we have replicated Fichte's original sentence structure to maintain his emphases.

We decided to translate plays on words literally and to footnote an explanation of the original twist, rather than to try and find an approximate English equivalent. This is a popular work of Fichte's, which contains a great deal of passionate language, polemic, jokes, and idiomatic expressions, all alongside some of Fichte's intimidating technical vocabulary. We have attempted to maintain the verve of Fichte's prose, as well as its playful and sardonic edge.

In order to keep the text readable, we have on occasion broken Fichte's often quite lengthy prose into several sentences. Certain grammatical constructions of the German language and, in particular, the gendered nouns and pronouns allow for longer sentences in German, and Fichte knew how to make use of German grammar. Hence, where the English translation would otherwise become vague or even unintelligible, we have inserted the antecedent in lieu of the pronoun and disentangled sentences into their components. We have updated punctuation in several places to guide the reader through the text better, but have retained Fichte's idiosyncratic use of dashes as it often reveals his thought process.

One peculiarity of Fichte's *Contribution*, especially in a work of political theory, is his frequent use of direct speech without a reporting verb or signal phrase. It is also not always clear who his interlocutor is. We have added quotation marks to indicate these passages, and sometimes specified who he seems to address. There are quite a number of technical terms Fichte employs in the *Contribution* that he adopts from Kant, and that themselves have a life after him in German Romanticism and Idealism. In all the cases of such terms, we have employed the standard translations from the Cambridge Edition of the Works of Immanuel Kant, Daniel Breazeale's translations of Fichte, and the SUNY Fichte series. At the end of the book, we include a glossary of major German words and their translation. Any exceptions from the standard translations are footnoted.

A few examples of important terms from Kant and Fichte used in this translation:

das Ich: The ground of Fichte's philosophy is human subjectivity, or the "I." The I is distinct from all empirical things in that it is free of all causation. In addition, the I also exhibits an end, that it manifest its freedom in the world—above all in our character—or, as Fichte says, the "I should be an I." The I, then, is the basis of the moral law and the value or significance of human life.

Willkür: In his philosophy, Kant distinguishes two types of free will. First, the *Wille* is a will free insofar as it follows the command of the moral law. However, the moral law does not exhaustively prescribe all human behavior, but rather leaves a good deal of decisions up to our discretion. Second, the *Willkür* is a will free insofar as it is not determined by natural inclinations, but freely makes a choice about how to act. *Willkür* is often translated as "arbitrary will" in Kant, Fichte, and Hegel translations, because this free choice is left to the arbitrary decision of the individual, when the moral law does not prescribe a particular course of action. In Kant's political philosophy (developed after the *Contribution*), as in Fichte's political philosophy, the purpose of the state is in part to protect the *Willkür* of its members.

Naturrecht: The translation of *Naturrecht* as "natural right," while standard, is odd in practice, because it poses a challenge for dealing with the cognates of *Recht*, such as *rechtlich* (legally). Whenever the word refers to "natural right" and not law in general, we have translated *rechtlich* as "rightfully" (rather than "legally"). We have rendered *naturrechtlich* with the expression "according to natural right."

Eigentum/Besitz: The German language distinguishes between *Eigentum* (property) and *Besitz* (possession). *Eigentum* is something that I legally own, whereas *Besitz* is something I merely possess or occupy for the time being; *Eigentum* is a right, while *Besitz* is a fact. Consequently, *Eigentümer* and *Besitzer* may not always be the same person or entity, and Fichte focuses on this distinction in the last chapter, where he talks about church property. He suggests that the church can occupy or possess goods, but, being only spiritual authority, it cannot own them. Because of the emphasis on this distinction in the last part of the work, we have carried the discriminating translation throughout the work, even where the word "possession" sounds odd. Readers of Rousseau and Kant will of course recognize this important distinction.

In what follows, Fichte's footnotes are indicated by asterisks and daggers. Editorial footnotes are numbered.

Chronology

1762   Fichte born May 19 in Rammenau, Saxony, the first child of ribbon weaver Christian Fichte and Johanna Maria Dorothea.

1774–80   Scholarship pupil in the Princely Secondary School at Pforta, near Naumburg (Schulpforta).

1780–84   Student at the universities of Jena, Wittenberg, and Leipzig; no degree earned.

1785–93   Private tutor in households in Leipzig, Zurich, and Eastern Prussia.

1789   The French Revolution begins; the Tennis Court Oath and the Storming of the Bastille.

1790   Reads Kant's *Critique of Pure Reason*, *Critique of Practical Reason*, and *Critique of the Power of Judgment*; gets engaged to Johanna Rahn, niece of the poet F. G. Klopstock.

1791   Travels to Warsaw for employment, then to Königsberg to ask Kant for financial support, then to Gdansk to work as a private tutor.

1792   Visits Kant in Königsberg; *Attempt at a Critique of All Revelation* is published with Kant's help; French royal family imprisoned in the Temple; National Convention abolishes the monarchy and establishes First French Republic.

1793   Returns to Zurich and marries Johanna Rahn; *Contribution to the Correction of the Public's Judgment of the French Revolution* and *Reclamation of the Freedom of Thought from the Princes of Europe*; execution of Louis XVI in January and of Marie Antoinette in October.

1794   Professor at the University of Jena as the successor of Karl L. Reinhold; *Foundations of the Entire Wissenschaftslehre* (parts 1 and 2); arrest and execution of Robespierre and the end of the Reign of Terror.

1795   *Foundations of the Entire Wissenschaftslehre* (part 3)

1796   Birth of his only child, I. H. Fichte, who later edits his father's work; *Foundations of Natural Right* (part 1).

1797   *Foundations of Natural Right* (part 2)

1798   *The System of Ethics* and *On the Basis of Our Belief in a Divine Governance of the World*

1798   November, beginning of the atheism dispute/controversy.

1799   Loses his professorship at Jena over charges of atheism; Napoleon is elected the First Consul of the Consulate.

1800   Moves to Berlin; *The Vocation of Man* and *The Closed Commercial State.*

1805   Professor in Erlangen.

1806   *Main Characteristics of the Present Age* and *Direction to the Blessed Life*; Napoleon's troops defeat Prussia at Jena and occupy Berlin.

1807   October, flees to Königsberg, where he is appointed professor, but then flees to Copenhagen when Napoleon's forces threaten to reach East Prussia; returns to Berlin after Peace of Tilsit.

1808   *Addresses to the German Nation*, a series of lectures delivered in Berlin.

1810   Professor and dean of the Philosophical Faculty at newly founded Humboldt University in Berlin.

1813   Prussian uprising against Napoleon.

1814   Dies January 29 in Berlin of fever caught from his wife, who contracted it while nursing Prussian soldiers.

Contribution to the Correction
of the Public's Judgments
on the French Revolution

BOOK ONE

On Judging the Legitimacy
of a Revolution

Preface

[203][1] The French Revolution seems to me to be important for the whole of humanity. I am not referring to the political consequences that it had for both the country itself and the neighboring states, and that it arguably would not have had without the unsolicited interference and imprudent self-confidence of these states. All that is in itself much, but it is little against the disproportionately more important matter.

As long as human beings do not become wiser and more just, all their attempts to become happy are in vain. Escaping from the despot's dungeon, they will murder themselves among each other with the ruins of their broken shackles. This would be too sad a lot, if their own misery or—if they are warned in time—others' misery could not lead them to belated wisdom and justice.

Thus, all events in the world seem to me [to be] instructional portrayals, which the great educator of humanity sets up so that humanity may learn what it is in need of knowing. Not that it learns *out of* history—in all of world history we will never find anything that we have not first put inside it ourselves. But through the judgment of real events, humanity may develop more easily by itself what lies within it. And thus, the French Revolution seems to me a rich painting about the grand text, "human rights and human worth."

The intention, however, is not that some few chosen ones know what is worth knowing, and that few among them act accordingly. The theory of man's duties, rights, and aspirations after death is not the school's trinket. The time must come where our nurses teach our minors[2] to speak about the first two points [man's duties and rights] according to the only

---

1. Square brackets [ ] refer to pagination from Johann Gottlieb Fichte, *Gesamtausgabe der Bayerischen Akademie der Wissenschaften*, Reihe 1, Band 1, *Werke 1791–1794*, ed. Hans Jacob and Reinhard Lauth (Stuttgart-Bad Cannstatt: Fromann-Holzboog, 1964).

2. *Unmündige*

true and accurate representations, because the scare word "that is wrong" is the only rod we need for [disciplining] them, and because these are [also] the first words that they utter. [204] May the school be content with the honorable custody of the weapons with which it defends this common good [the knowledge of man's duties and rights] against all remote sophistries. The weapons can only arise in the school and can only be diffused by it. The results themselves are common, like air and light. Only by imparting them [the results], or rather by lifting the sad prejudices, which have thus far impeded the development of that truth suppressed in the soul but not [yet] exterminated, will the school's own knowledge become truly clear, alive, and fruitful. As long as in the schools you talk about it with people of the trade according to the prescribed form, you will both be deceived precisely by this prescribed form, and if you only agree about the form, you present each other with some questions that may be exhausting for you to answer clearly. However, include the mother, seasoned by bearing and raising children, the warrior, who turned grey in danger, and the worthy countryman in your conversations about conscience, right and wrong, and your own concepts will gain in clarity, just as you clarify theirs.—Yet this is the least. What are these insights for, if they are not universally introduced into life? And how can they be introduced, if they are not shared by at least the greater half? It cannot remain the way it is now, for certainly some spark of divinity glows in our hearts that will point us to an almighty just being. Do we want to wait with the farmer until the stream that has broken free has torn away our huts? Do we want, amidst blood and corpses, to hold lectures about justice for the savage slave? Now is the time to acquaint the people with freedom, which it will find as soon as it knows it, so that the people may not seize injustice instead, falling back half its way and tearing us along. There are *no means* to protect [against] despotism. Maybe there are some means to coax the despot, who by inflicting evil upon us makes himself unhappier than us, to liberate himself from his long misery, to step down to us, and to become the first among equals. To prevent a violent revolution, there is a very reliable means, but it is the only one: to thoroughly teach the people about its rights and duties. To this end, the French Revolution offers us the instruction and the colors to enlighten the painting for stupid eyes; another, incomparably more important revolution, which I will not denote further here, has secured the material for us.[3]

---

3. Fichte is referring here to Kant's revolution in philosophy, as developed across his three *Critiques*.

The sign of the times has generally not gone unnoticed. Things have become the topic of the day, that were not [even] thought of before. [205] Conversations about human rights, about freedom and equality, about the holiness of contracts [and of] oaths, about the foundations and limits of a king's rights are occasionally replacing the conversations about new fashions and old adventures in illustrious and lackluster circles. We are beginning to learn.

However, the painting on display does not serve merely for instruction. It turns at the same time into a strict test of heads and hearts. On the one hand, the aversion to all independent thought, the inertness of the mind and its inability to follow just a short series of conclusions, the prejudices and contradictions that have spread across all our fragments of opinions; on the other hand, the effort to not let anything be changed about one's hitherto beloved existence, the lazy or destructive egoism, the shy timidity about the truth, or the violence with which one closes one's eyes when they enlighten us against our will—[these] never reveal themselves more manifestly than where there is talk about such evident and universally applicable topics as human rights and human duties are.

There are no means against the latter evil. Whoever fears the truth as his enemy will always know how to protest against her. Were she to follow him through all the nooks in which the shade-lover hides, he would always find a new one in the abyss of his heart. Whoever does not want to court the heavenly beauty without all the accoutrements does not deserve her at all.—It is not our purpose to get a certain principle into your head because it is *the* principle, but because it is true. If its opposite were true, we would teach you the opposite, because it would be true, entirely unconcerned about its content or its consequences. As long as you do not educate yourself towards this love for truth because it is truth you are of no use to us at all, for it is the first preparation for the love of justice for her own sake; it [the love of truth] is the first step towards goodness of character—do not boast about it, if you have not taken this step.

Against the former evil, against prejudices and inertness of the mind, there is a means: instruction and amicable help. I would like to be a friend to him, who needs such a friend and has not a better one around. Therefore, I wrote these pages.

I have sketched the course that my examination will further take, partially in the introduction and partially in the second chapter. This first volume was only intended as a trial, and therefore I have put down my pen after the first half of the book.[4] It depends on the public whether I will pick it back up and even finish this first book. [206] Meanwhile the French nation may wish to supply more abundant material for the second [book], which shall establish basic principles for the assessment of its constitution's wisdom.

Should these pages fall into the hands of real scholars, they will easily see which basic principles I assumed; why I did not choose a strictly systematic course, but pursued my argument[5] along a popular thread; why I never determined the propositions more sharply than required by the present occasion; why here and there I left more embellishment or fire in the presentation than would have been necessary for them; and that a strictly philosophical assessment will actually only be possible after completion of the first book. For the unlearned or partially learned reader, I additionally make a few, highly necessary remarks *about the careful use of this book.**

Even if I have assured my readers throughout what I have said thus far that I believe what I wrote down to be true, I would not deserve their trust. I wrote with the tone of certainty because it is falseness to pretend that one was doubting where one does not doubt. I have thought carefully about everything that I wrote, and thus I had reasons not to doubt. Whence it follows that I am not talking without discretion and am not lying. However, it does not follow that I am not *erring*. That, I do not know. I only know that I did not *want* to err. Yet even if I did err, I am not depriving my reader of anything. For I would not want him to accept my claims [solely] upon my word, but rather that he should think about their objects with me. I would throw this manuscript into the fire—even if I knew for certain that it contained the purest truth, presented in the most precise manner—if I knew at the same time that no single reader would assure himself of this truth by means of his own reflections. That which is indeed truth *for me*, because I have convinced myself of it, would only be opinion, illusions, prejudice, for him because

---

*Which I very much ask not to be skipped.

4. Fichte originally intended to write two books on the subject, but never finished the second. The first book consisted of two parts, or "booklets," the first of which included the preface, introduction, and chapters 1–3; the second booklet included chapters 4–6. Fichte suggests here that he put down his pen after completing the first booklet of the first book to await the public's reaction.

5. *Betrachtung*

he would not have judged himself. Even a divine gospel is truth to no one, who has not assured himself of its truth. Now, if my errors instigated the reader to discover the pure truth himself, and disclose it to me, he and I would be sufficiently rewarded. Even if my errors did not do that, and they only became an exercise in independent thought for the reader, the advantage would already be great enough. [207] Actually, no writer, who knows and loves his duty, has the goal of bringing the reader to believe in his opinions, but only to examine them. All our teaching must be aimed at the awakening of independent thinking, or [otherwise] we deliver a very dangerous gift [hidden] inside our most beautiful gift of humanity. Thus, everybody may judge for himself, and if he errs—perhaps in common with me—I am sorry; but in that case, he may not say that I have led him astray, but rather that he erred on his own. I wanted to relieve no one of this work of independent thinking—a writer should think *ahead* of his readers, but not *for* them.

Thus, even if I did err, the reader would not at all be bound to err with me. However, I owe him also this warning, that he may not let me say more than I am really saying. He finds principles in the course of this book that will [have to] be determined more closely; since the book has not been completed and important chapters are not in his hands yet, he can likewise expect that the principles that have been defined so far will receive more detailed specification by means of their further application, and I ask him—if he wants—to practice the application through his own attempts.

The reader would err most gravely, however, if he wanted to rush to apply these basic principles to his conduct towards the hitherto existing states. That the constitution of most states is not only faulty, but also most unjust, and that inalienable human rights—which human beings may not actually allow to have taken away from them—are infringed upon therein, thereof I am indeed deeply convinced, and I have worked, and will work, to likewise convince the reader of it. Even so, for the time being nothing may be done against them [the states], but to give to them what we may not allow to have taken from us by force, since they themselves certainly do not know what they are doing. As for ourselves, we have first of all to acquire knowledge of, and then deep love for justice, and to spread both around us as far as our sphere of influence reaches. Worthiness for freedom must grow from the bottom up, [while] the liberation without disorder may only come from above.

"Even if we made ourselves worthy of freedom, the monarchs will still not set us free."—Do not believe this, my reader. Until now, humanity is very far behind in what it truly needs, but unless I am very much mistaken, the time of breaking dawn is now, and the full day will follow it in due course. For the most part, your wise men are still blind leaders of a [even] blinder people—and your herdsmen should know more? They, who are largely raised in idleness and ignorance, or, if they do learn something, learn [only] a truth explicitly crafted for them. [208] They, who notoriously do not continue to work on their education, once they rule, who do not read a new pamphlet, but at most some watery sophistries, and who are all behind their time by at least the years of their reign? You may be certain that they lie down to rest peacefully after signing orders against freedom of thought and after battles, in which thousands wore themselves down, considering themselves to have spent a lordly day serving God and men. Talking does not help at all here, for who could scream loud enough to reach their ears and enter their hearts through their understanding? Only acting helps. Be just, you peoples, and your princes will not be able to endure to be unjust alone.

Only one more general remark, and then I will quietly leave the reader to his own contemplations!—My name does not concern the reader.[6] For, in this case, things do not depend at all on the reliability or unreliability of the testimony, but on the importance or unimportance of the reasons, which the reader must weigh on his own. Yet to me it was very important to keep in mind the thought of my age and of posterity in composing this work. My basic rule as a writer is to never write anything down that would make me blush before myself, and the test, which I perform for that purpose, is the question: Could you will that your age, and if possible all of posterity, knows that *you* have written this? I have submitted the present pamphlet to this test, and it passed. I may have erred. As soon as I discover these errors, or someone shows them to me, I will rush to recall them since erring is not a disgrace. I have spoken earnestly with one of Germany's sophists[7]—that is not disgraceful, but honorable. He, who loves truth's enemy, does not love truth. He shall be the first to whom I reveal my name if he prompts me with [good] reasons. To defend an error, which one has recognized as an error, by means of deceitful confusion, by malicious tricks, [or,] when nothing else

---

6. The *Contribution* was published anonymously.

7. The sophist is August Wilhelm Rehberg, 1757–1836, secretary to the Geheime Ratskollegium (Secret Council) in Hanover.

works, by removal of the foundation of all morality; to slander morality and her holiest product, the religion and the freedom of man—that is disgraceful, and that I did not do. Thus, my heart does not forbid me to reveal my name. However, at a time when one scholar is not afraid to charge another scholar with high treason in a review,[8] and when there could be princes who accept such a charge, the reader will understand that prudence forbids it to everyone who loves his tranquility. [209] Even so, I hereby give the public my word of honor, which I gave to myself, that I will confess to this writing either in my lifetime myself or after my death through someone else. The few who could identify me one way or another will surely understand that I did not forfeit the protection of my anonymity throughout these pages, even if my reasons are unknown to them.

The Author.

---

8. Rehberg leveled such an accusation in his review of Thomas Paine's *Rights of Man* in the *Allgemeine Literatur-Zeitung*, no. 274, October 18, 1792: "The Author of this pamphlet has been subjected to a criminal process due to its content. He teaches therein that all European countries must give themselves a new constitution after the French example. The people has a right to it. The present legitimate authorities in England are not only accused very harshly by him for constituting the nation's misfortune, but he makes very clear that one should not even have let the ruling house come over from the mainland, and that it is time to abolish the monarchy. However, all this is high treason, according to the editor's insight and opinion."

Introduction

The Basic Principles by Which One Ought to Judge Constitutional Changes

What has happened is a matter of knowing, not of judging. Indeed, we need judgment badly to locate this naked historical truth and to discern it. We need it partly to judge the physical possibility or impossibility of the ostensible fact itself, partly to judge the will or the capacity of the witness to recount it. Yet, once this truth has been determined, judgment has completed its business for everyone who has satisfied himself of it [the truth] and transfers the now refined and assured pure possession to memory.

However, something altogether different from the judgment of a fact's credibility is the judgment of the fact itself—the reflection upon it. In a judgment of the latter kind, the given fact, which has already been accepted as true based on other reasons, is compared to a law in order to justify either the former based on congruence with the latter, or the latter based on congruence with the former. In the first case, the law, according to which the fact is assessed, must precede the fact and be generally valid—acknowledged as such—and the latter must conform to it, for the law receives its validation not from the event itself, but the event from the law. [210] In the latter case, either the law itself or its greater or lesser general validity is to be found by means of comparison with the fact.

Nothing confuses our judgments more, and nothing makes us more incomprehensible to ourselves and to others, than when we overlook this important distinction, when we want to judge without actually knowing from what point of view we are judging, when, for certain facts, we appeal to laws, to generally valid truths, without knowing whether we are assessing the fact according to the law or the law according to the fact, whether we are assessing the protractor or the perpendicular line.

This is the richest source of that stale pedantry[1] in which not only our chivalrous gentlemen and ladies but also our most lauded writers get lost daily, whenever they judge the grand spectacle that France gave us in our day.

In judging a revolution—so that we may approach our object—only two questions may be raised, one about its *legitimacy*, the other about its *wisdom*. With regard to the first, it may be asked, either generally, Does a people actually have a right to change its constitution voluntarily?[2] or in particular, Does it have a right to do so in a certain specific manner, by certain persons, by certain means, according to certain basic principles? The second says as much: Are the means that have been chosen to achieve the intended goal the most appropriate? Which for the sake of accuracy is to be posed like this: Were they the most appropriate *under the given circumstances*?

According to which basic principles are we now going to have to judge these questions? Against what laws are we going to measure the given facts? Against laws that we will first develop from these facts—or if not from these, at least from other facts of experience—or against an eternal law, which would have applied, even if there could not have been an experience, and would apply, if one day all experience ceased to be? Do we want to say: right is what happened most often, and let the moral goodness be determined by the majority of actions, like the religious dogmas at councils by the majority of votes? Do we want to say: wise is what succeeds? Or do we rather want to combine both questions right away, waiting for success as the touchstone of both justice and wisdom, and then, once it materializes, call the robber a hero or [211] a criminal, the Socrates a wrongdoer or virtuous sage?

I know that many doubt the existence of eternal laws of truth and of right in general and will not admit to any truth but truth by the majority of votes, nor any moral goodness but goodness determined by the gentler or more intense titillation of nerves. I know that thereby they relinquish their spirituality and reasonable nature and turn them-

---

1. *Vernünfteleien*
2. *willkürlich*

selves into animals—which are determined by external impression through the senses—into machines—which incontestably determine how one cog wheel gears into the other—into trees—in which the circulation of juices produces the fruit of thought—that with this claim, they immediately turn themselves into all this, if only their thought machine is in the right setting. It is not my intention at all here to defend their humanity against them, and to prove to them that they are not unreasonable animals, but pure spirits. If the clock of their spirit ticks in time, they could not come across our question at all, could not participate in our examination at all. How should they arrive at ideas of wisdom, or of right?

But I also see that others, who either explicitly defend such primordial laws of the mental world or, if their examinations have not penetrated to this outermost boundary, at least silently accept them and build upon the consequences of their primordiality, have occasionally decided on a judgment according to laws of experience. They have on their side the educated public that wants to validate its expert knowledge, its beloved expert knowledge, the absent-minded and superficial [element] that avoids the work of thinking and wants to see everything with its eyes, hear with its ears, and touch with its hands, [and] the advantaged estates, who expect a favorable judgment based on prior experience—they have everything on their side. There seems to be no room left for the opposite opinion.—I want to be read. I want to find my way into the reader's soul. What should I do? Try, whether or not I can unite myself with the great crowd in some manner.

I.

Thus, the question whether a people has a right to change its constitution—or the more specific question whether it has a right to change it in a certain manner—[212] is to be answered based on experience, and the answer is really being sought by means of experience?—Most answers, which have been given to this question and are still being given daily, are influenced by empirical basic principles. This means here, in the most general sense of the words, *basic principles that are [either] clearly thought or unsuspectingly underlying our judgment, and that have been accepted by us based on the mere testimony of our senses without tracing them back to the first basic principles of all truth.* Such empirical basic principles, I say, have an influence on the answer to the above question in two ways, namely, in part *involuntarily*, in part *voluntarily*[3] and *with consciousness*.

Without our consciousness, empirical basic principles have an influence on the judgment that we render, because we do not perceive them as empirical basic principles, as principles that we accept in good faith from our senses, but as purely intellectual, eternally true basic principles.—Based on the reputation of our fathers or teachers, we accept without evidence principles as basic principles, which are not [actually basic principles], because their truth depends on the possibility of deducing them from even more basic principles. We step into the world and find our basic principles in all human beings with whom we become acquainted, because they, too, accepted the same [basic principles] based on their parents' or teachers' reputation. Nobody calls our attention to our lack of conviction and the need to reinspect them by means of an objection. Our faith[4] in the reputation of our teachers is complemented by the faith in the general consensus. Everywhere our experience confirms them precisely because everybody considers them to be universal laws and conforms his actions to them. We ourselves take them as the basis of our actions and our judgments [so that] with every action they become more intimately united with our I and eventually become interweaved with it to such an extent that they cannot be destroyed in any other way but along with it [the I].

This is the origin of the general opinion-systems of peoples, the results of which are commonly passed off as expressions of common sense, but a common sense that has its fashions just like our coats and hairstyles.—Twenty years ago, we considered unpressed cucumbers to be unhealthy, and today [we] consider pressed cucumbers to be unhealthy based on exactly those reasons, according to which most among us still believe until now that one human being could be the *master* of another human being, a citizen could be *entitled* to the assets of his fellow citizens by birth, [and] a prince is determined to make his subjects *happy*.

[213] Just try—I invite all those of you who combine Kantian thoroughness with Socratic popularity—try to wrest the first sentence from an uneducated owner of serfs, the second from an uneducated, ancient nobleman. Drive him into a corner with questions, with facile questions: he will accept your premises, he will concede all of them with deepest conviction. Now you draw the dreaded conclusion and you will be startled

---

3. *unwillkürlich, willkürlich*

4. *Glaube*

by how he, who saw so clearly before, is suddenly completely blind, [and] cannot grasp the tangible connection between your conclusion and your premises. Your conclusion indeed goes against *his* common sense.

Now such principles are unexamined, whether they are by *themselves* true or untrue, i.e., whether they can be deduced from the basic principles under which they stand or contradict them. Such principles are mere empirical basic principles, at least for him who accepted them based on the authority of his teachers, his fellow citizens, and his experience, and all judgments that he makes on their basis are judgments from experience. Over the course of this examination, I will cite multiple political prejudices of this kind—*prejudices* at least for him who did not examine them *afterwards*—and I will assess their rightness.[5]

This is precisely the unnoticed influence of sensibility, of the instrument of experience, on our *understanding* in the judgment at hand. It has an equally unnoticed and equally powerful influence on our will in this examination, and thereby on our judgment by means of the dark feeling of our interest.

Our judgment very often depends on the direction of our inclination, in particular in questions of the right. Injustices that befall *ourselves* seem much harsher to us than exactly the same injustices when they befall someone else. Indeed, our inclination frequently distorts our judgment to an even greater extent. Striving to present our self-interested claims to others and finally also to ourselves under an honorable mask, we turn them into *legal*[6] claims and scream about injustice, often when one does nothing but prevent us from being unjust ourselves. Hence, do not believe that we are trying to deceive you. We were deceived long before you. We ourselves believe, in complete seriousness, in the legitimacy of our claims. We are not making the first attempt to lie to you. Long before you, we have lied to ourselves.

One examines the given question based on empirical basic principles *voluntarily*[7] and with consciousness when one intends to answer it based on historical facts.—[214] It is difficult to believe that anyone who ever attempted to answer in this way actually knew what was being asked. However, this will only become completely clear in what follows.

---

5. This is a play on words in German. *Vorurteil* (prejudice) literally means that one judges before one actually knows. It ceases to be *Vorurteil*, if one examines the judgment afterwards (*nacher*).

6. *rechtlich*

7. *willkürlich*

Thus, we intend to answer the question at hand based on the suggested basic principles? Based on principles that we have accepted in good faith? However, if these principles themselves were now wrong, our answers predicated on them would therefore necessarily also be untrue.—Those whose reputation we have followed to form our system of opinions indeed took them to be true. But what if they erred? Our people and our age certainly take them to be true with us. But do we not know—we who know so many facts—do we not know that in Constantinople precisely that is generally accepted as true which in Rome is generally accepted as false? That several hundred years ago in Wittenberg and Geneva something was generally held to be right which is now generally held to be a pernicious falsity in the same place? If we were moved to different nations or into a different age, would we thereupon still want to maintain our current basic principles, which would then contradict the general manner of thought, contrary to our touchstone of truth? Or should then no longer be true for us, what was true for us until now [our basic principles]? Does our truth change according to age and circumstances?

What kind of answer were we actually searching for? One that holds only for our age, only for those human beings who agree with us in their opinions?—Then we could have saved ourselves the trouble of the examination, [for] they will answer the question without us exactly as we [will].—Or do we want such an answer that holds for all ages and peoples, for everything that is human? Then we have to build it upon universally valid basic principles.

Do we want to grant an influence to our *interest*, where *right* is in question, i.e., should our inclination become universal moral law for all of humanity?—It is true, Knight of the Golden Fleece, you who are nothing more than that, it is true, and nobody will deny it to you, that it would be very uncomfortable for you if the respect for your noble birth, for your title, and for your order suddenly vanished from the world and you were at once honored merely according to your personal worth, if all of your goods—the possession of which is based on unjust rights—were taken away from you.[8] It is true that you would become the most disdained and the poorest human being, that you would sink into the deepest misery. But pardon me—the question was not at all about your misery or nonmisery. [215] It was about our right. "What makes you miserable, can never be right," you opine.—But look here at your

---

8. The Order of the Golden Fleece was one of the most prominent knighthood orders in Europe, founded by Philip the Good in 1430.

slaves in bondage that have so far been oppressed by you: it would truly make them very happy to share among themselves even the small share of your treasures that you possess rightfully; to make you their slave, as they were yours until now; to take your sons and daughters as servants and maids, as you took theirs until now; to have you chase game in front of them, as they chased it in front of you until now. They are shouting at us: the rich [man], the privileged does not belong to the people. He does not have a part in universal human rights. That is *their* interest. Their conclusions are as thorough as yours. What makes them happy, could never be unjust, they opine. Should we grant [their pleas]?—Now then, allow us not to grant yours either.

To protest against this secret betrayal of sensibility is difficult even with the strongest will and the brightest mind. No nobleman,† no military person in monarchical states, no tradesman in the service of a court that has declared itself against the French Revolution‡ should be

---

†That is to say, [he] who is nothing more than a nobleman. The German audience admires in many men of the greatest houses the higher nobility, that of the spirit, and I certainly not less than anyone else. In this place, I will only mention the Baron of Knigge[9] and the noble author of the *Thoughts of a Danish Patriot on Standing Armies*, etc.[10]

‡Even less should such a person be a judge of incoming pamphlets in the most important intellectual journal of Europe, thereby an apparent interpreter of the national opinion.[11] I, at least, refuse to tolerate the judgment of any empiricist on this pamphlet, if it were found worthy of a complaint. He would be a judge on his own account. A speculative thinker [should] be my judge, or no one! Yet, even this rule has its exceptions, too. I value highly, for example, the pamphlet about the French Revolution by Herr *Brandes*, who is the *Geheimer Kanzleisekretär* [Secret Secretary of the Chancellery] in Hanover.[12] One can still hear the independently thinking and honest man, and does not notice dishonest twisting and turning.

9. Adolf Franz Friedrich Ludwig Freiherr von Knigge, 1752–96

10. Woldemar Friedrich Graf von Schmettau, *Patriotische Gendanken eines Dänen, über stehende Heere, politisches Gleichgewicht und Staatsrevolutionen* (Thoughts of a Danish Patriot on Standing Armies, the Political Balance of Power, and the Revolution of States), 1792.

11. Reference to Rehberg, who reviewed the most important pamphlets on the French Revolution in Jena's *Allgemeine Literatur-Zeitung* from 1870 on.

12. Ernst Brandes, *Politische Betrachtungen über die französische Revolution* (Political Considerations on the French Revolution), 1790; *Über einige bisherige Folgen der Französischen Revolution, in Rücksicht auf Deutschland* (On Several Previous Consequences of the French Revolution in Regard to Germany), 1792.

heard in this examination. [216] Does the common citizen, who sighs under harsh taxes contribute? [Or] the enslaved peasant, the battered soldier?—Or would we hear him, if he did? Only he can be judge here, who is neither oppressor nor oppressed, whose hands and inheritance are clean of the nations' robbery, whose head has not since youth been pressed into the conventional forms of our age, whose heart feels a warm but silent veneration for human worth and human rights.

These are sensibility's secret deceptions. Evidently, one relies on their testimonial whenever one wants to answer the question *based on history.*—Is it actually true? Should there really have been people, rightly thinking people, intellectuals, who have thought to have answered what *ought to* happen, in response to the question "What is happening?" or "What has happened?"—Impossible, we just did not understand them properly, they just did not understand themselves properly. Instead of engaging in strict arguments with them, which lies completely outside of our plan here, we only want to try to make their own words clear to them.

When they talk about an *ought*,[13] they hereby immediately predicate a *could-be-otherwise*[14] as well. What *must* be like this and absolutely cannot be otherwise, thereof no reasonable human being would examine whether it *ought to* be like this or otherwise. Thus, by the use of the word ["ought"], they immediately concede to some things their *independence from natural necessity.*

They can and will want to concede this independence, or this *freedom,* to no other thing but the decisions of reasonable beings, which in this respect may also be called *actions.* Thus, they recognize the free actions of reasonable beings.

Regarding these [free actions], they want to examine whether [the actions] ought to be like this or be otherwise, i.e., they want to hold the determined, given action up against a certain norm, and pass a judgment on the congruence of the former with the latter. Whence do they want to take this norm? Not from the action to which it [the norm] must comply, for the action ought to be assessed against the norm, not the norm against the action. Thus, from other free actions that are given by experience?—Maybe they want to deduce the *common* [element] in

13. *ein Sollen*
14. *Andersseinkönnen*

their [action's] determining ground and bring it into a *unity* as a law? If so, at least they may not be so unfair as to want to judge the acting, free being according to a law that he could not have made the basis of his action, because it was not known to him. [217] They will not want to judge the orthodoxy of patriarch Abraham according to the Prussian Edict on Religion,[15] [or] the legitimacy of the Canaanites' extermination by the Jewish people according to the Duke of Brunswick's manifestos against the Parisians.[16] They cannot expect anything more of this being but that he may have utilized the experience that is possible up to his age, and observed the law that is possible through its [experience's] multifariousness. Consequently, they have to prescribe for each age its own law for the free actions of reasonable beings, and according to them we have entirely different rights and duties today than our fathers a hundred years ago. According to them, the entire moral system of the spiritual world will have changed again in a hundred years due to heightened experience, and they themselves, should they reach such a high age, will then condemn what they now deem right, and deem right what they now condemn.—But, why do I say for every age!—They have to adopt a particular law for every individual person, since not everyone could possibly be as well-versed in history as they, and they would perhaps not expect of anyone that he derives rules of conduct from events he does not know about. Or is it a duty to become such an in-depth historian as they, so that we do not persist in this raw ignorance about our duties?

Finally, since their experience, after all, has an end somewhere, they have to reach a point where they cannot verify any previous experience. According to which laws do they want to judge then?—Or does the contemplation of free action in light of the ought cease entirely here? Does it cease, e.g., with the first decision of Adam, since they

---

15. This is an allusion to the Royal Edict of July 9, 1788, authored by Johann Christoph Wöllner, Minister of Education and Religious Affairs under Frederick William II of Prussia. The edict censored sermons and publications, requiring that they adhere to established Lutheran or Reformed orthodoxy. The edict was a response to the growth of Enlightenment writing about religion, and was challenged by several authors, including Fichte himself in his "Reclamation" essay of 1793.

16. Karl Wilhelm Ferdinand von Braunschweig, 1735–1806, was a Prussian general and the commander-in-chief of the Prussian-Austrian army. As commander-in-chief, he invaded France in 1792 and threatened the Parisian population with punishment if the king of France or his family were subjected to additional violence or insult.

could not possibly enumerate experiences for him from the time of the pre-Adamites to which he should have conformed?

The defenders of an empirical manner of answering the question of right would become entangled in these and vastly worse contradictions if they were not luckily inconsistent and their heart did not play the trick on them of feeling more rightly than their head thinks and their mouth speaks. We see after all that they judge the free actions of all peoples and ages pretty much according to the same basic principles, and [that they] hardly seem to fear a contradiction from the experience of future ages, [218] and that in practice they apply historical evidence or historical deduction—having falsely entitled it so—only as examples, as sensible representations of primordial principles.

Or do they perhaps sometimes confuse our question with an entirely different one: *Do I act prudently in this particular way?* As long as the first [question] is not fully answered, the second does not even take place.—However, it is clear to the natural, uneducated human reason that it is something entirely different to do one's duty than to seek one's advantage in a reasonable manner, and only the school was capable of the feat of darkening this clarity and blindfolding the sun. Even if one does not always want to admit it, everybody feels that it is frequently [a] duty to sacrifice one's properly understood advantage, that it is left entirely to our own choice[17] to sacrifice it also outside of this case, that we are not accountable to anyone for it, but ourselves at best, [and that], by contrast, the other may demand from us and desire as a debt whatever is duty bound. Both questions are therefore inherently different.

Now, if they really admit to such an *ought* that can be demanded according to a generally valid law, and consequently to a *may* or *may not*[18] that depends on this law, and if they do not merely play with words, then they admit at the same time that this law is neither to be deduced from experience nor to be confirmed by it. Rather, [in order to] make it the basis of a certain assessment of all experience, which is itself below it, it consequently has to be conceived as independent of all experience and superior to it. If they do not admit to such an ought, why do they intervene in an examination that is therefore absolutely futile for them [and] that according to them pertains to a phantasm? In that case, may they quietly let us pursue our business, and they pursue theirs!

---

17. *Willkür*

18. *das Dürfen oder nicht Dürfen*

ought implies can't

The question about ought and may, or what, as will become apparent immediately, is actually the question of right, does not belong in front of the tribunal of history at all. History's answer does not fit our question at all. It answers everything else that we want to know except that. And it is a laughable comparison[19] if we string together the answer that history provides and our question. Our question belongs in front of a different tribunal, which we will seek out.—Whether the second question, the one about prudence, belongs in front of it, and under which conditions it may belong in front of it, will manifest itself further below.

Thus, we desire to judge facts according to a law not borrowed from any facts and not contained in any. Now, whence do we think to take this law? Where do we think to find it? [219] Without doubt *in our self*, since it is not to be encountered *outside us*. To be specific, [we find it] in our self in so far as the self is not molded and cultivated by external things mediated by experience (for this is not our true self, but a foreign addition), but in its *pure, primordial* form; in our self, as it would be without all experience. The difficulty in doing so seems to be only that of isolating all foreign additions from our cultivation,[20] and of purifying the primordial form of our I.—If, however, we were to find something in us that can plainly not have originated from any experience, because it is of a completely different nature, then we could conclude confidently that this is our primordial form. Now, something of this kind we do actually find in the very law of the ought. Once it is present in us—and that it is present, is a fact—[we find that] it cannot be a foreign addition that has been added by nature, since it is entirely opposed to the nature of experience, but must be the pure form of our self. The existence of this law in us *as fact* therefore leads us to the primordial form of our I. And the law's appearance in fact is derived, in turn, from this primordial form of our I, as the *effect from its cause*.

In order to avoid even the most sneaking suspicion of a contradiction with myself, I will further note explicitly that the existence of such a law in us as fact, as well as all facts, is, however, *given* to our consciousness by (inner) experience. In individual cases, e.g., upon stimulation of a culpable inclination,[21] we become aware through experience of an inner voice in us, that yells at us: do not do it, it is not right.

---

19. *Eins fürs Andere*
20. *Bildung*
21. *Neigung*

Experience delivers individual expressions, individual effects of this law in our chest, but it does not therefore *bring about* the law. Experience plainly cannot do that.

This primordial, *unchangeable* form of our self now desires to bring its *changeable* forms, which are determined by experience and determine experience in turn, into agreement with itself, and is therefore called the *command*.[22] It [the primordial, unchangeable form] desires this continuously for all reasonable spirits, for it is the primordial form of *reason per se*, and is therefore called *law*. It can only desire this for actions that depend exclusively on reason, not on natural necessity, i.e., only for *free* actions, and is therefore called *moral law*. The most common names of its [the moral law's] expression in us, according to which even the most uninformed know it, are: *the conscience, the inner judge in us,* [220] *the thoughts that accuse and exculpate each other*, and the like.

What these laws command is generally called *right, a duty*. What it forbids [is called] *wrong, contrary to duty*. We *ought* [to do] the former, we *ought not* [to do] the latter.—If, as reasonable beings, we are as such and without all exceptions subject to this law, then we can *thus be subject to no other*. Wherever this law is silent, we are therefore subject to no law: we *may*. Everything that the law does not forbid, we may do. Whatever we may do, thereto we have a right, because this may *is lawful, a right*.

Indeed, even that in our nature without which the law would not be possible at all in it, as well as that which actually commands the law, alongside that which only is permitted by the law, [all these] belong under the inclusive category of *what is not forbidden* by the law. Therefore, we can say, we have the right to be reasonable beings, we have the right to do our duty, just as much as we can say, we have a right to do what the moral law permits.

However, a large, essential difference arises immediately here. For we have a right to do what the moral law merely permits. However, we also have the opposite right *not* to do it. The moral law is silent [here], and we are only subject to our arbitrary will.[23]—We also have a right to do our duty, but we do not have the opposite right not to do it. Likewise, we have the right to be free, moral beings, but we do not have the right not to be them. Hence the authorization is very different in these two cases: in the first [case], it is truly affirming, in the second merely

---

22. *Gebot*
23. *Willkür*

negating. "I have a right to do what the moral law permits" means: my doing or refraining depends merely on my arbitrary will. "I have a right to be free and to do my duty" only means: nothing [and] nobody has the right to prevent me from it. This distinction is infinitely important because of its consequences.

These are the basic principles, upon which all examinations about the legitimacy or illegitimacy or a free action have to be carried out, and other [principles] absolutely do not apply. The examination has to go back to the primordial form of our spirit, and must not stop at the spirit's colors, which chance, habit, or prejudice—involuntarily by mistake or voluntarily in the pursuit of oppression—breathe on it. (The examination must be carried out based on *a priori* principles, in fact on practical ones, and may absolutely not be based on empirical ones.) Who[ever] is not yet in agreement with himself on this, [221] is not mature [enough] for the assigned assessment. He will wander in the dark, and search his way with his fingertips; he will be swept away by the stream of his association of ideas, and will rely on good luck to be thrown on one island or another. He will stack unlike materials on top of each other as best he can in the order in which he fishes them from the surface of his memory. Neither he himself nor anyone else will understand him. He will receive the applause of the finer public, which recognizes itself in him. It was not my will to tell the story of authors who have written about this topic.

II.

The second question that could occur in the assessment of a revolution pertains to its wisdom, i.e., whether the best—at least under the circumstances the best—means were chosen to reach the intended goal.

And here, then, our know-it-all experts crowd closer together in the certain assumption that this question—a question about wisdom—belongs well and truly in front of their tribunal. "History, history is the lighthouse[24] of all tides and times," they cry, "the master teacher of peoples, the unerring herald[25] of the future." And without listening to their cries, I want to dissect the given question and see what other

---

24. *Seewarte*

25. *Verkünderin*

questions are contained in it. Then everyone will be able to take up what is his. And only after that a few words about its praised history.[26]

If the relationship of the chosen means to a [given] goal is to be tested, the goodness of the goal itself—and in our case the goodness of the goal insofar as it shall be made the basis of a constitution—is, above all things, to be assessed. The question "Which is the best final end[27] of the union of the state?"[28] depends on the answer to the following [question]: "What is the final end of each individual?" The answer to this question is purely moral and must be based on the moral law, which rules only over the human being as a human being and erects a final end for him. From this it follows, initially, [that] the exclusive condition of all morally possible constitutions [is] that its final end must not contradict each individual's final end, which is prescribed by the moral law, and that it must not hinder or disturb its attainment. A final end that sins against this basic rule is already reprehensible in itself, because it is unjust. Furthermore, if the entire union shall not be completely useless, the final end must also advance the highest final end of each individual. [222] This, however, is possible in various degrees, and, because this elevation proceeds into the infinite, no definite highest level can be specified. Therefore, in this regard, the goodness of the final end does not lend itself to being determined according to a fixed rule, but only according to possible degrees.[29]

Assuming that the final end of humanity in the particular and in the whole is not to be determined according to empirical laws but according to its primordial form, then there is nothing to do here for the historian, besides at most the business of providing us with material for the comparison of the [moral] degree[30] of various constitutions. But we fear that his search for this sort of material in the history of hitherto existing states will be very invidious, and that he will come back loaded with unusable spoil.

The second task is this: to compare the chosen means with the goal in order to see whether the former relates to the latter like cause

---

26. The antecedent of "its" is unclear and could refer either to the "question" or the "revolution."

27. *Endzweck*

28. *Staatsverbindung*

29. *Mehr oder Weniger*

30. *Mehr oder Weniger*

to its effect. In fact, this test is possible in two different ways: namely, either according to *clearly thought laws*, or [according to] *similar cases*.

If there is talk of means to achieve a certain final end in a societal union,[31] then the objects of these means are mainly the minds of human beings, in whom and by whom this final end is to be achieved. These, in turn, are stimulated, set into motion, determined to act according to certain universal rules that would presumably be called laws if we knew them more thoroughly. To be specific, I do not speak of that first fundamental law of humanity that always determines its free actions. Rather, I speak of those rules, according to which a human being can be determined not insofar as he is a primordial, pure human being, but rather as a human being cultivated by experience, by sensible addition, and in particular [those rules] according to which he shall be determined to accord with this primordial form. That is to say, just as all spirits are identical to one another according to the primordial form of reason,[32] all human beings are identical according to certain other sensible forms of spirit.[33] The differences that age, climate, [and] occupation produce in them are really minor against the sum of identical features, [and] must *cease to exist more and more with progressing culture* in the hands of wise constitutions. One learns them [the particular rules accounting for human diversity] easily, and the means to use them are small, negligible homespun remedies. The study of their universal forms, however, is not completed as easily.

Now, it is here where experience actually enters. [223] However, not the [experience] of how many great monarchies existed or on what day the Battle of Philippi took place,[34] but the kind that is much closer to us: the *empirical psychology*.[35]—Choose yourself as your most intimate company, follow yourself into the most secret corners of your heart, and coax all your secrets out of you: *get to know yourself*. This is the first basic principle of this psychology. The rules that you will derive from this introspection regarding the course of *your* instincts and inclinations, regarding the form of *your* sensible self, apply—you may believe

---

31. *Gesellschaftliche Verbindung*

32. *ursprüngliche Vernunftsformen*

33. *sinnliche Geistesformen*

34. 42 BC, when Brutus and Cassius, Caesar's murderers, were defeated by the triumvirate Antonius, Octavianus, and Lepidus.

35. *Erfahrungsseelenkunde*

assuredly—to everything with a human face. Herein they are all similar to you.—Do not leave unnoticed that I say "*herein*."[36] For you may be honestly resolved to always follow the voice of your conscience, you are able to be ashamed of yourself, and you are an honest man. [But] I do not advise you to confidently take everyone else to be the same. Maybe someone else holds nothing against himself, as long as it was helpful, and is just as firmly resolved to follow the voice of his interest [as you]. Selfishness is the mainspring of his actions, just as respect for the law is the mainspring of yours. But this you can be sure of, that these two very different mainsprings lead both of you to action in pretty much the same way.—From the history of your heart, you will perhaps still distantly recall the time when you were not much better than he is now. You will perhaps also still recall how and in what manner you were gradually converted to reason and were spiritually reborn. Precisely this course, he must go as well—not starting from this very point—if he should ever become a better human being. And you must help to lead him on this way, if you want to make him one.

The means chosen in a constitution for achieving its final end are now to be assessed according to the rules of this psychology, which will approach the rank of law through continuous wise observation. It is to be assessed according to the general analogy of the sensible human being whether the means can and will produce the desired effect on him. And this kind of assessment is the most thorough, the most infallible, and the most obvious. The historian of the common kind has nothing to do with it. Rather, it is the business of the observant independent thinker.

A second way of searching an answer to the present question is the *assessment according to similar cases*.[37] The basic principle of this assessment is the following: Similar causes have once produced certain effects, [224] consequently they will now produce similar effects. Now, this manner of contemplation appears on first sight to be purely historical, but various things about it have to be remembered.

First of all, it is only possible to show merely similar and never completely identical causes, [so that] consequently one may only reason to similar and never to identical effects. But how do you know what aspect of the required effect will be similar to the given and what aspect of it

---

36. *hierin*

37. See Rehberg, *Untersuchungen über die Französische Revolution* (Hannover: Ritscher, 1793), 1:12–13.

will be dissimilar to it? How will the dissimilar be constituted? History teaches you neither one of the two. Thus, if you want to know it, you have to look for it according to laws of reasons.

Next, on what does your inference, *that* similar causes will have similar effects, actually rest? If this inference is supposed to be lawful,[38] you have to silently assume that the effect is really connected with the causes by means of a law that is universal and valid for all cases, and that the effect will follow from the causes according to this law.

Thus, look, you defenders of the exclusive or preferential validity of this kind of assessment, look how far we agree with you, and where we depart from you. You assume a law and its universal validity unanimously together with us, but it is not important to you to find it. You only want to have the effect. Its connection with the cause concerns you the least. We are looking for the law itself, and only infer the effect from the given cause according to the law. You buy secondhand. We source our goods from the first. Who between us, do you think, will get them more earnestly and for a cheaper price? You observe at large, looking down from the observatory onto the clump of people crowded at the market. We go deeper into the particular, taking everyone in individually, and exploring each individual. Who, do you think, will learn more?

And what if you come across a case that has not occurred in your history before? What do you do then? I very much fear that this is indeed the case with the question about the means for achieving the only true goal of a constitution. I fear that you will look in vain for a common goal[39] in all hitherto existing states; in those states that fortuity has assembled, [and] that each age patched and mended with shy respect for the manes[40] of previous ages; in those [states] whose praiseworthy characteristic it is that they are inconsistent in the execution of some of its basic principles that would have crushed humanity entirely and extinguished all hope in it of an erstwhile resurrection; in those [states] in which one meets at most that unity that holds together the various species of carnivorous animals, where the weaker is eaten by the stronger and eats the yet weaker himself. I fear that you will not find news in your history of the effects of some mainsprings on the human being, [225] because history's heroes forgot to attach them to the human heart.

---

38. *gesetzlich*

39. *Zweckseinheit*

40. According to Roman mythology, *manes* are the deified souls of dead ancestors.

Therefore, you will have to be content with an *a priori* examination when[ever] the *a posteriori* should not be possible.

And, since we are already talking about this rich text, a few more words on it!—It is with humanity as a whole as it is with the individual. The former is shaped by the occurrences of its life,[41] like the latter. We have completely forgotten the events of our early childhood years. Are they therefore lost to us? Is the entire original individual tendency of our spirit therefore based any less on them, because we do not know them? If only the latter remains, what does the former concern us?—We cross over into boyhood, and our small deeds and afflictions are permanently engraved in our memory. Meanwhile, our cultivation moves forward by means of them [the memories], and as it moves forward we begin to feel ashamed of our childish ideas and foolishness. Precisely that which makes us wiser becomes abhorrent to us in our memory, due to the greater maturity that it gives us, and we would like to forget it if we could. The time in which we remember it indifferently comes later, comes only once those years have become foreign to us, and we no longer see ourselves as the same individual.—Humanity does not appear to have grown up to the age of learning shame yet. Otherwise, it would boast less of its childish feats, and attach a smaller value to enumerating them.

Only that which really remains in humanity as an acquired good is a true gain of its age and its experience. *How* it arrived at them concerns us less, and our curiosity would find little instruction about it in the common history either. They describe the scaffolding and the external machinery for us in all detailedness, [but] they could not see how one stone fits next to the other in front of the wonderful scaffolding. If anything, that is what we would have liked to know. Concerning the scaffolding, if only the building stood there, the scaffolding could be removed!§

---

§Since we are not writing a treatise against history here, the following may be noted: "Among other things, we need history to admire the wisdom of providence in the execution of its great plan."—But this is not true. You merely want to admire your own acumen. You have an idea by chance. That's *how* you [would] do it, if you were providence.—With disproportionately greater likelihood, one could point out the plan of an evil misanthropic being, which is aiming at humanity's greatest possible moral corruption and misery in the course of its fate. But that would not be true either. The only truth is arguably the following: that an infinite multifariousness exists, which in itself is neither good nor evil, but only becomes either of the two through the free application of reasonable beings, and that indeed it will not become better before *we* have become better.

41. *Dauer*

[226] Should one therefore let history die altogether? Oh no, it should only be taken out of your hands, you who remain children eternally and never know something other than *learning*; you who only ever let [things] be *given* to you and never know to *produce* yourself; [you] whose highest creative power never surpasses *imitation*. It should be consigned to the care of the true philosopher so that within the gaudy puppet play—the colors of which attract your eyes—he may provide the tangible evidence for you that all ways have been tried and that none has led to the destination, so that you finally cease to decry his way, the way of principles, against yours, the way of blind trial. It should be consigned to his care so that for you he may paint red some letters in the alphabet that you ought to learn so that you recognize them by their color until you will learn to recognize them by their inner character.

He shall need them for the enrichment and final anchoring of empirical psychology.—To get to know the human being on the whole, the human being under ordinary circumstances, no broad knowledge of history is required. For everyone, his own heart and the manners of acting of his neighbors both right and left is an inexhaustible text. However, what advantaged souls are capable of under extraordinary circumstances, daily experience does not teach. Advantaged souls under circumstances that develop and present their entire capability are not born every century. To get to know these, to get to know humanity in its finest dress, history's instruction is required.—Do you perhaps want to demonstrate to me how much we have gained in this regard from your treatment of history? Name the Plutarchs for me that you have educated for us.

Really, it is difficult to resist the movement of one's gall bladder or one's diaphragm, depending on whether the one or the other is more irritable in us, whenever one listens to our experts' declamations against the application of primordial rational basic principles in life, [or] to our empiricists' fierce attacks against our philosophers, [227] as if there was a forever irreconcilable conflict between theory and practice.[42]—But I ask you, according to what do *you* go about the businesses of your life? Do you leave them entirely to the blind wafting of fate or, since most of the time you speak very piously, to the direction of providence? Or do you, too, act in accordance with rules? In the first case, what is the purpose of your wordy warnings to the peoples not to let themselves be

---

42. See Rehberg, *Untersuchungen*, 2:407–8. Kant published his own response to the skepticism that theory can inform practice in his "Theory and Practice" essay a few months after the *Contribution*.

blinded by the philosophers' pretenses? You all, be quiet and let fortuity rule. If the philosophers win, they will have been right. If they do not win, they will have been wrong. It is not your concern to refute them. Fortuity will already sit in judgment over them.—In the second case, whence do you obtain your rules? From experience you say. But, doesn't this mean that you actually find them put into words for you by other men and that you accept them based on their authority? However, if it does mean this, I ask you: Whence did they take them? And you are not a step further.—However, if it does not mean this, surely you have to assess the experience first, bring the multifariousness of experience under certain unities, and thereby deduce your rules. This route that you take, in turn, cannot be derived from experience. Rather, its direction and its steps are predetermined for you by a primordial law of reason, which is known to you from school under the name of logic. Yet, even this law prescribes for you only the form of your assessment, not the point of view from which you want to assess the facts. You have to bring the multifariousness under certain specified unities, I say, and you will surely not deny me this, if you understand this expression. If not, then think about it for a little while. Now, how do you come by these concepts of unity?[43] Not by assessing that which is given in experience, since the [very] possibility of any assessment already presupposes them, as you must have grasped from what has been said. Thus, originally and prior to any experience, they must already have lain in your soul, and you have judged according to them without knowing it. Experience itself is a chest full of letters thrown among each other. Only the human spirit brings meaning to this chaos, composes an *Iliad* from them here, and a Schlenkertian historical drama there.[44]—Hence, you have done yourself a great injustice. You are more philosopher than you could believe yourself. [228] It is with you as with Master Jourdain in the comedy: all your life, you have been philosophizing without knowing a word about it.[45] Forgive us therefore always just one sin, which you have committed together with us.

---

43. *Einheitsbegriffe*

44. Friedrich Christian Schlenkert, 1757–1826 was a student in Pforta from 1771–76.

45. Jourdain was the protagonist in *Le bourgeois gentilhomme* (The Bourgeois Gentleman) by Molière (Jean-Baptiste Poquelin, 1622–73). In the play (act 2, scene 4), Mr. Jourdain learns from his master of philosophy that he has been speaking in prose his entire life.

I can perhaps tell you where the actual point of contention between you and us lies. Sure enough you do not want to part ways with reason completely, nor with your charitable friend, the beaten track.[46] You want to divide yourself between the two and therefore you get between two absolutely incompatible fields, into the uncomfortable situation of not being able to please anyone. Why don't you rather follow resolutely the sense of gratitude, which draws you to the latter, and then we know where we stand with you.

Perhaps you would like to be a little reasonable, only for heaven's sake not all the way.—Quite right, but why to the very threshold set by you? Why don't you already stop within it? Why don't you go a few more steps? You cannot offer a rational ground for it, since you abandon reason here. Now, how do you want to answer us on this question? How do you want to answer your allies, who agree with you on the matter itself, only not on the threshold? How do you want to answer them, who are resolute champions of the old, as it is? You are coming into conflict with the entire world and stand there alone and without answer.

But you stick to it. Our philosophical basic principles, you say, just do not let themselves be introduced in life. Our theories, you say, are indeed irrefutable, but they are *not realizable.*—Surely, you [can] mean this only under the condition *that everything should remain as it is now.* For otherwise your claim would indeed be too bold. But who says that it should remain like this, anyway? Who has hired you for mending and bungling anyway, for patching new pieces onto the old ragged coat, for washing [oneself] without wanting to get the skin wet? Who has denied that the machine will thereby come to a complete standstill, that the cracks will widen, that the Moor will surely remain a Moor?[47] Should we bear the [name of] ass, when you have botched it?

But you *want* everything to quite remain in the old way; thus, your resistance, thus your clamor about the unrealizability of our basic principles. Now then, at least be honest and say no longer: we *cannot* realize your basic principles. Rather say precisely as you mean it: we do not *want* to realize them.

[229] It's not only since today that you pursue this clamor about the unrealizability of that which does not please you. You have always

46. *Schlendrian*
47. *Mohr*

cried like this whenever a brave and resolute man stepped among you and told you how you should go about your affairs more prudently. Nevertheless, despite your clamor, some things have become real while you were proving its impossibility to yourself.—For instance, not so long ago you were calling out to a man who was going our way and had made only [the one] mistake that he did not follow it far enough: "proposez nous donc ce, qui est faisable." He replied to you very rightly that it should mean: "proposez nous ce, qu'on fait."[48] Since then you have been instructed by experience, the single [faculty] that can make you prudent, that his suggestions were not quite as inadvisable after all.

Rousseau, whom you have called a dreamer time and again [even] while his dreams came true before your eyes, dealt much too sparingly with you, you empiricists. That was his mistake. One will eventually talk to you much differently than he talked. Before your eyes—and to your embarrassment, I can add, if you do not know yet—inspired by Rousseau, the human spirit has completed a work that you would have declared to be the most impossible of all impossibilities, if [only] you had been capable of grasping its[49] idea: it [the human spirit] has measured itself.[50] While you are still nitpicking at the words of the record—noticing nothing, suspecting nothing, wrapping yourself in a few rags torn off of it as in a second lion skin, believing in all innocence and unselfconsciousness to follow its basic principles, although committing the ugliest violation of them—the spirit [of Rousseau and Kant] nourishes young powerful men in quiet. They foresee his influence on the system of human knowledge through all its parts and [foresee] the altogether new creation of the human manner of thinking, which the former work must produce, until they [the young men] will constitute it [the manner of thinking].[51] You will need to rub your eyes often in order to convince yourself whether you are seeing right whenever one of your impossibilities has come true again.

---

48. "Propose to us what is feasible. . . . Propose to us what we are to do." Fichte is paraphrasing a famous passage from the preface of Jean Jacque Rousseau's *Emile, or On Education* (1762).

49. In the German text, the antecedent *desselben* could also refer to Rousseau.

50. This is a reference to Kant's critique of reason.

51. Richard Schottky suggests that Fichte considers himself one of these young men completing Kant's work. Fichte, *Beitrag zur Berichtigung der Urteile des Publikums über die französische Revolution*, ed. Richard Schottky (Hamburg: Felix Meiner, 1973), 269n36.

Do you want to measure the man's force according to the boy's? Do you believe that the free man is not capable of more than the man in fetters was capable of? Do you judge the strength that a great decision will give us according to the strength we have every day? Thus, what do you want with your experience, anyway? Does it present us something other than children, men in shackles, and everyday people?

Precisely you are the competent judges of the limits of human force! Put under the yoke of authority when your neck was still the most bendable, [230] arduously pressed into an artificially conceived form of thinking that contradicts nature, deprived of selfhood[52] by the constant absorption of foreign basic principles, [by] the constant nestling under foreign plans, by the thousand needs of your bodies, ruined for the higher improvement of the spirit and [for] a strong, noble sense of your I—you are able to judge what man is capable of! Your force is the benchmark for human force in general! Have you ever heard the golden wing of genius whoosh?—not who inspires song, but who inspires deeds. Have you ever commanded your soul with a forceful "I *will*" and, after years of fighting, despite all sensible stimulation, despite all obstacles, presented its result and said, "*here it is*"? Do you feel capable of saying to the despot's face: "you can kill me, but not change my decision"? Have you?—if you cannot do this, leave this site, it is holy for you.

The human being *can* what it *ought*; if he says "I *cannot*," then he does not *will*.

III.

Without provisionally having examined in front of which tribunal we should institute legal proceedings, a judgment was completely impossible. Now that we have sorted it out, a new examination arises, prior to whose decision a thorough and coherent judgment is equally impossible: [namely,] the one about the rank order of the two competent tribunals and about their pronouncements' subordination among each other. I [will] make myself clearer.

An action can be very prudent, yet unjust. We can have a right to something, the exercise of which would, however, be very imprudent. For both tribunals speak entirely independently of each other, according

---

52. *entselbstet*

to entirely different laws, and on entirely different questions. Why then should the Yes or the No that fits the one [question], always also fit the other? Now, if we had brought our question in front of both tribunals with the intention of arranging our behavior according to the answer that we will obtain, and the one permits or [even] commands what the other dissuades, which one would we have to obey?

The pronouncement of reason, insofar as it pertains to the free actions of spiritual beings, is per se a valid universal *law*. Whatever reason commands must per se happen. Whatever it permits, must per se not be impeded. [231] [In contrast,] the voice of prudence is only *good advice*. If we are prudent, we will certainly heed it. However, if we are not as prudent as you, if we do not possess your sharp artful ability to calculate[53] advantages, that's indeed bad for us. But are you allowed to *compel* us to be prudent? Thus, if the moral law answered one of our questions, "you may not," then we must not do it, even if the voice of prudence cried ever so loudly, "do it, it is your highest advantage; if you refrained from it, your entire well-being would be foiled, you would sink into the deepest misery, the ruins of the universe would fall in over you." Let them fall and let yourself be buried in their lap, conscious that *you have not acted unjustly* and that you are *worthy* of a better fate.

If the moral law answers you, "you may," then go and consult with prudence; then examine your advantages, weigh them against each other, choose the one of best coinage,[54] and enjoy it in good conscience. Your heart blesses it for you.

However, if we had raised this question merely in order to judge the actions of someone else, how would we have to comport ourselves in the case of the different answers of the moral law and of prudence? If someone acted unjustly, his action deserves all our abomination and, if his injustice pertained to us, our revenge. If he acted only imprudently, his action deserves merely our criticism and he our pity and our good wishes. We cannot withdraw our respect from him, because he honored the law.

But—oh, it is a deep, hidden, ineradicable tendency of human corruption, that they [human beings] always prefer to be gracious rather than just, prefer to give alms rather than to pay debts. But we are gen-

53. *Rechenkunst*
54. *vollwichtig*

erous, we are looking for his own best [interest], and want to lead him back onto that road, even if it is by violent means.[55]

Now, do we know for certain what advances *his* well-being or *his* unhappiness? It is perhaps possible that *we* would feel very miserable in his situation, but do we know whether *he*, with his unique qualities, strengths, [and] predispositions, feels equally miserable? At other times, we think much of and depend much on the individual differences of human beings. Why then do we forget our own basic principle here? Do we even have a universal law for the assessment of happiness? Where is it to be found?

Where does the universal tendency in human beings come from, [the tendency] to measure the individual direction of others so readily according to one's own, to design plans for others so readily [232] that have no other mistake than [the fact] that they are merely suitable *for oneself*? The fearful [person] sketches for the brave [one] and the brave for the timid the way he would indeed walk himself. But woe betide the poor man who listens to such good advice! He will never occupy his station, he will constantly need a guardian, because he was immature[56] one single time. "That's what I would do, too, if I were Parmenio," said Alexander.[57] And in this moment, he was more philosopher than maybe throughout the whole remainder of his life. Be everything for yourself or you are nothing. Recognize in this tendency the sensible deformation of a basic tendency of our spiritual nature to bring about congruence in the types of action of rational beings as such.

But let us assume you could demonstrate what you would never [actually be able to] demonstrate, that he necessarily makes himself unhappy through his actions. You feel carried away by your generous hearts to hold him back on the brink of the abyss—do you not want to be patient at least until you have consulted among yourselves regarding *the legitimacy of your actions?*

---

55. *gewaltsame Mittel*

56. *unmündig*: In German, *un-mündig* is semantically related to *Vor-mund* (guardian). If you are not *mündig*, meaning you cannot speak for yourself, someone else will be your *Vor-mund* and speak for you. Cf. Kant's famous opening to his 1784 essay *What Is Enlightenment?*: "Enlightenment is man's emergence from his self-imposed immaturity [*Unmündigkeit*]." *Perpetual Peace and Other Essays*, trans. Ted Humphrey (Indianapolis: Hackett, 1983), 41.

57. Parmenio (d. 330 BC) was Alexander's (356–323 BC, King of Macedonia) field commander. On the event referenced here, compare Plutarch's *Parallel Lives*, ch. 29.

He shows a permission from the agreed law, which unites you and him. If this law is truly your commonly agreed upon [one], the permission he presents constitutes a *prohibition* for you. The law wills that he should be under no other law but it[self]. In the present case, it is silent, and consequently [it] releases him from all legality. And you want to impose a new law on him by means of your coercion? In that case *you* take back a permission that the law granted; then *you* want to tie him, whom the law wants free; then *you* are disobedient to the law; then *you* place your chair above the chair of the divinity, for even divinity makes no free being happy against its will. No, rational creature, you may not make anyone happy against his right because that is unjust.

O holy right, when will we recognize you for what you are, for a seal of divinity on our forehead, and prostrate [ourselves] before you and worship? When will you cover us, like a heavenly aegis, amidst the battle of all sensibility whose interest is sworn against us, and turn all our opponents into stone at the mere sight of you?[58] When will the armies rise and fall before the mere idea of you and the weapons slip from the strong man's grasp before the radiance of your majesty?

IV.

[233] In this introduction, dedicated to preliminary remarks, one may grant the following its place, too. It actually does not pertain to the basic principles of assessment, but to the right of a public assessment itself.

Regarding free political examinations, drivel is raised again these days, like the drivel of the past regarding religious ones, about *exoteric* and *esoteric* truths, i.e.—because you, uneducated public, are not supposed to understand it, they will perhaps be wary of saying it in German—about truths that everyone may know precisely because not much consolation follows from it and about other truths that—unfortunately!—are equally true, but which nobody should know that they are true. See, dear public, that's how your favorites stack the deck against you, and with childish unselfconsciousness, you are glad about the bread crumbs that they let you have from their lavishly spread table. Do not trust them. That which

---

58. The aegis was a shield wielded by Zeus, Athena, and Apollo, and bears the image of the Gorgon (or Medusa's head), a creature that could turn heroes to stone.

you take such warm delight in is only the exoteric. You should see the esoteric first, but that is not for you. "The thrones of princes will and must stand forever," they say. In fact, they think, "every administrator of the laws is called a prince." "Only a governed[59] people can be free," they say. In fact, they think, "governed by self-given laws."

That is another one of your old vices, cowardly souls, that you whisper into our ear with a secretive expression what you have detected. "But, but," you add, making a prudent face, "[make sure] that it does not get out, Mrs. Godmother."[60] That is not manly. What a man says, everyone may hear.

"But great harm would come about if everyone knew it." If you are not equipped to care for the well-being of the world, let this be your last concern. The truth is not exclusively the inheritance of the schools. It is a common good of humanity given to it by its common father as the most delightful endowment, as the most intimate means for uniting spirits with spirits. Everyone has the right to find it [the truth], and to relish and use it according to his receptivity to it. You may not impede him therein, because that is wrong. You may not deceive him, may not trick him, even if it was with the most benevolent intentions. You do not know what is beneficial for him. But you do know that you should absolutely never lie, absolutely never speak against your convictions. Indeed, we cannot coerce you [234] either to tell him the truth. You can keep your conviction entirely to yourself. We have neither a means nor a right to press it out of your soul.—But I want to tell it to him. Are you looking [at me] contemptuously because I am this gracious? Do I not have the right to do with mine what I want? Can you prevent it without injustice? Without injustice against me, although you contest my free use of my property, thus a human right? Without injustice against the other, although you would rob him of a freely offered means for the achievement of a higher spiritual culture? What[ever] may ensue from my message is not your concern. Your concern is only not to be unjust.

---

59. beherrschte

60. *Frau Gevatterin*: *Gevatterin* means "godmother," yet *Frau Gevatterin* appears to make specific reference to a character in a German fable. Frau Gevatterin is a good-hearted, yet naive she-wolf, who is deceived by a fox. Originating in the German oral tradition, the fable was included in the Grimms' collection of fables and fairy tales under the the the title "Der Fuchs und die Frau Gevatterin" (Gossip Wolf and the Fox).

But should so much dreadfulness truly ensue from it, or is it only your heated fantasy that sees giants in windmills?—Should the universal spread of truth, which elevates and refines our spirit, which instructs us about our rights and duties, which teaches us to find the best ways for how we can claim the former and make the fulfillment of the latter quite fruitful for the human species, have detrimental consequences? Maybe for those who want to maintain us forever in animality so that they can forever place a yoke on us and slaughter us in due course? And which [consequences does it] even [have] for them other than that they would maybe have to pick up a different trade? Do you fear this as a misery? Now, indeed, regarding this we do not agree with you. We do not fear this misery. Oh, may the clearest, most invigorating knowledge of truth spread among all human beings. May all falsities and prejudices be exterminated from the terrestrial globe. Then heaven would already be on earth.

A half knowledge, [those] isolated principles without overview of the whole that are only swimming on the surface of memory and that the mouth chats away without reason taking the slightest note of it—[those] could maybe cause harm, but this is not knowledge to begin with. We actually do not understand the sense of a principle that we have not developed from its basic principles and the consequences of which we have not surveyed.—But no, these do not cause harm either. They are like a dead chapter in the soul, without all influence. It is the passions that grab them [the isolated principles] under a euphemistic pretense; the passions that would find another pretense, if they did not have this one, or would remain the same without any pretense, if they found none at all.

Thus, have we done you injustice? If you knew something thoroughly but you had overlooked its consequences, you would [nevertheless] know that they, [235] like any truth's consequences, can be nothing but beneficial. At most you can have torn off a rag here and there in flying by, the foreign appearance of which frightened you so much that you instantly folded it like a holy relic before profane eyes. Thus, henceforth we will be less covetous of your esoteric truths. I assume [that] you give us in all faithfulness what you have and [that] the locked closets are only locked so that we do not see that they are empty.

See, benefactress, truth that invigorates humanity, this is how they treat you, those who call themselves your priests. Because they have never seen you, they defame you shamelessly. To them you are a misanthropic demon. They have carved a wooden image that they pray to instead of you. Only from that part from which Moses beheld his divinity do they show it to the people on high holy days, and pretend that anyone who touches their Ark of the Covenant must die. Oh, put an end to this trickery already. You yourself appear in our midst in your mild luster so that all peoples worship you.

Chapter One

Does a People Actually Have
the Right to Change Its Constitution?

Since Rousseau, it has been said again and again that *through time* all civil societies[1] have been based on a contract, a recent teacher of natural right maintains.[2] Yet, I desire to know against what giant [claim] this lance has been brandished. At the very least, Rousseau does not say this,* and if someone has said it since Rousseau, [236] this someone said something about which it is not worth the effort to rant. One can certainly tell by looking at our constitutions and all constitutions that history knows up to now that their formation was not the work of cool,

---

*One has to have made a very cursory foray into his *Social Contract*, or know it only from the citations of others, to find this in it. [In] book 1, chapter 1, he announces his topic like this: "*Comment* ce changement s'est il fait? Je l'ignore. Qu'est ce, qui peut le render *legitime*? Je crois pouvoir resoudre *cette* question."[3]—And, accordingly, he searches throughout the entire book for *right*, not for facts.—"But he always *talks* about the progress of humanity."—And what about it? Does that mislead the gentlemen? Perhaps you too narrate, "It happened that . . ." without always saying in advance, "in order to illustrate our principle by means of an example for you, weak intellects, who do not grasp this," thereby assuming it happened, as long as you do not lack the spiritual vitality for it.

1. *bürgerliche Gesellschaften*

2. *Naturrechtslehrer*

3. "How did this change come about? I do not know. What can make it legitimite? I do believe I can resolve that issue." Jean-Jacques Rousseau, *The Social Contract*, in *The Major Political Writings of Jean-Jacques Rousseau*, trans. John T. Scott (Chicago: University of Chicago Press, 2012), 163–64.

calculating deliberation, but the roll of fate or of forced oppression. They are all based on the *right of the stronger*, if it is permitted to repeat a blasphemy in order to make it hated.

However, it can be explained plausibly [and] without effort even to the weakest mind that a civil society can be *legitimately* based on nothing other than a contract among its members, and that every state proceeds absolutely unjustly and sins against the first right of humanity—the right of humanity *itself*—when it does not at the very least seek thereafter the consent of every single member to everything that ought to be legal in it.

For if the human being, as a rational being, stands plainly and exclusively under the moral law, he may stand under no other [law], and no being may dare to impose another [law] on him. Where his law liberates him, there he is entirely free. Where it grants him permission, it refers him to his arbitrary will[4] and in this case forbids him to acknowledge any other law but his arbitrary will. Yet precisely because he has been referred to his arbitrary will as the only ground for deciding his behavior regarding that which is permitted, he may also forbear that which is permitted. If it is important to another being that he forbears, the being may ask him to do so and he [in turn] has the absolute right to freely abstain from his strict right at the request. Yet he may not let himself be coerced.—He may freely *give* the execution of his right to the other.

He may also arrange an exchange of rights with him [the other being]. As it were, he may [even] *sell* his right.—You demand that I do not exercise some of my rights [237] because the exercise of them is disadvantageous to you. Well then, you have rights, too, the exercise of which is disadvantageous to me: you relinquish yours, and I relinquish mine.

Now in this contract, who imposes the law on me? Evidently, I myself. No human being can be bound, but by himself; no human being can be given a law, but by himself. If he allows a law to be imposed on him by a foreign will, he relinquishes his humanity and makes himself an animal. And that he may not.

In natural right,[5] we once used to believe—I may remind in passing—that we had to return to human beings' primordial state of nature. But, recently, we rant about this approach and find in it the origin of who knows what inconsistencies. And yet this way is the only right one: in order to discover the foundation of the binding character of all

---

4. *Willkühr*

5. *Naturrecht*

contracts, one has to conceive the human being as not yet bound by any external contracts, standing merely under the law of his nature, i.e., under the moral law. And that is the *state of nature.*—"But such a state of nature cannot be found in the real world, nor could it ever have been found."—Even if this were true, who tells you to search for our ideas in the real world, anyways? Do you have to see everything [with your own eyes]? It is regrettable, however, that it is not there! It *should* be there. Indeed, even our more sharp-witted teachers of natural right[6] believe that every human being is already obliged to the state from birth by virtue of the services that have already been provided and is [therefore] bound to it. Regrettably, we have always carried this principle out in practice before it had been established in theory. The state has asked no one among us for his consent, but it should have done so. And, until this request, we would have been in the state of nature, i.e., limited by no contract, we would have stood merely under the moral law. However, [more] about this when we will come along this way again!

Thus, a positive law becomes binding on us only as a result of us imposing it on ourselves. Our will, our decision, which is taken to be permanent, is the lawgiver and no one else. Another [lawgiver] is not possible. No foreign will is a law for us, even that of the divinity, if it could be different from the law of reason.

Yet, the Geheime Kanzleisekretär, Herr Rehberg,[7] makes an important discovery on this point. Namely, [he argues that] the *volonté générale* of Rousseau arises from a confusion with the moral nature of the human being, by virtue of which he [the human being] is not, nor could be, subject to any other law but that of practical reason.[8] [238]—I do not want to get into what Rousseau supposedly said or thought here. I only want to examine a little what Herr R. should have said. According to him, the legislation of practical reason[9] is not sufficient for the foundation of a state. The civil legislation[10] goes a step further, having to do with things that the former leaves to the arbitrary will.[11]—I think so, too, and

---

6. *Naturrechtslehrer*

7. August Wilhelm Rehberg, 1757–1836, had been Geheimer Kanzleisekretär (Secret Secretary of the Chancellery) in Hanover since 1786.

8. Rehberg, *Untersuchungen*, 1:8ff.

9. *Gesetzgebung der praktischen Vernunft*

10. *Bürgerliche Gesetzgebung*

11. *Willkür*

believe that Herr R. could have expanded this principle even further and actually have said: the moral law of reason is not the business of civil legislation. The former is absolutely complete without the latter, and the latter does something superfluous and harmful if it attempts to give the former a new sanction. The realm of civil legislation is that realm that has been left open by reason. The object of its discretion[12] are the *alienable rights of human beings*. Insofar Herr R. is right, and he may forgive us for having translated his opinion into somewhat more specific expressions, since he himself detests everything that is vague in others. But now he reasons that since this legislation is based on something inherently arbitrary[13] . . . Actually, I cannot even follow his reasoning clearly. But I ask this: Regardless what these laws pertain to, *whence arises their binding character after all?*—I do not know what kind of aversion Herr R. may have against the word "contract." He twists through entire pages to avoid it until finally, on p. 50,† he has to concede after all that *to a certain extent* civil society is to be viewed as a voluntary association.[14] I admit that I do not love the [expression] "to a certain extent" and its entire family. If you know something thoroughly and want to talk to us about it, speak specifically and draw a sharp boundary instead of your "to a certain extent." If you know nothing or do not dare to talk, leave it altogether. Don't do things by halves.—Thus, our question was where does the *binding character* of civil laws come from? I answer: from the voluntary adoption of them by the individual. And the right to acknowledge no law but that which one has given oneself is the basis of Rousseau's indivisible, inalienable *souveraineté*; [i.e., sovereignty is] not based on our rational nature itself but on the first postulate of our nature's law, [239] to be our *only* law. Neither acknowledging this right nor displaying its lack of grounding on primordial basic principles of pure reasons, Herr R. instead tells us plenty of things that we want to listen to another time. We asked him, "Stranger, *where* are you from?" and he told us a couple of fairytales about *who* he is in order that meanwhile we forget the uncomfortable question.

---

†Of his examination of the French Revolution.

12. *Verfügung*

13. *an sich Willkührliches*

14. Rehberg, *Untersuchungen*, 1:50: "The civil society in its origin can perhaps to a certain extent be viewed as a voluntary association among its equal members."

In order to let the public judge what is promised by the thoroughness of an author who impresses with his biting tone and does not cease to complain about vapid, shallow, unbearable prattle, I run through the first passage that I come across. [On] p. 45 he says: "Assuming a certain number of people, who lived independently next to one another, unites to collectively provide internal order among themselves and defense against external enemies."—Here he actually concedes a social contract not only to a certain extent, but completely. "One of the neighbors rejects the proposed union. Afterwards he nevertheless finds it beneficial to join the others. Yet, henceforth, he has no right to demand it."—To demand *what*? To join the others? It is his job to offer. Does he have no right to demand of himself that he go there and ask the society to be admitted into it? It is an author who otherwise has shown himself to be the master of his language, who indulges in such carelessness here.—He wants to say, "to demand the *admittance*." I ask, Did he actually have this right before? Did he have a legal entitlement to the society before the entire contract? Thus, one writes ambiguously—should I say due to ignorance or with deliberation?—in order to let a false principle slip through, turning this principle into a conclusion that would remain false even if its antecedent principle were correct. Rehberg continues: "now he has to put up with particularly structured conditions that will maybe be harder on him than the others." Are these particularly structured conditions harder on him than (these precise ones?) on the others? I thought the others did not stand under the same conditions; [rather I thought] they stood under other conditions that would be gentler *in themselves* and not (only relatively) gentler since they are harder on him. So much on the carelessness of the expression. Now about the matter itself! Why would he *have to*? And why *now*? If he had to now, he would also have had to before, in case it pleased the society to impose harder conditions on him. Were they perhaps not allowed to do so?—But he must neither now nor before. If he finds the conditions too hard, he has the complete right to refrain from joining the society. [240] He and the society are [like] two tradesmen who each estimate [the price of] their goods as high as they hope to get rid of them. Lucky for he who gains something in this trade. Who should have fixed the market price anyway?—The question is only whether there are rights that are in themselves inalienable, the alienation of which would make every contract unlawful and invalid. Herr R. will not be able to find an answer to this question in any of his examples. He will have to entangle himself into speculations with us or be silent.

I will have to come back more frequently to this author, who misunderstands the point of contention and the tribunal; who consistently reasons from that which *happens* to that which *ought to happen*; who again confuses everything that Rousseau and his successors have set apart and I set apart here; who seeks the origin of property in society;[15] and who binds us to the state from our birth, entirely without our cooperation.[16]

Now, if the binding character of social contracts arises only from the will of the parties to the contract, and if this will can change, it is clear that the question whether they can change their contract is completely identical to the question whether they could enter a contract at all. Every change to the first contract is a new contract, wherein the old is canceled[17] to such or such an extent or entirely, and, in turn, confirmed to such or such an extent. Changes and confirmations obtain their binding character from the consent of the parties to the second contract. Reasonably, such a question should therefore not arise to begin with.—It follows immediately from the above that all contracting parties have to be in agreement and no one could be coerced into membership. For otherwise a law would be imposed on him by something other than his will.

"But what if it were a condition of the contract that it be valid eternally and unchangeable?" I do not want to get into the question here whether such an eternally valid contract, which even the agreement of both parties could not revoke, would actually be contradictory. In order to make the examination more fruitful, plausible, and entertaining, I simply apply it to the present case and pose the question in this manner: Would an immutable constitution not somehow be contradictory and impossible? In particular, here, where the entire examination is guided by moral basic principles, one can only speak of moral contradiction [and] moral impossibilities. Thus, the question actually reads like this: Does the immutability [241] of any one constitution not somehow conflict with the purpose of humanity[18] established by the moral law?

Nothing in the sensible world, none of our activities, doings, and suffering, viewed as appearance,[19] has worth unless it affects culture. Pleasure in itself has no worth at all. At most, it obtains [worth] as a means for reviving and renewing our forces for culture.

---

15. Rehberg, *Untersuchungen*, 1:13–14.

16. Rehberg, *Untersuchungen*, 1:50–51.

17. *aufgehoben*

18. *Bestimmung der Menschheit*

19. *Erscheinung*

Culture is the exercise of all forces to the end of complete freedom, the complete independence from everything that is not we ourselves, our pure self. I [will] make myself clearer about this.

If our true final end[20] is established for us by, and in the form of, our pure self,‡ by the moral law in us, then everything in us that does not belong to this pure form, or everything that turns us into sensible beings, is not itself an end but merely a means to our higher spiritual ends. That is, it [everything in us that does not belong to pure form] should never determine us, but rather [it] should always be determined by the higher [element] in us, by reason. It should never be active, except at the behest of reason, and [should] not be active in any manner but according to the norm that the latter prescribes for it. We can say about sensibility what the savage in Marmontel says about danger in his death song:[21] "As soon as we were born, it [sensibility and danger] challenged us to a long, terrible duel over freedom or slavery. If you overcome [me], it said to us, I will be your slave. I will possibly be a very useful servant for you, but I always remain an unwilling servant, and as soon as you lift my yoke, I will rebel against my master and vanquisher. However, if I overcome you, I will insult you and dishonor you and trample you under foot. Since you [242] can be of no use to me, I will seek to destroy you entirely, according to the right of the conqueror."

Now, in this battle two things must happen to sensibility. In the first place, it should be tamed and subjugated; it should no longer command but serve; it should no longer arrogate to itself [the right] to dictate our ends or to condition them. This is the first action in the liberation of our I: the *taming* of sensibility.—But that is by far not everything that ought to happen. Not only should sensibility not be a commander, [but] it should also be a servant and, in particular, a skillful, suitable servant. It should be useful. This entails that one should find all its forces, form[22] them in all manners, and elevate and strengthen

---

‡The reader has to have brought these expressions to his mind in the introduction, or he does not understand this chapter and none of the following, and that by his own fault.

20. *Letzter Endzweck*

21. Jean François Marmontel, *Les Incas, ou la destruction de l'empire du Pérou; par M. Marmontel, Historiographe de France, l'un des Quarante de l'Académie Françoise* (Paris, 1777), 1:226.

22. *bilden*

[them] into the infinite. This is the second action in the liberation of our I: the *culture* of sensibility.

Two remarks here! First, when I speak of sensibility here, I do not merely understand what one perhaps usually denotes with the term, [i.e.,] the baser forces of temper, or even the mere bodily forces of human beings. [Rather,] in contrast to the pure I, everything belongs to sensibility that is not this pure I itself, i.e., all our forces of body and temper insofar as they can be determined by something external to us. Everything that is cultivatable, that can be practiced and strengthened, is included. It is the pure form of our I that is not capable of any cultivation. It is completely immutable. According to this sense of the word, cultivation of the spirit[23] or heart by means of the purest thinking or by means of the most sublime representations from religion therefore belongs to the cultivation of sensibility, of the sensible being in us, no less than, for instance, the training of the feet through dance.

Second, the suggested exercise and elevation of the sensible forces may perhaps lead someone to believe that the power of sensibility itself is thereby multiplied and [that] it is equipped with new weapons against reason. But that is not [the case]. Lawlessness is the primordial character of sensibility. In it alone lies its strength; [thus,] as this tool is wrested from it, it becomes increasingly powerless.—At least, all the cultivation described above takes place according to rules, if not according to laws. [It takes place] toward certain ends [and,] consequently, at least lawfully. By means of cultivation, the uniform of reason is put on sensibility. The weapons that the latter offers are harmless for [reason] itself and it is invulnerable against them.

Now, by means of the highest execution of both these rights of the vanquisher over sensibility, the human being would become *free*, i.e., dependent merely on himself, on his pure I. Every "I will" in his chest would have to correspond to a "there it is" [243] in the world of appearances. Without the exercise of the former [the execution of rights to vanquish sensibility], he could not even *will*. His actions would be determined by drives[24] external to him, as they affect his sensibility. He would be an instrument that is played in unison with the large concert of the material world and that always sounds the note which blind fate plays on him. After exercising the first right, he would be able to will independently, but, without asserting the second, his will would be *impo-*

---

23. *Bildung des Geistes*
24. *Antriebe*

tent. He would will, and that would be all. He would be a commander, but without servants; a king, but without subjects. He would still stand under the iron scepter of fate, would still be shackled to its chains, and his willing would be an impotent rattling of the chains. The first action of the vanquisher secures us the *willing*; the second—acquiring our force and turning it into a defense—secures us the *capability*.

Now, this culture for the sake of freedom is the only possible final end of the human being *insofar as he is part of the material world*. This highest sensible final end—which is however not the final end of the human being himself but the last means for achieving his highest spiritual final end—is the complete congruence of his will with the law of reason. Everything that human beings do or achieve must lend itself to being viewed as means to this final end in the material world. Otherwise, it is a doing without end, an irrational doing.

Sure enough, the course of the human species up to now has promoted this end.—But, I ask of you, illustrious guardians[25] of the latter, do not take this so prematurely as great praise for your wise direction. Wait a little longer before you cast me so confidently among the class of your flatterers. First, let me patiently examine [together] with you what I could reasonably want to say with this expression.—Namely, if I think about this course in hindsight and assume it could have had an end, I cannot reasonably attribute any other end to my considerations but the one being developed now, because it is the only possible one. Thereby, regarding the course's direction, I do not at all say that you or any being has determinately thought this end, but only that I determinately think this end for a possible assessment of its purposiveness.[26]—I wonder, "*If* this course had really been led by a rational being and the concept of this end had been the basis of its direction, would he then have chosen the most suitable means for achieving this end?" I do not say *that* it [244] has been like this. How would I know?—And now, what will I find in this assessment?

To begin with: nobody *is* cultivated, but everyone has *to cultivate himself*. All behavior that merely suffers is the exact opposite of culture. Cultivation takes place through independent activity[27] and aims at independent activity. Therefore, no cultural plan can be set up in

---

25. *Vormünder*: See footnote 56 in introduction. In the next several pages, Fichte conducts a dialogue with these *Vormünder*, referring to them as "you."

26. *Zwecksmässigkeit*

27. *Selbsttätigkeit*

such a manner that its achievement would be necessary. [Rather,] it [culture] affects freedom and depends on the use of freedom. Thus, the question reads like this: Have there been objects available upon which free beings could exercise their independent activity for the sake of culture's final end?

And what in the entire world of experience could be found that beings who want to be active could not practice their activity on it? Thus, this demand is easily met, since it is not intrusive. Who[ever] wants to cultivate himself, [may] cultivate himself on anything.—War, they say, cultivates. And it is true, it elevates our souls to heroic sensations and deeds, to contempt for danger and death, to disdain for goods that are daily exposed to robbery, [and] to more heartfelt compassion for everything that bears a human face, since shared danger or suffering draws them closer to us. But don't you dare take this as a praise for your bloodthirsty war addiction [or] as a submissive plea for the groaning humanity to continuously pit them against one another in bloody wars. War only elevates those souls to heroism who already have force in themselves, [while] it excites the base to robbery and oppression of the vulnerable and weak. It produces [both] heroes and cowardly thieves. And which probably in larger quantities?—If you were only judged according to this basic principle [that war cultivates], you would remain white, like snow,[28] even if you were as irritating as your age's lack of nerves allows. The harshest despotism cultivates. The slave hears the expression of irreversible doom in his despot's death sentence and honors himself more by the free submission of his will to the iron fate than anything in nature can do to dishonor him. This fate, which raises the slave from the dust and places him by the steps of the throne today yet hurls him back into his nothingness tomorrow, leaves nothing on the human being but the human being [itself] and grants the more noble Saracen and Turk that mild gentleness that breathes from their novels, as well as that sacrifice for foreigners and sufferers that governs their actions. [It is] precisely this fate that makes the baser Japanese into a resolute criminal, because their blamelessness[29] does not protect him.—Thus, you may even become despots. If only we wanted, we could refine ourselves even in the noose of your silky rope.

[245] Means toward [achieving] culture always exist.—And now the second question arises: Have they actually been used? Can the progress

---

28. That is, guiltless.

29. *Unsträflichkeit*

of the human race toward perfect freedom be demonstrated in its course so far?—Do not be afraid of this examination. We do not judge based on success, as you [do]. If no perceptible progress shows itself, you may say boldly: "this is your fault, you have not used the available means"— and we will have nothing thorough to reply to it and, since we are not sophists, [we will] reply with nothing at all.

But such progress does in fact show itself, and we should not expect anything different from human nature, which by all means cannot stand still. Ever since we could examine its course, the sensible forces of humanity have indeed been cultivated and strengthened in manifold ways. Should we now thank you for this, or who do we owe it to?

Have the possibility and the ease of our cultivation really been your final end in founding and governing your states? I inspect your own explanations about this, and, as far as I can go back, I hear you talk about the assertion of *your* rights and *your* honor and about the payback of *your* insults. Here it almost seems as if your plan was not aimed at *us* at all, as if it was aimed only at *you*, and as if we were included in the plan only as instruments for *your* ends. Or, when a rare magnanimity takes possession of your mouth, you talk a great deal about the well-being of your faithful subjects. Forgive us, if your magnanimity becomes a little suspicious to us whenever you pursue an end for us, namely, [the end of] sensible pleasure that we ourselves have given up entirely.

Yet, maybe you just do not know how to express yourself. Maybe your actions are better than your words. Therefore, I trace the best possible route through the inventive labyrinth of your crooked passages, through the deep, mysterious night that you spread over them, for a unity among the maxims of your actions, which I could attribute to them as the end. I search before God, conscientiously, and find: *absolute rule of your will inside*, and *expansion of your borders externally*. I apply the first end as a means to our highest final end, culture toward freedom, and I admit not to comprehend how it could elevate our independent activity if no one is acting independently but you; how it could be aimed at the liberation of our will, if no one in your entire country may have a will but you; how it may serve the production of pure selfhood, [246] if you are the only soul that sets millions of bodies into motion. I compare the second end with the final end, and, again, I am not discerning enough to see what it could offer our culture, [regardless of] whether your will puts itself in the place of a few thousand more or not. Do you think that it will greatly increase the concept of our worth, if our occupant possesses quite many herds?

Yet, indeed, nobody can understand all this, unless one is lucky enough to be inducted into the deep secrets of your politics,§ especially into its abyss, the secret of the balance [of power] of Europe. You want your will to be the sole ruler[30] in your states in order that, in case of danger to this balance, you can suddenly mobilize all their force against them. You want your state to be as powerful on the inside, as expansive on the outside as possible so that you have quite a large force to oppose this danger. The preservation of this balance is your ultimate final end,[31] and the former two ends are means for the achievement of the latter.

Thus, your true *ultimate* final end would be this? Allow me to doubt this for another moment. From whom does this balance have to fear so much evil, other than from the likes of you? Thus, after all, there must actually exist some among them who seek to disturb it. What then is the true final end of these malcontents? Without doubt precisely what you pass off as a means to your highest end goal—the most unlimited and extensive sole rule.

It must be possible to determine approximately how much power, which politics assigns to preserve this balance, each state must have if the scales should be kept in balance. If you are really concerned with nothing but the balance and you are being honest, you will find your precise boundary here. March up to this boundary and let the other march up to it in peace as well.—But the other has crossed this boundary. Now you have to cross it as well so that the broken balance may be restored?—If the scale [247] was leveled before, you would not have needed to let the other cross the boundary. You should have prevented it. You are suspected only to have permitted it in order that you would find a pretense to cross yours, because you secretly flatter yourself in the hope of besting him in this endeavor and to make a few steps further than he, in order that you, too, could disturb the balance in turn. In our times, one has seen unions of great powers that divided countries among

---

§A secret shiver runs through the above mentioned author especially when someone says that it only requires common sense in order to comprehend what has been so difficult for him until now. I concede to him that I am of the same opinion.—"But, the taste for thoroughness is running out; one will become superficial, whenever one says it out loud!"—Herr R. may let his opponents worry about this!

30. *alleinherrschend*
31. *Letzter Endzweck*

themselves in order to maintain the balance. This would have happened all the same if none of them had taken anything. Why then did they choose the former means in preference to the latter?—It may indeed be true that you are content with upholding this balance as long as you do not have enough force to become what you would rather be: disturber of the latter; and that you are content with preventing others from cancelling[32] the balance so that you can cancel it yourself one day. But it is a truth confirmed by a priori grounds and by the entire history: *the tendency of all monarchies is the unlimited sole rule internally and the universal monarchy externally.* Through claims about the threatened balance, our politicians very naively admit this themselves, presupposing about the other with certainty what they themselves are surely aware of. A minister has to laugh when he hears the other earnestly speak about this balance. They both have to laugh when we, with not an inch of land nor pension to gain, naively insert ourselves into their important examinations. Notably, if none of the new monarchies has approached the achievement of its end, they lacked indeed not in *willing*, but in *capability*.

But, assuming that this balance was really your final end goal, which demonstrably it is not, it does not therefore have to be ours. We will at least have to apply this goal to our final end as a means. We may at least ask: "Why should the balance be maintained at all?"

As soon as it [the balance] is upset, you say, a horrible war of one against all will break out and one will devour all.—In other words, for our sake, you fear greatly this one war, which would, once all peoples were united under the one head, [actually] bring about eternal peace? You fear this one, and in order to safeguard us against it, you entangle us in incessant [other wars]?—You fear our subjugation by a foreign power, and, in order to save us from this misfortune, you instead subjugate us yourselves? [248] Oh, do not lend us your manner of looking at things quite so confidently. That you prefer it when you are the ones who subjugate us rather than someone else is [easy] to believe. [But] why we should greatly prefer it, we don't know. You have a fond love for our freedom; you want it all to yourself.—The complete abolition of the balance [of powers] in Europe could never become as detrimental for the people[33] as the disastrous claim of it has been.

---

32. *aufheben*

33. *Völker*

But how and under what conditions is it necessary that this war, this universal conquest, follows from the abolition of the acclaimed balance? Who will mount it? One of the peoples, who are quite tired of your wars and would have liked to form[34] [itself] in peace and quiet already? Do you believe that the German artist and farmer cares very much whether the Lothringian or Alsatian artist and farmer henceforth finds his city and his village in the geography textbook's chapter on the German empire? Will he throw away etching needle and farming equipment in order to move them there [into the empire]? No. The monarch, who will be the most powerful after the abolition[35] of the balance [of powers], will mount this war. Thus, look at how you argue and how we argue against it.—In order that no *single* monarchy devours and subjugates everything, you say, several monarchies must exist that are strong enough to provide each other's counterweight, and, in order that they should be strong enough, each monarch must seek to ensure his sole rule internally and to expand his external borders from time to time.—In contrast, we argue like this: this constant striving after enlargement internally and externally is a great misfortune for the peoples.[36] If it is true that they must endure it in order to evade a disproportionately greater [misfortune], let us seek out the source of that greater misfortune and derive it, if it is possible. We find it in the unlimited, monarchical constitution. Every unlimited monarchy (you say it yourself) strives incessantly after universal monarchy. Let us clog this source, and our evil is removed at the foundation. When no one will want to attack us anymore, then we will no longer need to be armed. Then the horrible wars and the even more horrible constant readiness for war that we have to endure in order to prevent war will no longer be necessary. Then it will [also] no longer be necessary for you to work toward the sole rule of your will.—You say: since there ought to be unlimited monarchies, the human race ought to put up with a tremendous amount of miseries. We answer: since the human race does not want to put up with this tremendous amount of miseries, [249] there should be no unlimited monarchies. I know that you support your conclusions with standing armies, with heavy ordnances, with chains and punishments in fortresses, but they do not therefore seem to me to be the sturdier[37] ones.

---

34. *gebildet*

35. *Aufhebung*

36. *Völker*

37. *gründlicheren*

Honor to whom honor is due. Justice to everyone! The grinding of the complex wheelwork of this artificial, political machine of Europe has always kept the activities of the human race in suspense. It was an eternal war between quarreling forces on the inside and the outside. Inside, by means of the wonderful artifice[38] that is the subordination of the estates, the sovereign pressed on [the estate] that was nearest to him. This, in turn, [pressed] on that which was next beneath it, and like this all the way down to the slave who cultivates the field. Each of these forces resisted the impact and pressed upward in turn, and, in this way, this peculiar artifice, which sins against nature in its composition, maintained itself by means of the complex play of the machine and the elasticity of the human spirit. And, even though it originated from a single point, [it] brought forth the most diverse products—in Germany a federal republic, in France an unlimited monarchy. On the outside, where no subordination took place, action and reaction were determined and maintained by the constant tendency toward universal monarchy, which, even though it was not always consciously thought, was nonetheless the final goal of all endeavors. In the political ranks, it annihilated a Sweden, weakened an Austria and a Spain, and raised a Russia and Prussia out of nothing. Regarding moral phenomena, it gave humanity a new mainspring for heroic deeds: national pride without a nation. The contemplation of this complex play can offer a rousing mental celebration for the thinking observer, but it cannot satisfy and teach the wise man about that of which he is in need.

Thus, if we had gained in culture toward freedom not only *under* your political constitutions but also *by means of* them, we would not have had to thank you for it, since it was not your end and was indeed against it. It was your aim to annihilate all free will in humanity besides yours. We fought with you over this, and if we grew stronger throughout this fight, certainly no service was thereby done by you.—It is true—so full justice may be done to you—that you have, in fact, cultivated some of our forces purposely, yet not in order that we should become more useful for our ends but for yours. You dealt with us just as we should have dealt with ourselves. [250] You subjugated our sensibility and forced it to acknowledge a law. After you had subjugated it, you cultivated it in usefulness for all kinds of ends. So far, everything was well, and if you had stopped here, you would have become true guardians of an immature

---

38. *Kunststück*

humanity. But then your reason and not ours, your "I will" and not ours, was to become the supreme master who determines the ends for this tamed and cultivated sensibility. You had us taught in various sciences, the form and content of which were already furnished according to your intentions, in order that we should become more easily directed toward them [the intentions]. You had us learn various arts in order that we could relieve your boredom and that of those around you, or in order that we could provide the instruments of oppression in your hands, where your hands themselves could not reach, [namely,] the pomp with which you blind the mob's eyes. Finally, you educated millions—and this is the masterpiece that you are proudest of—in the art of swaying right and left on cue, linked together like Moors, only to suddenly separate again, and in the terrible skill of choking in order to use them against all who do not want to acknowledge your will as its law. That is, as far as I know, your purposeful merit on behalf of our culture.

In contrast, you have purposely hindered our culture from another side, slowed down our steps, and thrown traps in our tracks. I do not want to remind you of the deeds of the ideal of all monarchies, that which expressed its basic principles most firmly and coherently, i.e., the papacy. That is the kind of mischief you are not culpable for. Back then, you yourself were instruments in a foreign hand, like we are now in yours. But since you are freed, how far have your principles deviated from the principles of your great master, to whom only few among you show the owed gratitude?**—"In order to squash the last seed of independent activity in the human being, in order to make him entirely passive, one may make his opinion depend on a foreign authority"—[this] was the basic principle on which this horrible universal monarchy was founded, a principle that is more true than any [principle] invented by the wit of hell, a principle by which the unlimited monarchy inevitably stands or falls. He who is not allowed to determine what he wants to believe will never dare to determine what he wants to do. Yet he who liberates his understanding will before long liberate his will as well.—This saves your honor before the judgment of posterity, immortal *Frederick*.[39] [251] It elevates you from the class of trampling monarchs and places you among the honorable rank of the peoples' educators in freedom. Your clear-eyed spirit could not pass up this natural consequence unnoticed. Even so, you

---

**Oh well! One begins to acknowledge one's duty and to fulfill it.

39. Frederick II, 1712–86, King of Prussia, 1740–86.

wanted the understanding of your peoples [to be] *free*. Therefore, you had to will your peoples themselves [to be] free, and if they had seemed mature enough for freedom to you, you would have [instead] given them that which you only cultivate them for, sometimes under harsh breeding.—But you others, what do you do?—Indeed, you proceed consistently, maybe more consistently than you know yourself. For it would not be the first time that intuition led someone more rightly than his reasoning. If you want to rule, you must first subjugate the understanding of human beings; if the latter depends on your arbitrary will, everything else will follow without effort. The unlimited monarchy cannot exist next to unlimited freedom of thought. You know this, or feel it, and develop your measures accordingly. To give you an example, a courageous man rose from the midst of spiritual slavery[40] whom you would bury in your tomb of the living if he came now and took away the right to determine our opinions from the hand of the Roman despot and transferred it to a dead book.[41] This was enough to begin with, especially since this book left great room for spiritual freedom to play.[42] The trick with the book pleased you, but not the great room for play. What was done once could not be undone, yet for the future you chose your [own] measures. You forced everyone into that space that during the revival of spirits was taken up by his [the courageous man's spirit]. You fenced him in, like a charmed ghost under its spell, with distinctions and clauses, tied his civil honor and existence to these clauses, and said: "since unfortunately you are already here now, we will perhaps let you stay, but you shall not get any further than these pillars"[43]—and now you could be more certain than ever of our spiritual slavery. Our opinions were tied to a stiff, inflexible letter. If only you could have left us the living judge of opinions! Not irritated by any contradictions, he would have followed the course of the human race to some distance, and verily we would be further today.—This was your masterpiece! As long as we do not understand that nothing is true [merely] because it is written in a book, that, instead, the book is good, holy, divine when we want it, because what is written inside is true, you will be able to hold us back with this single chain.

---

40. *Geistessklaverei*

41. The allusion is to Martin Luther.

42. *Spielraum*

43. Fichte refers here again to Wöllner's Religious Edict. See footnote 15 in introduction.

[252] You have been faithful in all regards to this principle. You have arrayed border posts in all directions the human spirit could take, and these anoint the authorized foundational truths. You sat learned fighters[44] next to them, who will push back anyone who wants to go beyond. Since you could not always rely on the invulnerability of these rented warriors, you raised a civil fence between the posts for added security and placed visitors by the little gates. You may tolerate that we tussle about inside this fence. Whenever you are in a good mood, you perhaps even throw a few pennies for show among us in order to amuse yourself at the sight of us busily catching them. But woe betide him who ventures across this fence, or who wants to acknowledge no fence at all but that of the human spirit. If one slips through once in a while, this happens because neither you nor your visitors notice anything. Otherwise everything that aims to reinstate reason in its oppressed rights, to set humanity on its own feet and let it see with its own eyes, or—to give you an example that will instantly convince you—examinations like the present one, are foolishness and horror in your eyes.

This, then, is our reckoning with you about the progress in culture that we have made under your constitutions.—I [will] skip over your influence on our immediate moral cultivation. I do not want to remind you here of the moral corruption that spreads from your thrones all around you. According to its steep increase, one can calculate the miles one has to travel to your residences.

[253] If culture toward freedom†† is really the only possible final end of the state,[45] it is now evident that all state constitutions that have

---

†† [want to] address another possible misunderstanding here that I expect only from scholars, not the unlearned public.—It must be clear from the entire course of this treatise hitherto that I distinguish three kinds of *freedom*: the *transcendental*, which is the same in all rational spirits, [i.e.,] *the capability to be an originary independent cause*; the *cosmological*, [i.e.,] *the state of being truly dependent on nothing but oneself*—no spirit except the eternal possesses this freedom, yet it is the ultimate end of the culture of all finite spirits; [and] the *political*, [i.e.,] *the right to recognize no law but that which one has given oneself*. The last [kind] *ought to* be present in all states.—I hope that the kind of freedom I am talking about will nowhere remain ambiguous.—Should someone want to confound what I have set apart—maybe confound it in order to punish me for his own mistakes—this note will be a strong lock [to constrain] him.

44. *Klopffechter* refers to a medieval professional fencer who fights for show (originally at travelling markets). By Fichte's time, the term was used mostly figuratively and often mockingly to refer to someone who engages in a fight or argument for the sake of it.

45. *Staatsverbindung*

an entirely opposite end as their final end—i.e., slavery of all and the freedom of a single individual; culture for the sake of this one individual and the prevention of all kinds of culture that would lead to the freedom of many more—are not only capable of amendment, but must actually be amended. And now we stand before the second part of the question: If a constitution was given that aims at this final end by the most certain means, would it not be absolutely unchangeable?

If truly suitable means had been chosen, humanity would be approaching its grand purpose gradually. Each of its members would become ever freer and the use of those means whose ends have [already] been achieved would fall away. One cogwheel after the other in the machine of such a constitution would grind to a halt and be removed, because the [next] wheel would begin to set itself into motion by means of its own momentum. It [the machine] would become increasingly simpler. If the final end could ever be reached completely, no constitution would be necessary at all anymore. The machine would grind to a halt because no counterpressure would act on it. The universal law of reason would unite everyone in the highest unanimity of dispositions, and no other law would have to watch over their actions any more. No norm would have to determine how much right each should sacrifice for society, because no one would demand more than what would be necessary and no one would give less. No judge would have to decide on their disputes anymore, because they would always be in agreement.

Here, the admirer of humanity cannot even throw a fleeting glance without feeling his heart permeated by a gentle fire. I cannot fill in this sketch yet, [as] I am still grinding the colors. But already I ask you, do not let yourselves be frightened by that common saying, "so many heads, so many different dispositions." Not in the least does it contradict the other saying, "humanity must and should and will have only one final end, and the different ends, which different [people] set for themselves in order to reach it, will not only agree with each other, but also alleviate and support one another." [254] Do not let this invigorating prospect be spoiled by the resentful thought that it should never come true after all. Indeed, it will never come true entirely, but it is not merely a sweet dream, not merely a deceitful hope. It certainly rests on the necessary progress of humanity. It should, it will, it must ever approach this end. Before your eyes, humanity commenced a breakthrough at one end. Under a harsh battle with doom, which summoned all its forces against [humanity], humanity has accomplished something that, at the very least, is better than your despotic constitutions, which aim at the vilification of humanity. However, I do not want to jump ahead of my subject, do not want to reap before I sow.

No constitution is unchangeable; it is in their nature that they all change. A bad one that fights against the necessary final end of all constitutions must be changed. A good one that promotes the end goal changes itself. The former is a fire in rotten stubble that smokes but gives neither light nor warmth; it must be doused. The latter is a candle that consumes itself as it gleams and would go out if the day dawned.

A clause in the social contract [stipulating] that the contract shall be unchangeable would therefore be the harshest contradiction to the spirit of humanity. [Imagine] I promise never to change or allow to be changed anything about this state's constitution. This means I promise not to be a human being nor to tolerate anyone to be a human being as much as I can. I content myself with the rank of a clever animal. I bind myself and everyone else to stop at the level of culture to which we have advanced. Just as the beaver builds today like his ancestors built a thousand years ago, just as the bee today furnishes her cells like her race did millennia ago, so we and our ancestors will after millennia also arrange our manner of thinking, our theoretical, political, and moral maxims just like we do today.—And such a promise, if it were actually given, should be valid?—No, human being, you were not allowed to promise this; you do not have the right to relinquish your humanity. Your promise is illegitimate[46] and therefore ineffective.[47]

Could humanity have forgotten itself to such an extent that it would have surrendered the only prerogative that distinguishes its animality from other animals, [i.e.,] the prerogative of perfecting into infinity? [255] That it would have relinquished forever even the will to destroy the iron yoke of the despot?—No, do not abandon us, holy palladium of humanity, [or take away] these consoling thoughts: that a new perfection and a new bliss will spring forth for our brothers from every one of our works and every one our sufferings, that we work for them and not in vain; that in the place where we are now struggling and being tread on and—even worse than that—where we gravely err and fail, a race[48] will flourish one day that will always be allowed to do what it wills, because

---

46. *rechtswidrig*

47. *rechtsunkräftig*

48. *Geschlecht*

it wills nothing but the good. Meanwhile, we rejoice in higher regions about our posterity and find among their virtues that seed, now full-grown, that we recognize as ours, having planted it in them. Inspire us, hope of this time, with the sense of our dignity and show us our dignity at least in our predispositions, even if our present condition contradicts it. Pour boldness and high enthusiasm into our endeavors, and if it were to make us feel contrite, we will be sustained by the first thought, "I did my duty," and invigorated by the second, "no seed, which I sow, will be lost in the moral world. On the day of harvest, I will behold its fruits and weave immortal wreaths from them."

Jesus and Luther, the holy protective spirits of liberty, whom, during the days of your humiliation, you brought into the shackles of mankind with gigantic force and snapped wherever you reached, look down from higher spheres onto your posterity and delight in the seed that has already born fruit. Soon the third[49] will be united with you, who perfected your work and broke humanity's last, strongest shackle without humanity and possibly even himself knowing. We will bemoan his loss. You, by contrast, will cheerfully direct him to the seat waiting for him in your company, and the age that [actually] understands him and represents him will thank you.

---

49. Immanuel Kant

Chapter Two

Sketch of the Further Course
of the Examination

[256] He who derives his principles from primordial basic principles of reason through strict deduction is, in advance, certain of their truth as well as the untruth of all objections against them. He can know that what cannot exist alongside these principles must be false without even having entertained it. Thus, if in the foregoing chapter it has been proven by means of strict deduction from such basic principles—whether it has [indeed] been proven, I leave to the decision of more astute thinkers—*if*, however, it has been proven that the people's right to change its constitution is an inalienable, permanent human right, then all objections offered against the permanence of this right are certainly deceiving and based on false appearance. If we wanted to proceed with rigor, the examination about the legitimacy of revolutions in general, and therefore of each particular revolution, would now be closed. And everyone who is of a different opinion would either have to demonstrate a mistake in our assumptions or our deduction, or have to give up his opinion as false and untrue, even if he cannot track down the false appearance on which it is based. It is not superfluous to recall and [even] inculcate this on every suitable occasion, so that our public—[and] here I do not only mean the unphilosophical—will gradually become accustomed to uniting its convictions or opinions into a system governed by firm, durable principles and will lose its taste for patching together very dissimilar rags and for disputation against straw men.[1] That which follows from a

---

1. *Konsequenzmacherei*

proven principle by means of correct conclusions is true, and you will not frighten the resolute thinker with its dangerous appearance. Whatever contradicts it must be false and must be renounced, even if the axis of the earth seemed to run through it.

For now, however, this necessary consequence is merely a pious wish, and among the general public [it] may remain so for a very long time. Therefore, given the current state of things, one would provide the public very poor service if one abandoned it after having determined the first basic principles of the judgment and assigned to the public the troubles of applying the principles and of uniting its other opinions with these principles or correcting their opinions according to them. [257] Thus, we will do what according to the strict duty of a writer we would not have to do. We will seek out all possible objections against the permanence of this right and uncover their false appearance.

A *refutation* would have to proceed from primordial principles of reason, since the proof has proceeded from them. It would have to show that culture for the sake of freedom is not the only possible final end of civil society, that it is no inalienable human right to advance in this culture into infinity, and that a constitution's immutability does not contradict this progress into infinity.

Since such a refutation has not yet been possible—because, at least as far as I know, no one has yet arranged the foregoing principles in this combination—I have to engage with none. All I had to do was to show the future critic what he would have to achieve, which critics do not always know. And I did it.—Another refutation is not possible.

Misunderstandings, however, are possible, namely, when one says: "the right of a people to change its constitution must be alienable because *it actually has been alienated*." But such an objection reveals its author's utter incompetence in judging the case at hand, for it shows clearly that he does not even know what this is about. If we had claimed that it is against the law of natural necessity to alienate this right, that it *cannot* be alienated (that the alienation is *physically* impossible), then the answer that shows us that it *can* happen by reference to the fact that it *really does happen* would have been decidedly victorious. However, since we did not claim the latter, but merely that it is against the law of morality, that it *ought* not to happen (that it is *morally* impossible), an objection taken from an entirely different world does not pertain to us. Unfortunately, some things happen in the real world that should not happen; but [the fact] that it happens does not make it right.

Even so, one insists that the right has been alienated, and so we must gradually and step-by-step divest this claim from its false appearance and show, not merely in general, that it must be false.

Such an alienation could have taken place only *by means of contract*—even *Herr Rehberg* admits this to a certain extent, where he believes that no one will notice entirely. Should someone want to be even harsher, I ask him [258] to stick to the beginning of my first chapter until I will have uncovered the very last sophistries against this principle. The right could have been alienated *to members of the state* itself or to *someone outside the state*; within the state by means of the contract of *all with all* or by means of the contract of *the commoner estates with the privileged estates, guilds,* or *one privileged person,* the *sovereign*; outside the state, *to other states,* in this case *entirely* or *in part*.

In examining this objection, we will have to answer the following two questions, the first of which is historical: Did it really take place, can such a contract be verified? The second is to be answered based on natural law: Should it have happened *in this case*, and was it allowed? Following our reminder above, the reader already knows in advance how the answers will turn out. He knows that we do not advance this examination in order to correct our basic principles, but in order to clarify them by means of application. Thus, if he hopes to find more convenient explanations for his preconceived opinions in the following chapters, we recommend him with all sincerity to throw this book away, if he has not thrown it away yet.

Chapter Three

Is the Right to Change the Constitution Alienable through the Contract of All with All?

The way from darkness to light passes through the twilight. I can lead my readers on no other path but the one nature leads. In the foregoing, I have spoken of a people's right to change its constitution and have not defined the concept of the people. What is otherwise a great mistake is not a mistake at all when it follows from the nature of things.—Whenever the largest society, the whole of humanity—or the entire realm of spirits, if we want—is seen in light of the moral law alone, it must be viewed as an individual. The law is the same, and, on its territory, there is only [259] *one* will. Several individuals exist only at that point where the moral law lets us go over into the domain of the arbitrary will.[1] In this domain, the contract rules. Several [individuals] enter into it. If the concept of the people is *still* undefined at the end of this chapter, I am wrong.

Throughout this entire chapter, I assume that all members of the state, as such, are equal and that no one has promised more in the civil contract than all [others] promised him. I do not thereby want to establish *that* it is this way or should be surreptitiously. I will talk about this in the following chapters. In the present [chapter], I merely examine what would follow from this [assumption about equality] for the mutability of the constitution, *if* it were this way.

The right to change the constitution could have been given away by means of the contract of all with all in two ways: either all had

---

1. *Willkühr*

promised all never to alter the contract at all or all promised all not to change it without every individual's consent.

Regarding the first promise, it has already been shown above in regard to its *matter* or object, the immutability of a constitution, that it is absolutely not allowed, because it is at odds with the highest final end of humanity. In view of the *form*, if all had made this promise to all, it would be their common will. The people would have made a promise to itself. Now, if later on it becomes the common will, the will of all, to alter the constitution, who would then have the right to raise an objection against it? Such a putative contract violates the formal condition of all contracts that it involve at least two moral persons. In this case there would only be one: the people. This requirement is therefore in itself impossible and contradictory, and only the second [type of promise] remains, that is to say, [the possibility] that in the civil contract the agreement was made that the constitution should not be altered without the common will, without the will of all, or that all would have promised each not to alter the constitution without his explicit consent.

It seems to be both in the nature of things and in our own principles, determined above, that such a promise would have to have been given in the civil contract and that it would have to be valid and binding. And this is true or possibly not, depending on how one takes it. However, since it is not our style to let the reader take things however he wants, we must first of all dissect the hypothesis a bit.—Such a promise actually contains in itself the following two: all would *not repeal*[2] *anything old* without the consent of every individual, and they would not force any of the [260] citizens to *accept* the *new* put in its place without his consent.

The second part of the promise, that no one should be bound by new arrangements without his consent, cannot reasonably be given through a contract at all. As has been shown above, the opposite would infringe upon the first of all human rights. He who promises me by contract not to offend against any inalienable human right inherent in me promises me nothing. He was not allowed to do that prior to any contract. The state may have promised it or not. No new arrangement binds the citizen of the old constitution without his consent, not by virtue of the contract but by virtue of human rights.

---

2. *aufheben*

The question about the first part of the promise seems, at first glance, to be easy and to be answered in the following way. I predict that most of my readers who are thinking with me will give such an answer: the institutions of the state are conditions of the civil contract, they will say. All have joined with all to fulfill these conditions. If some will repeal the conditions without the consent of the others, they unilaterally break the contract and act against the obligation that they assumed through the contract. It thus goes without saying that no institution within the state can be repealed without the consent of all.

If these conclusions were entirely true, our theory would run the great risk not quite to be pushed aside, but at least to deserve the allegation of not being applicable in life. Regardless of how precisely it has been shown that every constitution—by virtue of the progress of culture required by the moral law—must from time to time be altered and improved, when could such an improvement ever come about in the real world if every member of the state first had to give his consent to the smallest change? And what would our proof have been but the work of the schools, an example of pedantry?—But before concluding so quickly, let us first dig a little deeper into the nature of the contract than is generally done.

If no contract happens concerning natural human rights (as [indeed] it does not take place), I obtain a right over someone by means of a contract that I did not have according to the law of reason alone. In addition, he [incurs] an obligation toward me that he did not have according to this law either. What is it that places this obligation on him? His will, for nothing can bind when the [261] moral law is silent but our own will. My *right* is based on his *obligation* [and] therefore ultimately on his will, on which the latter is based. If he does not have the will, I do not get the right. A disingenuous promise does not grant a right.—One should not be frightened by the apparent harshness of these sentences. It *is* this way and, one may say, how it is. Morality, the sacredness of contracts, will know how to save itself in light of our conclusions.

I offer a promise in turn. I truly have the will to keep it, thereby imposing an obligation on myself and giving the other a right. He did not have the will and gave me no right. Did he betray me? Have I been insidiously bilked out of my right?

"According to natural right, I have no perfect right to the truthfulness of the other. If he makes me a disingenuous promise, I cannot complain of harm until he tempts me into his service," says the most sharp-witted and consistent teacher of natural right that we have had up to now.* The following should be regarded as commentary and, where necessary, as correction of these sentences.[3]

When I gave him my truthful promise, did I assume, perhaps, that he was lying, or did I instead assume that he meant it as sincerely as I did? If I had supposed that he was lying, would I have promised him earnestly? Would I have had the will to keep my promise? Thus my will was conditional. The *right* that I have given him with my *will* is conditional. If he was lying, he obtained no right, because I obtained none.—*No contract was actually entered*, because [262] *no right was granted* and *no obligation incurred*.

You tell me: even if *he* did lie, *I* myself do not want to be a liar. His faithlessness shall not cancel[4] *my* faith. I want to honestly keep what I promised.—And it is good on you to do that, but you must not confuse the concepts. You must not go over from the boundaries of the natural right to morality. In this case, you pay him no debt [since] you owed him nothing. [Instead,] you give him something. You keep your promise not because his right demands it from you—he did not have one—but because your self-respect demands it. You are not worried about becoming contemptuous of *him*. You are worried about becoming contemptuous of *yourself*.

Thus, truthfulness is the exclusive condition of every contract. If one of the two [parties] does not want to keep his word—and even more so, if neither wants to—no contract is entered.

Both are sincere in the hour of the promise. There is a contract between them. They go forth, and *one* of the *two*, or *both*, reconsider and in their hearts take back their will. The contract is repealed. The promises are undone because right and obligation are repealed.

So far, the entire affair remains within the domain of the inner tribunal. Each knows how he himself means it, but no one knows how the other means it. No being knows whether a contract really *exists* or *not* except for the one [being] that constitutes the common inner tribunal for both, the executive power of the moral law, God.

Herr Schmalz in his *pure natural right* will forgive me for paying tribute to him here. That I am working not from his basic principles but from mine, will be apparent to the adept.

3. Here Fichte refers to Theodor Anton Heinrich Schmalz, *Das reine Naturrecht* [The Pure Natural Right] (Königsberg: Friedrich Nicolovius, 1792), especially §§43, 104, 107.

4. *aufheben*

Now, one of them performs what he promised, and thereafter the business passes over into the world of appearances.—What follows from this and what does not follow? Without a doubt, he makes clear and visible through his action that he was sincere and that he believed the other to be likewise sincere, that he *believes* to be in a genuine contract with the other and to have given him a right over himself and to have received a right over the other. But does he actually *receive* this right over the other through his action? Or, if he did not have it before or only partially had it, does he merely *confirm* it? How would that be possible? If the other could still doubt the actuality of his will, then his will that the other should perform [his part of the contract] is not binding, and the will does not become more binding once its actuality is confirmed in the world of appearances. In the former and the latter cases, it is merely his will that binds. A foreign will never does. Or again—in order to close any possible loopholes—[263] does he perhaps, through the external signs of his [own] truthfulness, obtain the perfect right to the other's truthfulness? That is, does he perhaps, through his [own] performance, bind the other to *actually will* what he promised and to commit himself with *his own will*? If I never have a perfect right to the other's truthfulness, how can I obtain it through my own truthfulness? Does my morality bind the other to the same morality? I am not at all the executioner of the moral law; that's God. He has to punish falseness. I am only the executioner of my rights granted to me by the moral law, and the supervision of the other's purity of heart does not belong among these rights.

Thus, even by performing my side [of the bargain], I obtain no right to the other's performance, unless his free will, the direction of which I do not know, has granted me that right and continues to grant it.—But through the other's breach of promise, I am shortened of my service. According to such basic principles, how can anyone still dare to make a contract?—We shall go only one step further with the application of these principles and everything will be clear and the difficulty satisfactorily resolved.

I performed my service believing that the other has a right to my performance; that it was not *mine* but *his*; that my powers[5] that I used in the process, [and] the fruits of this exercise of power are the property of the other. I erred in this: they were *mine*, since the other had no right over me, because he granted me no right over himself.

---

5. *Kräfte*

Before the eyes of the supreme judge of all morality they were mine. No finite spirit could have known whose they were. [Now assume] the other does not perform his service and what was previously known only to the supreme judge now becomes clear in the world of appearances as well. As a result of his omission, my service does not *become* mine *again.* [Rather,] it was mine from the beginning and it merely becomes known that it is mine. I retain my property. The product of my performance is mine. The product of my exercise of power, too, which is a net loss, is my property. It is not my concern that it is lost, [since] it should not be lost. It is to be found in the other's powers; in those I find my share. I can compel him to a full restitution of damage. After all this, I have lost nothing through the other's breach of promise, and he gained nothing. We are both restored to the condition that existed prior to our agreement. Everything is undone and that is how it should be, for no contract existed between us.

[264] Only through his completed performance, does the other absorb my service into his property. It *was* his through my free will. Yet no one knew that it was [his] except for the knower of hearts,[6] who knew that he would perform his service. Through his performance as well, he demonstrated in the world of appearances that it was his.—The contract is sealed before the invisible tribunal as soon as both genuinely will the promised service. In the world of appearances, [however,] the contract does not come into force until both services are completely fulfilled. The moment that implements [the contract] here, resolves it.

Let us apply this to an ongoing association for mutual services such as the civil contract.—All have given all a right over each, and, in turn, each received a right over them. At least, this must be presupposed, since it is to be assumed that they are honest people. They have shown in the world of appearances that they were [indeed honest people]. They all have, each individually, performed their services through action, through omission, [and] through subjecting themselves to the lawful fine whenever they neglected to act when they should have or acted where they should have refrained. As long as no one shows a change of will through words or actions, it is to be assumed that he is in the contract.

Now one person changes his will and from this moment onward, he is no longer part of the contract. He no longer has a right to the state, the state no right over him. He shows his changed will either through

---

6. *Herzenskündiger*

an overt declaration or by refraining from the contracted help and not submitting to the lawful fine in case of omission.† What is henceforth his relationship to the state and the state's to him? Do both parties still have reciprocal rights and duties, and [if so,] which?

Obviously, vis-à-vis each other they have been restored to the pure state of nature. The only law still common to them is the moral law. [265] We have seen above what is right according to this law in the case of omitted services after one has performed one's part: retraction of the performance's product and restitution of damages.

But does this situation really occur here? If all have equal rights and equal duties in a civil contract—and this alone is the subject of the present chapter—and everyone faithfully performs what he should according to time, place, and circumstances—in the case of omission through atonement—then I do not see how they would ever have to get even with each other. Up to this moment you have rendered me what you owed. I rendered you what I owed. From this moment on you do not perform a service anymore, and neither do I. Equal for equal evens out. We are square. It is possible, if you are great calculators of *utility*, that I am quite behind in this regard. But we are not talking about utility here; we are talking about *right*. If I had come into a situation, where I had to do much more for your utility than you could do for mine, then it was my duty to do it; it was *your right*. I may not file a suit for restitution, since, according to the contract, what I did for you was never my property, but yours. What you did for me, you may demand back?—It is legally my property.

This last comment, then, fully reveals the false appearance of all sophistries that are derived from the long chapter of good deeds that the citizen owes to the state against the citizen's right to change his

---

†Only this much in the footnote!—Somebody may point out that, if this was how it worked, everyone facing a penalty would leave the association and consequently punishment would be utterly impossible. And I reply logically: anybody who wants may do that and then the state cannot punish him without [committing] the greatest injustice. No one can reasonably submit to the punishment except in order to be allowed to remain part of the state.—What follows from this for the death penalty? Oh, it does not require this detour to show that every death sentence for civil offences is murder. [However,] if the citizen offends against inalienable human rights in society (not merely contractual rights), he is no longer a *citizen*; he is an *enemy*. And society does not make him *atone*. It *avenges* itself on him, i.e., it treats him according to the law that he established.

constitution. These sophists all speak of thankfulness, of fairness. They all speak of gentle donations. [But] this is not what such a judgment is about. It is strictly about right and about claims for restitution. Let us first settle this account, then we will see how much we have left to give away.—Thus, one of them reminds us, having just finished his laments about the meaningless sermons and dull, ridiculous ideas of the orators who confuse morality and politics, that culture, which we owe to our good mother, should not be used to mutilate itself.[7] But—let us leave the children to play with their mother and talk about this like men!

[266] Which, then, would be the service for which the state could file a restitution suit? Your entire property, some say, since the state granted it to you on the condition that you should be its members. At least your landed estate, others say, because the land belongs to the state. But effectively the latter are not any more generous than the former. While the former strip us down naked, the latter relegates us into the air, for land and sea are already occupied and even the lands that are still undiscovered have already been given away by the pope by virtue of his divine rights.[8] If these threats were entirely serious, we would freely abandon our desire ever to step into civil society. An examination of the legal foundation of property in general and of landed estates in particular will make the matter clearer.

Originally, we are our own property. No one is our master and no one can become our master. We carry our letter of emancipation, given to us under divine seal, deep in our chest. He himself set us free and said: henceforth be no one's slave. Which being would be allowed to take possession of us?[9]

We are *our* property, I say, and thereby I assume we are twofold, a proprietor[10] and property. The pure *I* in us, reason, is master over our sensibility, all our spiritual and physical powers; reason may use them as means to any discretionary end.

All around us are things that are not their own property because they are not free. Originally, however, they are not ours either, because they do not immediately belong to our sensible I.

---

7. Rehberg, *Untersuchungen*, 1:63–64, 80.

8. The bull *Inter caetera divinia*, decreed by pope Alexander VI in 1493, divided the entire globe into a Spanish and a Portuguese domain for colonisation.

9. Cf. Schmalz, *Das reine Naturrecht*, 29–30.

10. *Eigentümer*

We have the right to use our own sensible powers to any discretionary end that is not forbidden by the law of reason. The law of reason does not forbid [us] to use those things with our powers that are not their own property as means to our ends, nor to make them suitable for being this. Thus, we have the right to apply our powers to these things.

If we have given things the shape of means to our ends, no other being can employ them without either using for himself the effect[11] of our powers, and consequently our powers themselves, which are originally our property, [267] or destroying this shape, i.e., impeding our powers in their free effect. (That the immediate effectiveness[12] of our powers is over, does not matter. As long as the effect lasts, our effectiveness lasts.) This, however, no rational being may do, for the moral law forbids him to disturb the free effect of any free being and this prohibition corresponds to a right in us to prevent such a disturbance.—Thus, we have the right to exclude everyone else from the use of a thing that we have formed by means of our powers, that we have given our shape. And in regard to things this right is called *property*.

This formation[13] of things by means of one's power is the true legal foundation of property, but also the only one based on natural law.‡ Thus, Herr *Rehberg* should have found it less naive, reading that Schlözer writes in his *Reports on the State:*[15] he who does not work, ought not to eat either.[16]—He who does not work, may eat if I want to give him something to eat, but he has not legal claim to food. He may not use another's powers for himself. If no one is so good as to do it for him voluntarily, he will have to use his own powers in order to find or prepare something or die from starvation, and that as a matter of law.

But human beings cannot produce anything new, create anything, Herr *Rehberg* notes. The matter, to which human beings give form, must

---

‡That which *Herr Schmalz* calls "accession" is ultimately founded on formation.[14]

11. *die Wirkung* (outcome)

12. *das Wirken* (process)

13. *Bildung*

14. Schmalz, *Das reine Naturrecht*, 42.

15. August Ludwig von Schlözer, 1735–1809, German historian and political critic who published his own popular periodical, *Staatsanzeigen* (Reports on the State) from 1782 to 1793.

16. Rehberg, *Untersuchungen*, 1:27.

already have existed. Thus, even if I can lay a legally founded claim to the form, it is never possible to prove ownership over the matter.[17]—We were genuinely sorry that Herr R. [268] drew a wrong conclusion from the only comment in his entire book that was astute and could have led to instructive discussion. That is because he applies this comment to landed property. And since per this comment no one can be owner of the land according to natural law, he thinks one must have this right from the state.

Herr R. by far did not deduce enough from his basic principle. Not only is the land matter that we cannot produce. Matter, which exists entirely without our effort, forms the basis of everything that can possibly become our property.—The clothing I am wearing was indeed the rightful property of the tailor who made it, which he transferred to me through contract. The cloth for it was the property of the weaver before it got to the tailor. The wool from which it was made [was] the property of the flock owner. His flock was born to him by sheep that he inherited or purchased through contract. The first sheep became the property of him, who tamed and fed it, but where did the first sheep itself come from? It was organized matter without anyone's contribution. If the state conferred the sheep on the first occupant, then without a doubt I also possess my clothing merely as a privilege from the state. If I leave the association, the state will have it taken off me.

However, above all, how does the state obtain a right that none of the individual members who constitute it has? As you say, no one has a property right over matter. But when all unite their rights, such a right is supposed to arise? Do you assemble multiple identical parts into a whole that is [then] of a different nature than the parts? Do you think, if everyone pours rum into the bowl, it will become punch?—That is illogical.

It is completely correct that not only no property right over matter can be substantiated *as such*, but also the contradiction in such a right can be palpably demonstrated. Such a right contradicts the concept of *raw matter according to the meaning of the natural law*. That is, if no other manner of appropriation is possible but formation, then necessarily everything that is not yet formed, that is raw, not yet appropriated, is no one's property. We have the *right of appropriation* over raw matter, the *right of property* over matter that has been modified by us. The first

---

17. Rehberg, *Untersuchungen*, 1:12–13.

designates the moral possibility; the second the moral and physical reality. If you cannot take the matter from us without also taking the form and if you are not allowed take this form from us, then we do not want to argue with you about the possession of matter *thought of* as distinct from the form, since you cannot *really* separate it. If it is not our property, [269] it is not yours either. And since you have to leave us the form, you will have to leave us the matter as well.—One can accurately say, if not strictly philosophically at least metaphorically, that God is the owner of raw matter; that we are enfeoffed by him with it, each with the entire matter that exists; that the law of freedom in our chest is the letter of enfeoffment; and that he transfers the real possession to us when the formation takes place.[18] Thus, one could have found this old thought less trivial. Only this enfeoffment must not be transferred to us as inheritance from Adam or from the three sons of Noah. We did not inherit it. Everyone received it directly, together with the gift of moral freedom.

And should it be any different? If raw matter, as such, could be someone's property, how should we ever come into property? What should we appropriate to ourselves? To look for a proof of property rights over matter means to want to abolish property altogether.

To apply these principles to landed property: every human being has an original right of appropriation over the entire earth. That no one may exercise this right to its complete extent is provided for partly by each individual's weakness and partly by [the fact] that each individual has the identical right—what one has already occupied, the next can no longer occupy. That all human beings have a legal claim to an identical share of the land and that the earth should be divided among them in equal portions—which some French writers claim—would only follow if everyone had not only the *right of appropriation*, but also the actual *right of property* over the ground. However, since someone first makes something his property through appropriation by means of his labor, it is clear that he who works more may also possess more and that he who does not work legally possesses nothing at all.—Imagine a bunch of people who arrive on a deserted, uncultivated island with farming equipment and draft cattle. Each one sets his plough into the earth where he wants. Wherever his [plough] stands, no one else's can stand. Everyone ploughs

---

18. The letter or deed of enfeoffment contained the pledge of service on the part of the serf to the lord, and the granting of land to the serf by the lord.

as much land as he can and whoever has made the largest piece arable by the evening, will legally possess the largest piece.—Now the entire island has been ploughed. Whoever slept away the day will not possess anything, and that as a matter of right.

Herr R., raising the question§ whence we *derive* the right** [270] to labor on the objects that do not belong to us—a question that I have answered above and that was already answered thoroughly before, e.g., in *Herr Schmalz's* natural right†† —slips in an emphasized "exclusively." This is supposed to settle it, but does not even tip the scale by a hair-breadth. If I have a piece of raw matter directly in my hands, everyone else is obviously excluded, for he cannot labor on it without wresting it from me, and he may not do that. If he had grabbed it faster, though I wanted to pick it up from the ground, it would be in his hands and *I* would be excluded. When it was still lying on the floor, we both had an equal right to it. Now I have the exclusionary right or, as Herr R. would say, the *exclusive*‡‡ right to labor on it. I hold it directly in my hands.

However, he [Rehberg] does not speak of such things that can be held directly in one's hands, although he generally speaks about objects. Those must have escaped his thoroughness. His example is taken from land. He asks, "If I want to sow a field but someone else, who [271] does not have a suitable field or prefers this one, wants to labor on it as well, what should be the grounds for deciding?"[21]—If the piece of land over which the question emerges is indeed *a field* (or is this word only written here in order to relieve the other [words] that are tired?),

---

§Page 13 of his above-mentioned book.

**After all, one can hear what the people are talking about.

††A book that Herr R. either should have read before writing his or should have refuted, if he did read it.[19]

‡‡*Exclusive* as in *excludable*, as if the person laboring on [the piece of raw matter] demanded to *be* excluded himself rather than to exclude everyone else.—It would be inappropriate hairsplitting to push such a comment on any other author. [Yet] it serves him right, who uses this tone against others. Metiri—quemque suo modulo ac pede verum est.[20]

19. Schmalz, *Das reine Naturrecht*, §§39–42, §§55–63.

20. Horace, *Epistles*, trans. James Lonsdale and Samuel Lee (London: Macmillan, 1873), 1.7: "It is meet that every man should measure himself by his own rule and foot."

21. Rehberg, *Untersuchungen*, 1:13.

the decision is easy and one may say that whoever asks like this, does not merit an answer. A field has been ploughed. Someone must have ploughed it[, and,] according to natural right, this someone is the owner, and no one else would want to take the futile and unlawful trouble to labor on it once more. Every field has an owner as surely as it is a field, for it is no longer raw matter, but has a form. Herr R. indeed wants to *sow* said field (if all this, and possibly his entire book, has not been written merely for the sake of the popular copia dicendi[22]), therefore it must really be freshly ploughed. This, I should think, would be reason enough to exclude each other from laboring on it.—Yet, we do not want to avail ourselves of the clumsiness of our opponent by means of a lawyer's trick. We want to examine in order to instruct. Even if the field was not freshly ploughed, even if it had not been [ploughed] in a number of years, the first person who labored on it, or his representative, still always remains the rightful owner as long as even the slightest effect of the first labor is in the ground—and when could that ever disappear? If the external traces of the first labor have disappeared, he who takes possession of the field without knowing of the erstwhile labor is certainly an honest but not a rightful occupant. Upon the objection of the true owner, he must refrain from laboring on [the field].

Herr R.'s next question permits a more accurate interpretation, and we want to accept it, regardless of how suspicious the question becomes by virtue of its proximity with the first. He asks, "How would it be possible for me to prove based exclusively on reason that this ground on which both are standing belongs to one rather than the other?"[23] We shall assume that "ground" means here what it ought to mean, if we are to engage the question: not an arable, but a raw piece of land that has never been labored on. And then the question deserves an answer.—What then is that ground of which he speaks? This one and same ground on which both are supposed to stand? How does he delimit it? Where does he cut it off from the other ground that is no longer the same ground [as that] on which they are both standing? Did not his imagination perhaps play a trick on him here by quietly planting fence lines, moats, lynchets, [and] border stones on it? [272] Those cannot be there, otherwise the ground would already be occupied, and would belong either to one or

---

22. copiousness in speaking

23. Rehberg, *Untersuchungen*, 1:13.

the other or to neither of the two but exclusively[24] to a third. Therefore, apologies for [calling it] *the ground*. Let's rather speak *about a place*! The two of them cannot stand in one and the same place. That is against the law of impenetrability[25] of matter. One person is excluded from the place on which another stands. He cannot stand there without pushing the other one away, and he may not do that. Everyone is rightful and exclusionary owner of the place on which he stands as long as this place did not already have a previous owner. He became the owner by standing on the place. However, his property does not reach further than he can cover with his body.—Now one of them digs a trench. This trench is his; it is the product of his labor. He was entitled to dig the trench by virtue of his reasonable nature. You say that he cannot prove his ownership over the slice of earth.—That bothers him very little. At least the trench that he has fashioned from the slice of earth is his; you may take the slice, but leave him the trench!—His neighbor digs a trench right next to his. He may do that but he cannot dig [one] where the first already dug without destroying the latter's trench, and that he may not.—Thus we can satisfactorily answer that question why, on nonoccupied ground, the place on which someone stands and the trench that someone dug belongs to him and not to someone who does not stand on it and who did not dig it. And in this moment, we made one of Herr R.'s impossibilities real.

In general, the rightful owner of the *last* form is the owner of the thing.—[Imagine,] I give a piece of gold that I rightfully own—be it through my own labor or through contract—to a goldsmith with the commission to make me a cup from it. I promised him a certain wage for it. A contract appears to exist between us. He brings the cup, but I do not give him his wage. No contract existed between us. His labor was his and remains his.—But the gold is surely mine?—I may take it back, if I can, without taking the cup as well or destroying it. If he wants to recompense me for my loss, it is right and well, but I do not have a legal claim to my cup. He is the rightful occupant of the last form, since he gave my gold its form with my authorization. If he were

---

24. *ausschliessend*: See Fichte's previous note in which he discusses the difference between "auschliessend" (exclusive) and "ausschliesslich" (exclusionary). In order to avoid the grammatical awkwardness, we have decided to forgo the distinction in this sentence.

25. *Gesetz der Undurchdringlichkeit*

the wrongful occupant of the latter—had he made my gold into the cup without my consent—he would have to give me back the gold with or without the form.

[273] All this makes evident that the source of property rights is not the state but the rational nature of human beings as such, and that we can indeed own something according to natural right alone and exclude all others legally from owning the same.

Yet, we ask, how can this help us, who have been born in the state? Admittedly, we could have acquired property for ourselves according to pure natural right and *thereby* could have made it entirely independent of the state. But we have not acquired ours in this way. We owe it to the state's regulation and will have to give it back to the state if we leave the association.—We will see if this fear is well founded.

Sure enough, we were born poor, naked, and helpless. We will speak later about what the state allegedly did for the development of our powers, [i.e.,] the state's claim that we would still be poor, naked, and helpless in this moment had it not developed our powers! For now, allow me to jump over the years of bumbling animality. [I assume] that our powers are developed and that we can help ourselves. I will be ready to acknowledge the state's achievements in this development later, if they can be shown.—Thus, our powers are developed. We want to appropriate something, direct our eyes around us, and everything has an owner except air and light, for the simple reason that they are not susceptible to any foreign form. We would wander around the globe without finding anything upon which we could assert our right of appropriation, which extends to all raw matter. There is hardly any raw matter left. Do we perhaps want to reproach the state for this, as if it had already taken everything and left nothing for us? No, we would thereby reveal great ineptitude and show that we do not understand this situation at all. It is not the state that has already taken possession of everything. It is the individuals. Do we want to argue with them for not having waited on us—for not having anticipated us—before we got there? Do we want to demand a right in the world of appearances, before we ever appeared? It is indeed sad for us that all places are already taken, but it's just too bad that we were not born earlier. We may not push someone from his place because we need one. Thus, we must see how we make do. That's our concern.

Now, they say, this is where the state enters. The state places us for the time being in shared rule over our parents' property, if they have any, and as heirs after their death.—It would be very magnanimous of the state [274] to redress an evil that, as we just granted, it did not cause. But allow me to ask for the time being, only for the sake of arousing attention: Whence does the state have the right to grant me first the shared rule and then the complete rule over foreign property? Can all have a right that no individual has? Didn't I say already that no punch can result when everyone has poured only rum into the bowl?

We will see how the shared rule of children over the property of their parents is intended according to basic principles of natural right when we discuss culture. Now about inheritance! According to natural right, they say, no inheritance takes place.[26] Eh? In fact, a very large, extensive [inheritance takes place], but one has to know to grasp the concepts purely and not to let the imagination mix into them foreign features borrowed from habit.

As soon as someone exits from the world of appearances, he loses his rights in it. His property practically becomes raw matter again, because no one is the occupant of its form. All of humanity is the rightful heir to every deceased, since all of humanity has the unrestricted right of appropriation over everything that has no occupant. Whoever properly appropriates it first will be the rightful owner.—In this way, nature provided for those whom she brings forth later by gradually recalling the old occupants from the scene. Nature and moral law are in the most perfect agreement here. The former is here what it should always be: servant of the latter.—You should not push anyone off his place, the law says. But I have to have a place, you say. Here is your place, nature says, and pushes off whom you were not allowed to push off.§§

When human beings became citizens, they said, "we do not like this running after possessions, which is ultimately in vain, [nor] this strife and animosity that must arise over it," and they spoke well. [They agreed that] henceforth everyone takes what is closest to him and thus he spares himself and others the trip. [275] He takes what was in his father's hut and around his father's hut. The rest of us relinquish our right of appropriation over this no longer occupied possession if he,

---

§§The teacher of natural law praised at the beginning of the chapter may not interpret this and the following [comment] as if I were recounting a historical fact, as if—to use his expression—this had happened *in time*. I cannot find any information on this in my notebook.

26. Rehberg, *Untersuchungen*, 1:59

for his part, relinquish his right of appropriation over the belongings of every other deceased citizen.—Accordingly, you do not enjoy civil inheritance law for free. You gave up an alienable human right—[the right] to inherit from any deceased, if you can—for it. Now, if you really did not occupy [any land] as long as you lived in the state, you fulfilled your obligation and the state its. Your patrimony is yours according to the contract that you fulfilled. You can own it in good conscience, even if you leave the state. If the state demands it [the patrimony] back, you may demand everything from the state that you could have appropriated from the inheritance of deceased citizen during this time. It [the state] will certainly leave it [your patrimony] to you.

The second manner in which we acquire property in the state is through labor by means of a contract. Mere labor rarely or never yields a property in the state, because raw matter rarely or never exists. Whatever we want to labor on already has a form. We are not allowed to labor on it without the consent of the owner of the last form. If the owner commissions us with further labor on the thing in exchange for compensation for our employed power, which is originally our property, then that portion of his property that he surrenders to us becomes ours by virtue of [both] contract and labor. He sells it to us.—If he consents for us to labor on the thing with our discretion[27] (the act of taking something is already an employed effort) without demanding something from us in exchange, the thing itself becomes ours likewise through contract and labor. For we cannot force him to keep his promise before we applied any effort to it. He could have never had the will to give it to us, or changed it, and then it would not be ours according to the discussion above. However, since he does not absorb anything into his property, he does not sell it to us. He gives it to us.—Inheritance and labor contract comprise all the manners in which we may obtain a possession in the state. Trade is merely an exchange contract over possessions, the ownership of which already presupposes inheritance or labor contract.

"These contracts, however, are made in the state, under the protection of the state, [and] by virtue of the existence of the state, the first contract of which constitutes the foundation of all possible subsequent contracts. Therefore, we owe everything that we obtain [through those contracts] to the state."—This is a lot at once and concluded rashly! We need time to disentangle these things.

---

27. *willkürlich*

First of all, I have to issue a reprimand over a confusion of terms here, which, as far as I know, has persisted universally until this day and has woven itself so far into the interior of language[28] [276] that it is difficult to find a word to put an end to it. The word "society,"[29] in particular, is the source of this tiresome misunderstanding. One uses the word as if it were homonymous both for human beings that are in a contract in general and for human beings that are especially in a civil contract with the state. Thereby, one sneaks around an important consideration: how are the people constituted that live around, beside, among each other without being in any contract, let alone in a civil contract? Regarding the word "society," I distinguish between two main meanings: on the one hand, it expresses a physical relationship between multiple individuals, which can be none other than their relation to one another in space. On the other hand, it expresses a moral relationship, the relation of mutual rights and obligations towards one another. In the latter sense, one uses the word and has these rights and duties determined either through contract in general or through the particular social contract. And thus every society came into being—and necessarily so—through a contract. Without a contract no society is possible.

Why, though, has the first meaning of the word "society" been forgotten?—[Because] beings that are not merely bodies can never as [mere] bodies be in space without a moral relationship between them.—Right! But this [justification] is the fault of an old, wrong understanding of human beings' state of nature, of the war of all against all that was supposed to be right, [and] of the right of the stronger that supposedly reigned on this ground. It was said that two individuals could not approach each other within a foot's breadth without each obtaining the perfect right to declare the other a fine find, to capture and roast him. If neither one of them was quite certain whether he would be the strongest, they would have to tell each other: "My dear, do not eat me; I will not eat you either." And henceforth, it is said, it is no longer rightful to eat one another since, after all, they promised each other. And although they would have had the inherent, complete right to eat one another, they do not have the right not to keep their word. A thorough philosophy![30] Even

---

28. *das Innere der Sprache*

29. *Gesellschaft*: May be translated as either "society" or "company" in English, depending on the context.

30. Fichte here summarizes and dismisses Thomas Hobbes's famous account of the state of nature in the *Leviathan* as the war of all against all, devoid of justice.

in those systems, where this understanding [of the state of nature] has been entirely rejected, its immediate and distant consequences still show.

Human beings, however, can—i.e., it is morally possible—live in "society" in the first sense of the word—i.e., around, beside, between, among each other—without being in a society in *your* second sense, in a contract. In this case, they are not without mutual rights and obligations. Their common law, which defines these [rights and obligations] sharply enough, is the law of freedom. The basic principle [is]: [277] hinder no one's freedom insofar as his freedom does not hinder yours.—"But *would* human beings actually submit to this basic principle without coercive laws? Would they not increasingly ask for what they are capable of rather than for what they are allowed?"—I know that you always appeal to human beings' primordial wickedness, of which I cannot convince myself. But let's grant it. [Let's assume that] the coercive laws are valid in the state of nature as well. I may legally coerce anyone who hinders my freedom to restore it [my freedom] and all of its effects.—"You *may*, but will you always *be able to*? Will you always be the stronger?"—[You talk] only about what I *would* or *will* [do]; I talk about what I *ought* [to do]. If the moral law ruled over nature, I *would* always be the stronger when I am right, because in that case I *should* be. You constantly place me in the realm of natural necessity. A little patience and I will have wrested this objection from your heart without engaging your hypothesis of what human beings' state of nature *would really be*.

Moreover, human beings can be in a society, in your second meaning of the word—i.e., in a contract in general—without living in a state, in a civil contract. What is generally rightful according to a contract is not first determined through a special type of contract, the civil [contract]. That would (let us recall in passing, for those who will find it more plausible this way) be evidently circular: we make a contract that the contract should be valid in the first place, and the same contract is valid because, according to our contract, contracts are valid in the first place. It is, as has been shown above, precisely determined by the moral law: mutual performance, or restoration of a unilateral service and compensation. I do not obtain the right to insist on it from the state. [Rather,] I obtained it together with the gift of freedom as my endowment from the common father of spirits.

I did not take on this discussion merely for amusement but to draw an important conclusion from it.—If the state can neither take away nor grant the rights that are originally ours, then all these relationships must in fact persist in civil society. A right that I have as a human being, I can never have as a citizen, *by virtue of being a citizen*. A right that I should have as a citizen, I cannot already have had as a human being. It is therefore a great fallacy to believe that human beings' state of nature is suspended[31] by the civil contract. The state of nature may never be suspended. It extends through the state [278] uninterrupted.—The human being in the state can be considered in various relationships. First, [he may be considered] in isolation, alone with his conscience and with the highest executioner of all his pronouncements. This is his highest level to which all his other relationships are subordinated. No stranger can be his judge here (the deity is not foreign to him). The law that the invisible judge of this tribunal administers is the moral law, insofar as it refers only to the world of spirits. In this first relationship, he is *spirit*.—Next, he is to be considered in society, living among others of his kind. In this relationship the moral law is his law to the extent that it determines the world of appearances and is called natural law. Before this external tribunal, everyone is his judge who lives around him. In this relationship, he is a *human being*.—Now, he enters into contracts. The realm of contracts is [part of] the world of appearances insofar as the latter is not completely determined by the moral law. His law in the realm of contracts is the *free* (free from the law) will.[32] If he violates the other's freedom by withdrawing his will, his will is no longer free. It retreats under the [moral] law and is judged according to the law. He can enter such contracts as frequently and as variously as he wants. Among them, he can also enter the special contract of one with all and all with one, which is called the civil contract. The domain of this contract is a discretionary portion of the realm of the free will. Laws and rights [in the civil contract] are the same as in contract in general, of which it represents one type. Insofar as he is part of this contract, he is called a citizen.—In order to visualize the circumference and the ratio of these different realms, let us draw a circle. [Let us assume that] this entire disk is the realm of conscience. Within its perimeter, draw a much smaller one. This one encompasses the visible world; that portion of the realm of conscience in which the law of nature—the law of perfect obligation, subordinated to conscience—judges as well. Within this second circle, draw a third, smaller one. Within its perimeter, subordinated to conscience and natural law, contract law judges as well. Drawn within this

---

31. *aufgehoben*
32. *Willkühr*

third one, a fourth, smaller circle within this third one yields the space in which the special social contract judges, subordinated to the above judges. In order to illustrate my thoughts, I take the liberty to add the following figure. [279]

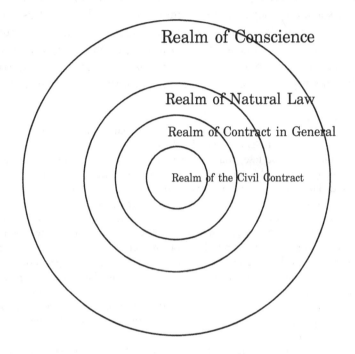

Only this must still be noted, that the realm of the superior tribunals passes invisibly through the domains of the inferior [tribunals]. Even in its own realm, the natural law only pertains to such objects that have been left free by conscience, *and so forth*. The enclosed circles do not contain *the same* as the outer [circles] contain within their perimeters. Rather, entirely different objects fall within these perimeters, across which their jurisdiction stretches. In order to make it totally clear, we would have to cut out four such circles and place them on top of each other. The realm of conscience contains everything, that of the civil contract [contains] the least. It must be permissible for anyone to withdraw from the center towards the perimeter, even from the realm of natural law if he wants to live on a deserted island. However, he never leaves the realm of conscience, if he is not an animal.—Now one can judge on what authority the state—whose realm is enclosed in the narrowest space—encroaches over its borders and seeks to conquer the domain of contracts in general, perhaps that of the natural law and, God willing, even that of conscience.***

[280] Whatever I have acquired throughout my life in the state by means of some contract is therefore mine as *human being*, not as *citizen*. Did I not have to be a moral person in order to be able to enter a contract? Am I, viewed as a citizen, a moral person? Do I, as a citizen, have a free will? Oh no. Only when I am taken together with everyone, does this moral person come into being. Thus, the will of the state first

---

***It is only by differentiating these various realms that the fallacies of that Greek sophist and his worthy student emerge.[33]—"If you win your first lawsuit, you pay me a hundred talents. If you lose, you never pay me anything," the former said to the latter and taught him in his art. The teacher needed money. The date of payment was delayed. He went and arraigned his student in court. "In either case, judges, he will pay me the hundred talents," he said, "either by dint of your ruling, if you order him to pay, [or] by dint of our contract, if he wins the lawsuit." "No," replied the worthy student, "I do not pay anything in either case. [I] do not pay if you rule in my favor by dint of your ruling. [I] do not pay either if you rule against me by dint of our contract, because in that case I did not win my first legal action." The judges—they were Athenians—issued a gag order, where they could not render a decision. Every reader—forgive me, if I make unexpected examinations occasionally—who has understood the theory above settles this quarrel on first sight. Whoever cannot settle this quarrel, has not understood the theory and should think through it until he can settle it!

Who doesn't see that the old and the young sophist are muddying their quarrel by wanting to jump from one realm to the other, and that the old [sophist] had intended such a confusion with the peculiar conditions of the contract? Everyone wants to escape into the domain of the state when the other is after him in the realm of contracts, and into the realm of contracts when the other is after him in the domain of the state. And if this is permitted, they will never meet each other. If only you, Athenian judges, had sent them to the right tribunal! No Areopagus decides what is right in the case of contracts [because] this law is older than the tribunal.[34] Their present quarrel does not belong before your judgment seat. It is not a civil lawsuit. Let them go, and if the conditions of the contract are fulfilled in a true lawsuit, then not you but the matter itself passes the judgment. Then the teacher may come and beg the state *not for a decision on what is right, but for the protection under civil contract of his natural* rights. Then you have a deal. Now, not yet.

33. Protagoras, c. 481–411 BC; his student was called Euathlos.

34. The Areopagus was a council of elders with jurisdictional function in ancient Greece, prior to Solon's democratic reforms.

comes into being through the will of all. If I am able to enter a contract at all, I have to enter it as a human being. As a citizen, I cannot. The other, who entered into the contract with me, likewise entered it as a human being for the same reason.

Even if I had entered the contract with the state, I could only have entered it as a human being. This is almost more obvious in this case than in the previous. The two voluntary decisions that belong to a contract [281] are that of the state and mine. If my will had been included in the will of the state, there would have been only one will. The state would have entered a contract with itself, which is self-contradictory. If I performed, and the state performed, the contract is fulfilled. My performance would belong to the state, and the state's to me.

But, they say, if the state did not do [that], you could not count on the holiness of the contracts that you may still enter as a human being. If the other did not keep his word, you would indeed have the authority, according to natural law, to compel him to the restitution of services and compensation, but you would not always be the stronger [one]. Now, the state [has taken] your place. It helps you to enforce your right, which you may still call a human right when someone offends it. Awe of the state is the reason that rights are rarely violated.—And thus, we are approaching the objection, which we promised above to refute.

Against whom did the state protect my right? Against a foreigner or a fellow citizen? If it protected my right against a foreigner, it was bound to it by the very contract. At the time, I was in the contract. In one way or another—be it merely by the fact that I did not put obstacles in its way—I myself was part of the protective body. I helped to protect the rights of other fellow citizens. I did my part. The state did its part. This is now over. Our contract is completed and each keeps what is his.—If I leave the contract, the state's duty to protect my right is indeed cancelled completely, because my duty to help protect others' right is cancelled. Then I must see how to help myself.

If the state protected my right against a fellow citizen, I repeat the above but add much more.—I entered a contract with a fellow citizen, as a human being with another human being. The law of nature and no other is our law here. He hurts me and thereby places himself in the relationship of an enemy toward me. I have the right to treat him with hostility until my property has been fully restored. You do not want me to treat your fellow citizen with hostility? Well then, help enforce my right peacefully. As soon as you take his side by opposing my rightful prosecution of him, the affair becomes your affair. Henceforth you are all *one* moral person, charged before the tribunal of natural law. And I am the second moral person, who [282] sues. I am not a citizen now. Grant me my right peacefully or I will wage war on you. [Whether] I am your fellow citizen or I am a foreigner; [whether] I left your state or I was never part of it to begin with does not matter here. In this action I am not a citizen at all. "What? You, individually, want to inflict war on the entire state? You are certainly the weaker [party]." So? Did you unite to be unjust, and does one join your association in order to rob [others] unpunished? If you philosophize like this, I abandon you here and continue my path onward.

It has now been demonstrated that all property that we acquired in the state and that was protected by the latter remains rightfully ours even if we leave the state. Now we stand before the second object, concerning which the state threatens us with a restitution suit, the *culture* that we acquire in the state. As terrible as the first lawsuit may have been, this one is much worse. If we had indeed been stripped naked, as threatened, and expelled from the land and the sea, maybe we would have found a means to escape into the air, where we would have been allowed to exist peacefully. But, in order to divest us of all our physical and spiritual capabilities, there is no other means but to hit us over the head with a big hammer.

Thus, the state demands back our culture, claiming that it is its. If we cannot give it back to it, we will remain fettered to the state without any rescue. We admit that the state has found a means—the best, most charitable [means], it will say—to chain us to it forever. What do we want to say? [Do we want to] demand back the rights of humanity? After all, we owe it, if not the possibility of being human, at least the very consciousness of this humanity.—"Honor the humanity in me," you say. "You ingrate," replies the state, "would you be a human being, if I had not made you one? Do you raise claims against me that I myself asserted in you in the first place? Oh, had I not allowed you to know that you are more than an animal, I would not have as much trouble with you now."

"Thus, O state, you have formed me for your final ends, that I will be more useful for your ends, not for mine. You have treated me like a piece of raw matter that ought to be useful to you. Now I give myself my own ends and want to pursue them myself." "That's not what you formed me for," you say.—"Now, then, I do not have this kind of culture from you and will not give it back. If you leave me this [culture], I will give you my word never to use this [culture] for *your* ends."

[283] "Thus, the education that you gave me, you only gave me under the condition that it should always be yours? Did you ask me whether I accept this condition? Did I think about the matter and say, 'yes'?"—[Imagine] I come down into a pilgrim's inn hungry. Just in front of my seat, I find a red lentil dish. I take it eagerly and thank the anonymous, generous donor in my heart. You fall out of your nook, grab me, and say: "You are mine. Why did you taste this dish? It was the buying price for your heavenly birthright."[35]—This is neither generous, nor just.

But if you had really asked me, I would have replied. If we had really entered a contract, what could it have been about? You would have told me, "I want to mold you from a suffering animal into an independent human being," and I would have promised you in turn never to act independently. You would have told me, "I want to take you to where you could judge independently," and I would have promised solemnly never to judge independently. After all, you admitted that I am still uneducated; otherwise, for what would you have wanted to educate me? "However, as soon as you get to work, I am to judge your constitution and endorse it? How, my dear, can I do that at present? Complete your work first. Mold me into a reasonable human first, then we will see. You might indeed have the secondary aim to place me, with the culture that you give me, in the position to find your constitution fine and admirable and to learn to love it from conviction. But you cannot bind me [by contract] to this [appreciation] in advance, unless, perhaps, you do not want to cultivate me but to distort and refine me; unless you do not want to sharpen my eyesight but put colored glasses over them. Give me the promised culture. If it brings me to love your constitution, you obtain your goal. If it does not bring me to love your constitution, either the professed culture is good for nothing or you did not keep your word. Or, if your culture is good, your constitution must be good for nothing.

---

35. This is an allusion to the biblical scene (Genesis 25:29–34) in which Esau returns hungry from a hunt and sells his birthright to his younger brother Jacob for a meal of red lentil stew.

Can I apply your gift better than to your own improvement?"—But why do I even reply to the people in their vein? Why do I wrestle with the sophists on their own turf? After all, they digest greater contradictions than this one. [Instead] I [shall] talk to the impartial truth-seeker.

Culture cannot be hung over a human being like a coat over the naked shoulders of a paralytic. Use your hands, grab it and hold on to it, and nestle the garb into all the distinct curves of your figure, or [284] you will always show nakedness and be cold. In the end, if I make something of myself, I owe what I am to myself. If I am only something with, in, or attached to others—a household tool who cleans the room and, in turn, derives his greatest charm from the room itself, or an épée that only wounds in the busy hand, or a flute whose sweet sounds are first breathed into it by the mouth of the virtuoso—you can be sure that I will not walk out of the room, escape from your hand, or pull away from your mouth myself. "If you, O state, have made me for it and I have let myself be made for it, you might answer for this in front of a different tribunal. I, at least, will never hold you accountable." He who turns his culture against the state did not obtain it from the state, and he who obtains his culture from the state does not turn it against the state.

Should I tell my readers everything? Should I apply the distinction between society and state that we just developed above here as well? Neither the former nor the latter can provide culture, because nobody is being cultivated.[36] The former provides disproportionately more culture and disproportionately more useful means toward culture than the latter. The influence of each on our culture is proportionate to their respective realms.

Here, I do not want to recall the basic feature in the sensible nature of human beings, that we abandon its entire strength before helplessness and feel nothing but compassion for this weakness at the sight of it. Is it the state that reared this trait inside of us? I do not want to recall the human being's animalistic instinct to love that which is born from him or from his wife. Is it the state, who inculcated it in us? I do not want to recollect that the moment of the appearance of another human being is necessarily a moment of joy for a human being, because the former relieves him of a pressing burden and an agonizing pain. [I] do

---

36. *kultiviert*

not want to mention that the first gulp from my mother's breast placed me in the sweet relationship of mutual comfort with another human being. She gave me nourishment and I relieved her of a burden.†††   Is it the state, who gave this holy law of nature?—[285] All this, I do not want to mention here, because I do not want to view man as animal here, but as spirit. I do not want to talk about the traits of his sensible nature but about his rights.

My first step into the world of appearances takes place at a stranger's hand. And this hand, by offering itself to me, grants me fully valid entitlements to itself. So, did you pull me out in order to let me perish helplessly? I could perish without you, [thus] you promised me preservation. If you do not keep your word, I will sue you for all the sufferings that I endure since you pulled me out into daylight, until my passing. I may sue, because I carry within me the imprint of reason that is perhaps well known to you.

My first weeping is a cry to the world of spirits, that once again one of them has entered into the world of appearances and wants to assert his rights in it. [It] is a solemn declaration and announcement of these rights for the whole of nature, a solemn occupation of them. I could not occupy them in any other way but through this impotent weeping, [for] I am not capable of anything else. You, who hear me, should recognize my rights in me and hasten near to protect them until I can protect them myself. You are protecting the rights of all of humanity in me.

---

†††Maybe your mother has found other means to relieve herself of that burden. She did not want to accept anything from you, so she would not have to give anything to you. But let it go! Perhaps you had a wet nurse. Go and thank her or cry a tear over a grave if she's dead. Even if she might have been a contemptible being in everyone's eyes, even if, with her milk, she might have poured the poison into your body that is tearing your nerves until this moment and will tear them until the grave—that is little. She still did what your mother did not want to do. She tied to your heart the only end point of the great chain, which goes out into eternity and which, starting from her, the first point, will eventually connect all beings—that of free, mutual giving and taking.

Drive in, sharp arrow, and tear at the heart of every mother that you meet. But do not fly away without the soothing balm—the highest possible compensation for the injuries caused, betterment in the future, or, where the latter is not possible, the well-founded conviction that one would act differently in the present case, warning and exhortation for others—that, and that alone, will undo what has been done. And then you still might wound deeply in order to lance and heal old, nasty injuries.

This is the legal ground of parental authority. If someone, who wears a human face, is unable to claim his human rights, the whole of humanity has the right and duty to exercise them on his behalf. They [the infant's human rights] become the common concern and their assertion the common duty of the entire [human] race. In violating these rights, the entire [human] race is violated. Something to which humanity is collectively entitled becomes the subject of whoever takes possession of it first. The unreasonable thing itself becomes property. The being incapable of the use of reason cannot itself become property, [286] but his rights become property of whoever takes possession of them. One takes possession of rights here through the exercise of them. The midwife who birthed me and brought me into the world of appearances exercised my first right. I was entitled to a place in space. I could not have occupied it myself. She did it on my behalf when she laid me down where I could not stand myself. If she had not promised my parents through contract to surrender her right over me back to them, or if she had not acted according to this contract in my parents' name in the first place, my rights would have been hers by virtue of this first exercise of them. As such, however, they are my parents' [rights]. I may rightfully occupy the rights of any child, regardless how foreign it is to me, if I catch the child upon its entry into the world and no contract binds me to give it back. Parents commonly take possession of their children's rights because they are nearest at [the time of] their arrival. They anticipate and have already made arrangements for their welcome into the world in advance. Thus, it is accidental. According to the law of nature, they do not have an exclusive right to their children *as* the latter's parents. They only turn their right of appropriation, which they have in common with all of humanity, into a property right through occupation.—I leave it to the reader to apply this theory to the insane and beseech him to test thereby whether he grasped it [the theory] correctly.

If I have turned the rights of a rational being, who is not [currently] using his reason, into my own, they remain mine against any stranger's objection simply because they are mine. You demand [to take] this immature[37] child, whose rights I have rightfully appropriated, into your protection. And [even] if you were his begetter or his bearer, I may [still] tell you "no." This immature child, if he were not immature but in command of his reason, would perhaps have the right to tell you, "I do

---

37. *unmündig*

not want your protection." Had he [the child] the right without doubt, then I have it insofar as his rights are mine. And, as the executioner of his rights, I tell you, "I do not want your protection." If you want to make a contract with me over his rights, you may do that and I may do that. But no one but the child himself has the right to legally demand his rights back from me. As his reason develops, he will exercise one [right] after the other on his own; step-by-step he will detach himself from my I in order to form his own. And that will be cue enough for me not to interfere with a stranger's rights. If I do interfere, he will legally restrain me.—I know that the state has always passed a number of regulations regarding these points. But I also know that the state has always [287] tried to habituate us in every way [possible] to be a machine, rather than an independent being.

If I took on the child's right, I likewise took on his duties, through which alone he has rights. I act entirely from within his soul, and my reason fully takes the place of his. I took on his obligation toward others. This child caused you harm; your damage must be compensated. You cannot turn to the child, [for] he is not in command of his reason. [Instead,] you turn to me, who committed to have reason in his place. I am, as it were, collateral for him. I also take on his much greater obligation toward himself: his relationship to the moral law itself. The child is called to work toward the highest final end of all moral beings through culture. In order to be able to do that, he must, above all things, be able to live in the world of appearances, into which he was received. I owe him subsistence, because he owes subsistence to himself, and I am acting in his place. In exchange, I have the right to absorb the products of his developing powers into my property, because his powers are mine. This is joint property[38] in the state of nature, which would more aptly be called joint usufruct,[39] because no one can have actual property who cannot occupy it, and a child cannot do that. He has the duty and right to seek out and apply the means toward culture. I took on his duties and rights in his place, and thus he has the perfect right to demand these means, insofar as they are under my control, [back] from me. It is not goodwill; rather, it is my non-neglectable duty to do my utmost to work toward culture for him. —You may say—I recall this only in passing—that had the state not benevolently interceded and made this the parents' civic

---

38. *Miteigentum*

39. *Mitgenuss*

duty, no one would concern himself with the guardianship over minors,[40] since, according to your own estimation, the burden is much greater than the small advantage. But here your distrust toward human nature manifests itself again. After first denigrating human nature with your civic ordinances that incessantly infringe upon foreign boundaries, you do not cease to slander it [now]. All of human nature's basic traits are good, and they only become harmful through their degeneracy. Everyone prefers to be superior, to protect rather than to be protected. Thereby he elevates himself and obtains a certain importance in his own eyes. Everyone likes to re-present[41] himself in the other and to shape their characteristic peculiarities with his own imprint. [288] These splendid traits, as long as they do not encroach upon others' liberty, would always drive us to attend to the immature and to re-present ourselves in them and to elevate ourselves in our own eyes. If only you had not discovered the unfortunate secret of making the shame of humiliation honorable and the pretense before other people's eyes more pleasant than the honor in our own. In short, if only you had not extinguished the noble pride from our soul to put your petty vanity in its place.

This is what my guardians did for me, and they did nothing but their duty. But they themselves lived in society, and everyone who had a point of commonality with them also educated me. Every word they said served to develop my capacities. Thanks be to the benevolent nature and the lucky coincidence that I was born in society, even if they [the people that educated him] did not intend that. Thanks be also to their good hearts, if they did intend it! In that case, they gave alms to the poor out of free goodness. They did not pay a debt. And I give what alone can be given in return for gifts: my gratitude.—But, what does the state have to do with any of this? If the state cannot demonstrate that society exists altogether only through the state itself, the merits of society are not the state's [to claim]. The state, however, cannot demonstrate that. We have already demonstrated that [instead] the state itself exists by virtue of society. The state may owe society what it owes. We will compensate it [society] even without the state's mediation.

But my horizon broadens. I cross the threshold of the higher spiritual culture.[42] I find elementary and secondary schools that are ready to accept me. Don't those at least exist because of the state's ordinances? It

---

40. *Unmündige*

41. *wieder darstellen*

42. *Geisteskultur*

would not be difficult to show that even those are institutions not of the state but of society and that their existence is founded not on the civil contract but on other special contracts among smaller and larger societies. Only those [features] in these institutions that weigh down the spirit and paralyze its free momentum—monastic discipline, supervision over all kinds of orthodoxies, devotion to the old [merely] *because* it is old, mandatory textbooks and courses—can be attributed to the care of the state. But I don't want to be a stickler for details. Once at least, I want to let the state have its way and let it ascribe everything that is good in society to itself and everything that is bad to our resistance to its salutary regulations. It may have endowed those institutions, appointed the teachers to them, and payed them. [289] I do not even want to remind the state that, in spite of its wise care, I would never have become either learned or smart, if I had not used my own powers. The state may even have the ability to make human beings wise against their will and may offer us glistening samples of this [ability] in its lofty pillars, those upon whom it will perhaps use its best tricks—the children of princes and the aristocracy.

So did the state appoint and remunerate our teachers? Did the state's summons pour out over them the ability to penetrate our interior and to instill their spirit and their tender interest in us as if we were children of *their* spirit? Was it the state's niggardly pay that compensated them for the thousand inconveniences of their position, for all the sorrows and enduring troubles they bore? That paid them for the assertion of the human spirit at the level it had achieved, or perhaps also for the mighty push forward that they gave it? Oh, believe the state anything else but this. No appointment makes someone a teacher of humanity if his bright, flexible spirit and his heart beating warm for human worth have not made him one long ago. The appointment can do nothing but fill an empty seat with a man who, unless he already received the higher calling, ousts someone worthier and occupies his position in vain. The free communication of truth is the most beautiful bond that holds the world of spirits together. It is a secret that no one knows but those who have received it. The truth is the common patrimony of this higher world, free like the ether, and to be enjoyed by myriads at once without being consumed. You handed me my share of it not as my property but as a sacred deposit that is to be passed down to your future descendants. I will and I must deliver. I did well if it proliferated in my hands. This is the only way that I can pay for my place in the world of spirits. Indeed, I am repaying a debt, but not to you, O state. Your realm does not belong to the world with which I have to settle. You speak about remuneration? Your instructions are not valid in the same world, and the teacher of humanity is paid with a coin that you did not mint. As often as the teacher imparts the truth to someone else, he sees it in a different light, and every student whom he converts to the truth shows him a new facet of it. All the joys and rewards that you could give him are nothing compared to those he tastes every day anew—to bring about unanimity of thought and to merge an[other] human spirit with his own. The prospects you could offer him for this short life span are nothing compared to [290] his [prospect] that the fruits of his labor will subsist into eternity and that nothing in the endless succession of causes and effects toward the perfection of the human race that he brought into it will decay. The disciple is not greater than the master if he is nothing but a disciple and apprentice and can do nothing but imitate. But great and happy would be the master who could make all his students greater than he was himself. What a seed of human worth and human happiness, arising from the grain he threw, must be dawning before his eyes! My name may be lost and its syllables may not roll over the tongues of posterity if only my existence constitutes a link in the great chain of the perfection of my brotherly race into which other links tie into eternity. No one needs to know [my name], as long as it is that way.

No, ancestral[43] spirits, whose shadows float around me invisibly— Greeks and Romans, whose lingering writings my spirit dabbled with first—you who imperceptibly breathed this boldness, this contempt for deceit, danger and death, this feeling for everything that is strong and great into my soul; and you other teachers, some of whom are still alive, with whose helping hand I still seek daily to penetrate into the nature of our spirit and its concepts and to unfetter myself ever more from deep-rooted prejudices—the dishonorable thought that I paid you with a few miserable pennies for your writing is distant from me. This very minute, my spirit flies longingly to your unknown graves or the cities where you dwell, from which I am separated by countries and seas. Emotional yet manly, I want to thank you at your grave or shake your hand, to tell you that you are my fathers [and that] parts of your spirits have passed over into mine. And you, my oral teachers, especially you, venerable G***[44]—whose straight, harmonious chain of thought through

---

43. *Vorwelt*, in German, is a play on the word *Nachwelt*, posterity; it refers to the world that comes before (*Vor-*) as compared to the world that comes after (*Nach-*).

44. Johann Gottfried Geißler, 1726–1800, was the headmaster in Schulpforta from 1779 to 1786. Fichte attended the famous boarding school in 1774.

flowered fields first woke my spirit from its long slumber and it found itself—maybe I will still be able to thank you, and that will be the pay you content yourself with.

Thus, it is in vain that the state demands back a culture that it neither gave to me nor could have given. In vain the state complains that I turn a gift against it that is not from it. Everyone has the perfect right to leave the state as soon as he wants to. He is not held back by the civil contract, which is valid only as long as everyone wills it and the bill for which can be settled at any moment. Nor is he held back by the special contracts over his property or the culture he acquired. His property remains his. [291] His culture, which furthermore cannot be taken from him, does not give the state the authority to complain about a violation of a contract or about ungratefulness.

If one person can leave the state, several persons can. Those [who leave] now stand against each other, and against the state they left according to natural right alone. If those who seceded want to unite more closely among themselves and enter a new civil contract on whatever conditions, then, according to natural right, they have the perfect right to do that in the realm they have withdrawn to.—A new state came into being. The revolution, which at this point involves only a part [of the citizenry], is completed. Every revolution consists of the renouncing of the old contract and the unification through a new one. Both [steps] are legitimate [and] consequently every revolution, in which both [steps] take place in a legitimate manner—i.e., from free will—[is legitimate] as well.

Until now, two states exist beside and within each other that relate as all states relate to one another, i.e., as individuals without special contracts, subject to the law of natural right alone.—But here I come across the powerful objection about the harmfulness of a state within a state, a case that would evidently occur here. I have broken away and have entered into the new association. My adjacent neighbors are still in the old association, and thus all is mixed up across the entire, incalculable stretch. What kind of confusion and disorder will not arise from this?

But don't always ask first what *will* come of it, but examine, above all the things, what you *may* or *may not* do to avert it. You may not prevent me from leaving your association and entering a new one, [for] you would violate a human right in me. Equally, I may not force you to give up your old [association] and to enter the new one with me. Then I would violate a human right in you. Therefore, we both have to adapt as well as we can and endure what we may not prevent. It could be that states find it inconvenient to see another state arise within it. But that is not the question here. The question is whether the state may rightfully prevent it, and to this I answer "no."

But, I beg you, is it really necessary, or even probable, that this much harm will follow? You, who greatly fear the danger of such a relationship, have you never before thought about your own situation, never discovered that a hundredfold danger constantly surrounds you?

[292] Through almost all countries of Europe, a powerful, hostile state is spreading that is permanently at war with all others and that pushes down very heavily on the citizens in some: it is Judaism.[45] I do not believe, and hope to demonstrate in what follows, that the latter becomes so horrible not because it forms a separate and tightly knotted state, but because this state is founded upon the hatred of the entire human race. [It is] a people among which the most insignificant [member] holds his ancestors in higher regard than we hold our entire history, and who considers an emir,[46] who is older than they all are, to be their patriarch—a legend that we have included among our articles of faith ourselves. This people sees everywhere the descendants of those who expelled them from their dearly beloved fatherland. It condemned itself, and is condemned [by others], to the retail trade that numbs the body and kills the spirit toward any noble feeling. By the most binding [institution] that humanity knows, its religion, it is excluded from our meals, our abundance of joy, and the sweet exchange of cheerfulness from heart to heart with us. It isolates itself from all of us with respect to its duties and rights and even with respect to the soul of the Lord.—From such a people one should perhaps be able to expect something else than we currently see. The absolute king may not take my paternal hut, and my rights are protected against the almighty minister, but the first Jew who feels like it can plunder me unpunished. You witness all this and you cannot deny it. And you speak sugar-sweet words of tolerance, human rights, and civil rights, while you violate the first human rights in us. You cannot satisfy your loving acceptance of those who do not believe in Jesus Christ through titles, dignities, and honorable appointments that you give them, while publicly insulting those who, unlike you, believe in him, and take away their civil honor and the bread they earned with dignity. Do you not, here, recall the state within the state? Does the understandable thought not occur to you that the Jews—who without

---

45. *Judentum*
46. Abraham

you are citizens of a state that is more fixed and powerful than all of yours—will trample your remaining citizens entirely under foot if you grant them the right of citizenship in your states as well?‡‡‡

---

‡‡‡The stench of intolerance is as remote from these pages as it is from my heart! The Jew, who penetrates from the sturdy—one wants to say insurmountable—barricade that lies before him to the *universal love of justice, human beings, and truth*, is a hero and a saint. I do not know if people like that existed or exist. I want to believe it as soon as I see it, but no one shall sell me lovely appearances for reality!—The Jews may not believe in Jesus Christ, [and they] may not believe in any God at all, as long as they do not believe in two different moral laws and in a misanthropic God. They must have human rights, even if they do not concede the same to us, because they *are* human beings and their injustice does not permit us to become like them. Do not force a Jew against his will and do not let it happen when you are the closest to prevent it. You simply owe him that. If you ate yesterday and are hungry again and have bread only for this day, then give it to the Jew, who hungers next to you, if he did not eat yesterday. And you do well in this. But in order to grant them rights of citizenship, I see no other means but to cut off their heads at night and to put other [heads] on them that have not even one Jewish idea in them. In order to protect ourselves against them, I see, in turn, no other means but to conquer their beloved land for them and to send them all there.

The prevailing tolerance towards Jews in states where there is no tolerance toward independent thinkers [Selbstdenker] shows crystal clear what the actual intention is. The maintenance of your faith is so close to your fatherly heart. Behold these Jews: they don't even believe in Jesus Christ. You don't need to tolerate that, [yet] I see that you heap good deeds on them. "Oh, they have superstition,[47] and that is enough for me. You may believe in Zoroaster or Confucius, in Moses or Mohammed, in the pope, Luther, or Calvin. That's all equally valid for me as long as you believe in a foreign reason. But you want to reason *yourself*, and I will never tolerate that. Be immature, otherwise you are too much for me." I do not want to suggest that we should prosecute the Jews for their faith, but that no one should be prosecuted for their faith.

I know that one may attack morality and its most holy product, religion, more easily before various learned tribunals than the Jewish nation. I can tell them that no Jew has ever defrauded me, because I never got involved with one, and that, on several occasions, I have come to the defense of Jews who were being teased at my own peril and to my own disadvantage. Thus, I do not speak out of private animosity. What I say I hold to be true. I said it *in this way* because I deemed it necessary. I add that the treatment of the Jews by many new writers appears very inconsistent to me and that I believe I have a right to say *what* and *how* I think.

Whoever does not like what was said, should not rail against, slander, [or] be offended about the *above facts*, but *refute* them.

47. *Aberglauben*: The German word for superstition literally means "wrong/erroneous faith."

[293] Alongside these, another almost equally dreadful state weaves itself through militaristic monarchies: the military. Their estate is tough through [294] strict discipline[48] and the laws written in blood that are tied to it. Through this discipline and law, they [members of the military] find honor in their humiliation and find compensation for other burdens in offenses against the citizen and peasant committed with impunity. The crudest half-barbarian believes to put on with his uniform a certain superiority over the shy peasant, who is happy when he can endure the former's teasing, offenses, and insults without also being dragged before his worthy commander and beaten. The noble youth, who has more ancestors but not more education, considers his sword belt to be an authorization letter to look down scoffing upon the merchant, the worthy scholar, [and] the deserving statesman, who would probably defeat him in a proof of ancestors, to tease them, and to push them. Or they would heal our youths, who have [now] dedicated themselves to the sciences, from their possible bad habits with foot kicks.§§§

The aristocracy is less dangerous since it is no longer the exclusive occupant of all riches and of the sparse culture of immature peoples. Yet it is still a real state within a state, separated by its guild spirit, by its intermarriage, and by the exclusive right to certain services. At best [it is] useful only where the people still requires a wall against despotism. I will not mention the persistent, horrible violence of hierarchy, because I [295] write predominantly for Protestant countries. However, if our clergy does not—through their exclusive subordination to chief consistories,

---

§§§Everyone familiar with a certain strong garrison knows that this trait can be proven with multiple facts. By the way, I add that precisely this estate splendidly maintains and fosters many a noble virtue: that quick and courageous resolve, manly and frank candor, the zest of social life, are found almost exclusively among educated officers in this age. I pay tribute with heartfelt admiration to all worthy men I know or don't know in this estate. But the judgment in general here does not rest on the greater or smaller number of facts but on reasons. This one estate is withdrawn from the common court of law and brought before a special [court]. The laws of this court are very different from the universal laws of morality and punish harshly what is hardly a mistake according to the latter and overlook misdemeanors that the latter would penalize strictly. This estate, then, sustains a separate interest and a separate morality, and it becomes a dangerous state within the state. Whoever evades the temptations of such a constitution is all the nobler of a man, but he does not disprove the rule. He only constitutes an exception.

48. *Manneszucht*

consistories, and superintendents, through their separate law courts, and through the maxims prevailing here and there—declare much to Gad and Askalon, so as not to give the Philistine any joy;[49] in short, if, through their separate state, they do not oppress the excluded citizen more publicly and strongly, then this only proves that the Reformation really did bring a better spirit into Christianity. And didn't our clergy succeed equally well [as the Catholics] in delaying the progress of the human spirit and in opposing important improvements?—Smaller taunting is carried out by the guilds of artists and craftsmen, which are felt less only because one has to fight with bigger nuisances.

All these are states within states that have not only a separate interest, but also one opposed to all other citizens. [These are] truths that I only mention in passing here, but if I ever see my reader again, I will have to trace them back to their basic principles in the following chapter. They are indeed hostile states. Why do we not recall its basic principle here?

No state becomes dangerous as a result of being within another state in terms of space but as a result of having an interest opposed to the other. Now, if all states are standing under the law of natural right, like isolated human beings, and this law absolutely forbids everyone to hinder the lawful freedom of others, insofar as they do not hinder his, then such a conflict cannot arise at all unless the members in one or both of the states have joined with each other to be unjust. They should not do that, [and] therefore they ought to complain not about the pressure of the circumstances but about their own ill will. If only they were all just, they could, mingled yet separated from one another, pursue their various businesses.

Have you ever noticed that, in the various regions of the German empire, the oppressed and exhausted estates of greater and smaller despots weave through the blessed fields of mild and humane princes? And yet, the shriveled slave tills calmly next to the strong farmer? Have you never stepped from the region of a certain imperial city [296]—in which the well-fed, educated, and learned farmer did not find it novel to be your equal, since he is a human being—across borders marked everywhere with, instead of a coat of arms, the image of a hand under an axe and of a man tied to a cart, where you encountered dried-out mummies in rags that, seeing your whole attire, pulled off the rest of their headpiece

49. An allusion to 2 Samuel 1:20.

before they even came into your view? The latter live calmly beside and among the former and now bleed out the last drop of blood for those who took the earlier ones [drops of blood]. There are doubtlessly very different states in the same space, and no conflict arises between them. Thus, those who left the old association, may unite through a new one and may strengthen their union through the voluntary assent of others. They have the perfect right to it. If, finally, the old association has no more supporters and all have turned voluntarily to the new one, the *entire* revolution has been legitimately accomplished.

And here I put my pen down. I will pick it back up, if I should find that I have not worked in vain and if the public for once disproves the familiar accusation that it is not mature enough for such examinations through action. If not, I will run my course in a different sphere.

Chapter Four

On Privileged Classes in General, in Relation to the Right of Changing the State

[299] Until now, our path has led along the smooth high road of natural right. From now on, it winds through the dark sunken roads of Gothic opinions and through the hedges and bushes of half-barbaric politics. Here I must ask the reader, who has followed along up to this point, for a renewal of his leniency and courage. It is no small feat to do justice to certain opinions in front of the tribunal of reason that are not accustomed to speak in the language of reason themselves. [It is not easy] to stand their ineloquence in good stead, to be the defendant's attorney and the just judge at the same time. At least, it is not my will to proceed unfairly. According to the judge's maxim—to take everyone to be as credible as possible—I will attribute to the defendant the best reasons that can be found anywhere. If their cause still does not prevail, there will be little doubt about its defeat if they make do with bad reasons.

Distinguished citizens of the state are those to whom the remaining citizens have pledged themselves to particular service that the former will not give back. [They pledge] perhaps in exchange for other service on the part of the distinguished, who will not get [anything] back from the other remaining citizens either. Let us not be miserly here about the return service of the distinguished [citizens]. Their condescension to accept the marks of respect from the lesser citizens and to place a worth on them, or their efforts to utilize the prerogatives that we allowed them to employ our services and to consume the earnings we surrender

---

1. *Willkühr*

107

to them may even be [regarded as] such return services, if they want us to regard them that way. That these mutual rights and obligations can only be founded on contract and that the validity or invalidity of this special contract rests on the basic principles of contracts in general, which we developed above, is immediately apparent to everyone without further examination.

Most objections that have been made to the validity of this kind of contract seem to have been founded on doubts about whether the mutual services between the distinguished and the remaining citizens can indeed be viewed as equally valid, or whether the true inner worth of the one perhaps outweighs the other's [worth] disproportionately. [300] Whether, through their service, the former really repays the latter or whether the former perhaps remains in debt to the latter. Whether an exchange of advantages really takes place or whether one of the two is perhaps advantaged beyond all measure. The suspicion that the latter is most of the time really the case is the reason that the distinguished [citizens] are also called *privileged*. And, since I don't want to deny that I harbor the same suspicion, one may allow me to begin using this designation from here on until I will justify it. According to our basic principles determined and developed above, the advantage beyond all measure takes place most certainly where an inalienable human right has been alienated. No substitute of equal worth is even possible for such [a human right]. We may not forsake such [a right] as long as we remain human beings. A contract in which it is forsaken is already inherently invalid and void. Following our reflections above, we can therefore establish as the exclusive condition for the validity of any contract of privilege: *that no inalienable human right must be alienated through it*. This condition extends far, but it is the only one. We can give away our alienable rights in the manner and under the conditions we want. We can give them away for free. The other has to do nothing but accept them and the contract is fulfilled and established in the world of appearances.

It is an inalienable right of the human being to repeal any of his contracts as soon as he wants, even unilaterally. Immutability and eternal validity of any contract is the most severe offense to the right of humanity itself. In the case of the civil contract in particular, this has already been proven above based on its substance, [i.e.,] based on its end. For all contracts in general, it can be deduced without difficulty from the above determined principles about the form of the contract itself.

Specifically, the reciprocally free arbitrary will[1] is the foundation of right and obligation in the contract. It has been proven above that a contract can take place only about things that are objects of our arbitrary will, which is mutable, but not over such [things] in respect of which our will[2] ought to be determined immutably by the moral law. I explained in the same place that the mutual rights and obligations, and consequently the contract itself, are repealed as soon as *one* of us changes his arbitrary will over the object of the contract. Thus, it remains here only to answer the question whether a human being perhaps has the right to bind himself in advance [301] *never to change his arbitrary will* on a certain object—perhaps in the same manner in which he is bound never to change his will to do his duty. On the answer to this question depends the answer to the following question: whether the immutability of a contract is consistent with the inalienable right of humanity or not. Since the continuation of the right and the obligation of a contract can be based on nothing but the continuation of the free arbitrary will, the immutability of a contract necessarily presupposes the promise that one never wants to change one's arbitrary will on the object of the contract. This means that as I enter an immutable contract, I pledge never to change my present will on the objects included in the contract.

The *arbitrary will* itself, insofar as and because it is arbitrary, is entirely exempt from the binding law of reason. Its direction depends on physical causes, which determine the extent of our insight.[3] I always embrace the decision that appears to be the most useful and beneficial, and, because of the permission from the moral law, I have the complete right thereto. My arbitrary will necessarily changes as my insight increases and decreases. The promise not to change one's arbitrary will would be a promise not to augment and perfect one's insight. But no human being may give such a promise. Everyone has *the duty*, and therefore also the *inalienable right*, to work on his perfection into eternity and always to follow his best insight. Thus, he also has the inalienable right to change his arbitrary will in accordance with the degree of his perfection, but in no way does he have the right to bind himself never to will to change

---

1. *Willkür*

2. *Wille*

3. *Einsicht*

it. The clause in a contract, of whatever nature it may be, that says that it [the will] ought to be unchangeable is therefore completely empty and meaningless, because it violates an inalienable human right. It is entirely as if it [the clause] did not exist.

Even so, the unilateral repeal of even the most disadvantageous contract is subject to the same conditions as all unilateral repeals of contracts. Regardless of how much you are advantaged, not only do you not have *the* right to demand the restitution of that which the other has already absorbed into his property with your good will, but also, in fact, you have to replace him the damage that he demonstrably incurs by relying on the continuation of your good will, now withdrawn. What's past is passed. For the future, you might take better measures. You gave away rights that you had no use for. Now you learned to use them better. Demand back the exercise of them, but do not punish the misuse that has been made of [302] your thoughtless kindness before. You have only yourself to blame. You sold noble assets in exchange for a lentil dish. You have indeed been taken advantage of. Once you notice this, take them [the assets] back and do not taste his lentil dish anymore. It would be most unjust to compel you to remain a fool because you were a fool once. But it is not unjust at all that you should bear the consequences of your previous foolishness.

Thus, as soon as the unprivileged citizen begins to notice that he is being taken advantage of by the contract with the privileged, he has the complete right to repeal the disadvantageous contract. He releases the latter from his promise and takes his [promise] back in turn. Either he cancels the services to which the latter had obligated himself entirely, because he believes he can do without them, or he thinks about obtaining them for a cheaper price. Perhaps he no longer finds it brings honor to himself when a handful of noblemen and princes form a magnificent court at his expense, or [he finds it] no longer conducive to the well-being of his soul when a flock of bigwigs fatten themselves up on the marrow of his estates, or perhaps he offers the few military services he needs for more bearable conditions. He will transfer those services to whoever gives him the mildest [conditions]. Who would be allowed to refuse this to the state?

"To the state," I said, and so I stand before a powerful objection: the privileged individual is a citizen of the state as well. Therefore, without his consent, nothing generally binding can be agreed upon regarding the abolition of his privileges. But this is not true. The privileged individual, insofar as he is privileged, is not a citizen. You say, he has entered a contract with the remaining citizens. Could he do that as a citizen of the state who has no will of his own and who first becomes a moral person in association with the others? He was a party to the agreement when he entered the contract. That is what he is when the contract is to be repealed by the other party. He will [have to] acquiesce to being silent as long as they consult about the repeal of the contract. Once this matter is decided, he will get back his right to vote as a citizen of the state. If it will come into question how and under what conditions the administrative offices [previously] run by him ought to be filled again, then he may voice his opinion. If, for example, the question of nobility came up, he may perhaps say, "there ought to be noblemen in our state." But he may not say, "I want to be a nobleman in our state."

But our privileged behave differently. When we cancel the contract with them and want to transfer their possible services to others under milder conditions, they show us their personal entitlement [303] to control these services, excluding all others, a prohibition for everyone else to concern themselves with [the services]. And if they get away with it, we are worse off than before. We must continue to accept these services from them. We may not cancel them, because they rely on performing them. We may assign them to no one else, [since] they rely on them *exclusively*. We cannot haggle with them[, because] they prevent all competition. They estimate the price for their services as high as they want, and we can do nothing but pay. For example, we no longer want those decorations on our public buildings that are nothing but mere decorations.

"No," they say, "decorations like that are necessary because we are there to pick these decorations. If *they* no longer exist, *we* will no longer exist."

"Alright," we say, "but why should you exist?"

"Because decorations are necessary," they reply.

"We want to abolish useless things."

"No," they say, "these things are not useless at all; they are useful to *us*."

"Yes, but what are *you* useful for?"

"*We* are useful to use those things."

—And [like this] we are not a single step further with them. Thus, we must examine, without listening to them any further, what kind of entitlement that actually is which they show us.

They, only they, are exclusively entitled. Who, then, are these "they?" How are they distinguished from all others who are not "they"? What is their exclusive feature? It is not founded on the presumed contract that we want to repeal. Supposedly, their right is older than any contract entered with them. Consequently, it must be an inborn, a hereditary right. However, we know of no inborn rights but the universal human rights, and none of these are exclusive. Thus, their right must, after all, be *acquired*, if not by them, nevertheless by someone else who would have transferred it to them. In particular, it must be acquired *by contract*, since a right over persons can be acquired in no other way.—We do not want to search for this contract here. It is apparent from the above that we would have the complete right to repeal and annihilate the contractual obligation from our side. At this point, we only want to talk about the peculiar transfer of rights, the legal validity of which is presupposed here.

Every right over persons rests on an obligation on the other's part. And since we are not speaking here about a natural human right but about an acquired civil right, [it rests on] an obligation that is not imposed by the law of reason but by one's own free arbitrary will. And therefore it presupposes a contract. "The right is *transferred*" means that *one party appoints* [304] *another person to the contract instead of himself.* That this must take place at least with the *knowledge* of the obligated party is obvious. Otherwise, how would he know to whom he must render his obligation? That it must also take place through his *will*, follows in our system immediately from the fact that the contract would have endured only through his enduring will, even with the first actual contracting party [remaining]. But we can grant all this to the opponent. If the appointed party has been appointed to the contract under the *same* conditions [as the previous party], he may always say that [this transfer] should make no difference to the other party, as long this second party remains *one and the same person.*

But, in the case of the transfer of rights that is at stake here, [i.e.,] in the case of the *inheritance of rights* in our states, the person does not remain one and the same. He who accepted the obligation is also said to have appointed another to the contract in his place. If it is really a contract between a privileged and a disadvantaged party, it is entirely to be expected that the representative of the privileged entered into the contract voluntarily and gladly. But did the representative of the disadvantaged [party] enter it just as voluntarily? Or could the disadvantaged [party] perhaps transfer his obligation to another [person] at his own discretion,[4] without asking whether he wants to accept it? Or, in other words, is the latter bound by a foreign will? *A foreign will never binds.* That is the first principle of all contract law. The privileged [party] can continue to deny that the disadvantaged [party] may repeal the contract as soon as he wants while he is alive. When the disadvantaged party dies, his obligation certainly ceases, since he can no longer satisfy it. Whoever exits from the world of appearances, forfeits his rights in it and sheds his obligations. The privileged [party] can pursue him into the other world and assert his claims there, if he can. He can simply no longer be found in this. But to grab the first available [person] and tell him, "I had demands on someone. He dodged them by dying. I must be satisfied. Come, *you* ought to vouch for him."—How should that be acceptable?—

"But he appointed you," you say.

"Then I regret that you let yourself be deceived. He had no right to command me. Nobody has that [right] but I myself."

"But you are his son."

"But not therefore his property."

"As the custodian of your rights during your immaturity, he included you in the contract with me."

"He was allowed to do that until the point where I [305] became mature, but no longer. Now I am mature and myself the custodian of my rights and [I] grant you no right over me."

Under the title *inheritance law*, Herr Rehberg* conflates the right to inherit *things*—that are not their own property—and the right to inherit obligations from *persons*—who are all surely their own property—without further distinction. Did this occur through hardly conceivable ignorance or through the clearly premediated intention to confuse the examination and to obtain surreptitiously the assent, which he could not hope to compel with reasons? I should think that the two rights—the first well-founded and the second invented and contradicting reason—are quite evidently distinct. The legal ground of the civil, exclusive law

---

*P. 32 of his pamphlet cited above.[5]

4. *Willkürlich*

5. Rehberg, *Untersuchungen*.

of inheritance has been developed above. It is founded on a contract among all citizens to relinquish their *common* right of inheritance over the goods of *every* deceased person in exchange for the *exclusive* right of inheritance over the goods of *certain* deceased persons. They did not have to inquire into the object of the contract, the goods. They were very certain that the latter would not object against this regulation.—[By analogy,] the legal ground of a right of inheritance over persons' acquired obligations could only rest on a contract among the privileged citizens to relinquish their *common* right of inheritance over the obligations of *all* disadvantaged and oppressed [citizens] in exchange for the *exclusive* right of inheritance over the obligations of *certain* disadvantaged and oppressed [citizens]. And this supposed common right of inheritance itself, alienated in exchange for an exclusive [right of inheritance]—if it is not founded on the right of the stronger, on the legally binding war of all against all, if that contract is not supposed to be the contract of highway robbers, who peacefully share their loot in a den so as not to attack each other with the sword and kill each other, which perhaps it ought not to be after all—on what, I say, could this common right of inheritance be founded but on a prior contract with the disadvantaged [citizens] never to demand the rights back that they gave up? Aside from the fact that, according to the above, such a contract would not have the force of law, since the inalienable human right to change one's arbitrary will is alienated in it, where should more disadvantaged citizens come from after the death of the first? Where should the obligations to be inherited emerge from? Do we want to give as little regard to the persons who will be inherited [306] as we give to the things in an inheritance contract of things? Doubtless, in a system where no equality among human beings is granted but equality before God in relation to the church, this question, too, will be answered "yes" without thought. And if it was asked whether human beings themselves cannot be inherited, exchanged, sold, and given away as property, following this system, one would have to answer "yes" as well.

Montesquieu says that whenever one says evident things, one cons [the reader] the least.[6] And it is in no way unknown to me that I present things here that tremendously offend the fragmented common opinion of peoples—otherwise also called by its more honest name,

---

6. Charles de Secondat Montesquieu, *Spirit of the Laws*, bk. 25, ch. 13.

common sense. But what do I care? Make the effort to return to the basic principles and to dismantle those. Or, if you have to allow them to stand, rest assured that everything that follows from them through proper inference is necessarily correct and [that] your opinion, which contradicts it, is necessarily false, even if all human beings had been of your opinion from the beginning of time until now. Since the [time of] the first law-giving people that we know of, since the [ancient] Egyptians, it has indeed been assumed in all states that the son is responsible for the father's obligations and therefore thoughtless people follow the authorities and believe it must indeed be true. But in several of the states that implanted their opinions in us along with their laws, it was also deemed rightful for the father to abandon his newborn child or to punish his grown [child] with death, without anyone having the right to ask him why. Why haven't we maintained the latter opinion alongside the former? Does the same principle not underlie both, namely, that the child is the father's property, which he can control at his discretion? Is it perhaps harsher to leave a young child to die, who has not become fully conscious of itself yet [and] that perchance [307] feels less at his death than a choked pigeon? Or is it harsher to suddenly deprive a grown [child] of all the laboriousness of life through his quick death than it is to coerce that same child, in full possession of his power and his rights, for fear of death to be a livelong serf? That is because Christianity has disseminated a different opinion—for you it is nothing more than opinion—of the immortal soul of man and of the influence of the life spent here in this world, especially his last hours, on the fate of this soul in the other life, [an opinion] that opposes such an arbitrary[7] disposal of *human life*. Christianity, or rather its servants who have been sold to despotism, forgot to disseminate an opinion that opposes a [similar] arbitrary disposal of *human freedom*. And the philosopher simply cannot command popular opinion in the same manner as the spirited divine envoy.—In regard to the first fragment of your incoherent opinion, you were open to persuasion by a milder human religion. In regard to the second, you are still determined by the crude mode of thinking of half-savages who just took the first step to wean themselves off human flesh. This mode of thinking seeks to take advantage of the depressing situation of a fellow citizen who simply does not make a good meal. It

---

7. *Willkürlich*

demands the promise of lifelong slavery with the complete renunciation of even the desire for freedom. Once the frightened man has promised this, this mode of thinking makes him promise the subservience of his children to the children of the oppressor and then, once he has promised that as well with fear in his heart, it makes him promise the same subservience for the third, then for the forth, then for the fifth link, and then for all possible generations into eternity. Can this mode of thinking be anything but [that of half-savages]? And can anyone promise this but in the face of the burning stake and the spit on which he shall be roasted? There you see your authorities!

Even the steadfast Herr R. does not want to deny all insight of those men who feel indignation in their heart upon applying such basic principles to the contemporary state of the world. And he does not want to construe their melancholic sentiments in an extreme way. But his goodwill does not last long.[8] He says, "one simply destroys all possibility of a [308] civil order, if that which an ancestor did perhaps out of necessity (which he bound himself to, he wants to say),† even if it was one million years ago, would not bind his heir. No state could exist if children or other heirs were not forced to take the place of the deceased."[10] Should this mean that none of the presently existing states could exist in the way it is now, if each constitution does not also remain in the way it is now, then he is entirely right and his acumen was not needed for us to discover this. However, should this mean that, without this organization, no civil association is thinkable at all and that it is included as an attribute in the concept [of the civil association], it would follow that the civil association itself is entirely irrational and illegitimate and that none must be tolerated.—A civil association ought to exist. It is Herr R.'s conclusion that, since this is not possible without injustice, injustices must be committed. On the contrary, I would argue thus: no injustices ought to be committed. Since no civil association is possible without injustices, no civil association must exist. In this case, the adjudication of our conflict would depend on the answer to the question

---

†P. 60—Almost no line written by this man, who ceaselessly complains about vague chatter,[9] can be copied without having to correct his formulations.

8. Rehberg, *Untersuchungen*, 1:59.

9. Rehberg, *Untersuchungen*, 1:63–64.

10. Rehberg, *Untersuchungen*, 1:60–61.

whether it is the ultimate final end of the human race to live in civil society or to do right. The verification of R's claim itself—that no civil constitution is possible at all without an arrangement for bequeathing civil obligations—does not belong here. I am not speaking about the possible arrangements of particular constitutions yet, but about the exclusive conditions for the moral possibility of all constitutions in general.

Hitherto we have examined the validity of contracts of privilege in respect to *their* form. We found not only that no inheritance of privileges takes place (as is purported), but also that even the immediate, first contracting party can repeal any contract as soon as he wants, due to the fact that he believes himself to be disadvantaged. [309] Recall that, in this case, the person who unilaterally repeals [the contract] is obligated to restitution and compensation. To be able to estimate this compensation, we now have to undertake another examination of the contracts of privilege in respect to their possible *matter*, i.e., of the objects of such contracts. Right away, we must mention *one* conceivable object of such a contract in advance, before its turn in our discussion. Namely, one may believe, the commoners in the state could have exclusively surrendered by contract their right to change something about the constitution to the privileged class of the citizenry, or perhaps to *one* privileged [person]. If such a contract was made, all other contracts of privilege would thereby become confirmed and inviolable for the excluded citizens, as if they [these contracts] were a part of the constitution. If the commoners were not allowed to break this [contract] without foregoing compensation, they could not repeal any of the other contracts of privilege either. This is because no equivalent compensation is possible for the repeal of the first [contract] except the maintenance of the other contracts, [and] consequently the contract at hand, too.—But such a contract is already void and invalid in itself precisely because it makes all other contracts of privilege unchangeable for a portion of the citizens, and therefore it repeals the inalienable human right to change one's arbitrary will.—If I relinquish entirely my right to change anything about this constitution and transfer it to someone else, this means that I do not want to change my free arbitrary will about the obligations that are imposed on me by it [the constitution]; that I want to hold that which I deem necessary and useful today to be so as long as a certain other person holds it so. And isn't such a promise surely irrational? Such a contract is practically no contract at all. Thus, it does not prevent any member of the state from repealing his contract of privilege.

Only alienable rights can be given up—in all contracts in general [and] therefore in this [contract] as well. A guide for locating all alienable rights, if such [a guide itself] can be located, would therefore be a reliable means of thoroughly listing all possible objects of contracts of privilege as well as of all contracts in general.

On the whole, alienable rights are modifications of inalienable rights. The latter can be exercised in manifold ways. The free being has the right to every manner of exercise. But precisely because there are multiple [ways of exercising these rights], none of them are inherently inalienable. If I don't exercise it [my right] in this manner, I exercise it in another way. Indeed, I must exercise it in some way, for the primordial right[11] is inalienable.

[310] All primordial rights of humanity can be traced back to the following two classes: *rights of unchangeable spirituality*[12] and *rights of the changeable sensibility*.[13] The form of my pure I is determined immutably by the moral law in me: I ought to be an I—an independent being, a person. I ought always to will my duty, [and] therefore I have the right to be a person and to *will* my duty. The rights are inalienable and no alienable rights spring forth from them because my I is not capable of modification in this respect.—Everything in me that is not this pure I itself, is sensibility (in the broadest meaning of the word, part of the material world) [and] therefore changeable. I have the right to form this changeable I into the given form of the pure I through gradual laboring on it (which constitutes a modification). I have the right to *do* my duty. Since the pure form of my I is determined immutably, the form that is to be brought out in my sensible I is also determined immutably (in particular, in the idea). The right to do my duty is only exercisable in *one* way and not capable of any modification. Therefore, no alienable rights spring forth from it. A number of modifications are, however, still left in my sensible I, which cannot be related to the unchangeable forms of the pure I. These modifications are not regulated by the immutable moral law, and therefore their determination is at the discretion of my arbitrary will, which itself is changeable. Since it [my arbitrary will] is this way [changeable], it can determine those modifications in manifold

---

11. *Urrecht*

12. *Recht der unveränderlichen Geistigkeit*

13. *Recht der veränderlichen Sinnlichkeit*

ways. It has a right to every manner of those [modifications], but all are in themselves alienable. It is only here, that we enter the domain of the alienable rights.

This arbitrary will modifies either my inner forces—that which goes on in my mind—or my external, bodily forces. I may, with regard to the former, direct my considerations to a certain point, think about this or about another object, and judge. In this way, I may bring myself to desire this, detest that, admire this person, disrespect that person, love this person, hate that person. Since all these are changeable deter-minations of my mind, the rights to them would not be inalienable in a moral sense, but they are in a physical [sense]. They may perhaps be alienated, but they cannot be because no foreign being could know whether I performed my accepted obligation toward him or not. One could say, metaphorically, that they [the rights] are often alienated to ourselves, to our power of judgment.[14] Our power of judgment often advises us to detach our thoughts from this [311] object and to direct it to that. And the free arbitrary will transforms this good advice into a law for us.‡—Thus, no legally binding promise takes place concerning our will not to think beyond certain things or beyond certain boundaries, our will to be kind to someone else, love him, admire him. For how, granting this was entirely subject to our arbitrary will, could the other ever make certain that we kept our word?

Accordingly, no rights alienable by contract remain but those regarding the use of our bodily forces, regarding our external actions.

Our actions are directed at *persons* or *things*. In the case of persons, we either exercise a *natural* or an *acquired* right. The former, the right to self-defense under coercion, the right to war, can be surrendered to someone else, but [only] with two limitations. We must reserve the right—or rather, it necessarily remains ours even without explicitly reserving it—[first,] to defend ourselves against a swift assault that endangers an irreplaceable possession, our life, and does not allow us to wait for out-

---

‡Unfortunately, this is entirely unintelligible for all those who have never become aware of a law-giving free arbitrary will but have been consistently guided by the blind power of imagination, according to the stream of their association of ideas. But this is not my fault!—Human beings' recollection of thought [*Gedankenerinnerung*] is free, too. And whoever has not liberated it, is certainly receptive to no other kind of freedom.

14. *Urteilskraft*

side help, and [second,] to defend ourselves against the highest defender of our rights *always* in person. In general, no one has ever doubted the first of these rights, despite the fact that it has been noticeably violated in multiple states by [exploiting] that fear of the law, by that demand of a proof of [actual] self-defense, which is as apparent to everyone as danger in the hour of fear is. The second has been withheld in most states entirely and some have tried to convince us with every means—especially with reasons borrowed from the Christian religion—to silently endure all injustices that our defenders do not want to avenge or, since they inflicted it on us themselves, cannot avenge, to willingly surrender ourselves to the hand of our shearer or our slaughterer. But just because it [the second right] has been suppressed, it is not therefore less solidly founded.—You defend us against all violence by other [people]. That is right and good. But if now you either use direct violence against us yourself or [312] make others' violence your own by omitting the defense you promised, which we may not undertake ourselves, who should defend us against you? You cannot be your own judge. If we are not allowed to secure our rights against you ourselves, we have entirely given up our right to self-defense, insofar it relates to you. We are not allowed to do that because only the manner of exercising this right—e.g., whether it ought to take place through us or through our representative—is alienable but not the right itself. *Whether* and *how* this defense against the highest power in the state is possible without disorder and disintegration, I don't have to examine here yet. I only had to show *that* it takes place and necessarily must take place. Incidentally, since this defense of our rights against others is a burdensome duty itself and in no way a benefit, it is not inconceivable how he [the defender of our rights], whom we relieve of this trouble, could thereby suffer and demand compensation of the same from us. [Our compensation] for the lost benefit would have to be offset by the intrinsically unjust and legally invalid impunity of his violence against us, or the no less unjust and legally invalid excess compensation that he perhaps extorts from our adversaries and keeps for himself. This, however, would obviously be a request for us to allow him to be unjust with impunity in the future, too, and consequently it should be dismissed without further consideration. Or does he perhaps fear the confiscation of what he obtains from us for his defense, which exceeds the value of [our] corresponding effort probably by far? We do not yet confiscate his pay immediately with the repeal of his commission. We will come to talk about this pay in due time and will discover how to determine it by law.—*One* kind of remuneration, we must, however, consider right away, because, according to our plan, we will not cover it in what follows. We said above that no binding promise to will to love or admire someone is possible because the other party could never know whether one has satisfied one's obligation or not. But activities which by their nature attract the love and the admiration of human beings are possible. And almost nothing makes one more honorable than the lofty occupation of defending the defenseless and protecting the oppressed from violence. Our protector hitherto could say that at least the respect that is necessarily associated with this occupation that has become a need through the habit of enjoying it, and the continuous possession of which he is entitled to rely on thanks to our contract, will be taken from him through the repeal of the contract. We reply to him: nothing [313] is more dishonorable than injustices committed in such a position, [namely,] oppression of defenseless innocence by a power instituted to defend the same. If we robbed him of the possibility of attracting the admiration of other nations, then we have also withdrawn the temptation to publicly dishonor himself before them, to become their curse and their abomination. Equal for equal cancels out.—But *he* alone is certain of his incorruptibility, his impartiality, his courage, and his power. *He* would certainly never have dishonored himself.—Now, then, in any case it would not have been his task, but the faithful fulfillment of his task, that makes him honorable. If he had done everything possible to fulfill it, he would still only have done what we could expect from him, what he owed to do according to his commission. The free performance of noble deeds, which are not demanded by any commandment, confers even more honor. He is now free. There will still be violent oppressors of the defenseless, humanity will always suffer, here and there. If he now deploys his power to boldly resist the unjust and mighty, to help humanity out of the abyss of misery on his shoulders, he will truly not miss out on our admiration. There is never a lack of occasions to acquire reverence. More often, there is a lack of men who want to achieve it through effort and exhaustion.

Acquired rights over persons are acquired through contract. We have the right to enter contracts and can alienate these rights *entirely* or *partly*. I said, "entirely." However, since this alienation itself is only possible through contract, it is clear that the alienation of this right must have been preceded by at least the one-time exercise of this right. Otherwise such an alienation would be absurd, because, as has been shown above, no natural human right, but only particular modifications of it, can be alienated. One party promises the other: "As long as I will be in the present contract with you, I do not want to enter another contract either with you or with anyone else." Judging by its form, such a contract is entirely valid. Judging by its content [it is] terrifying due to its monstrous extent. And if it is at the same time thought to be immutable—as it should be thought by the peasant, who is tied to the landed estate—then the contract will completely reduce the human being to an animal. Even without considering this immutability invalid in itself, the disadvantaged [person] relinquishes every demand on the privileged for better conditions [and] all help from others, who might want to treat him better, as long as it is impossible for him to make himself entirely independent of his oppressor. [314] The world becomes uninhabited to him and without a being of his kind. A moment of greatest fear, which might never return, is hastily seized in such a contract and is, so long as it depends on the oppressor, eternalized.

The right to enter contracts is *partially* alienated when one party promises not to enter a contract either only with certain persons or only over certain objects. Whether promises of this kind are in themselves valid cannot be a question, since the legal validity of the promise to enter no contract at all could not even be contested. There is nothing further to say about excepting certain persons from the right to enter a contract with others. With regard to objects, contracts (except the marriage contract, which, as is generally known, is everywhere restricted in manifold ways and which the serf cannot enter without permission from his lord at all) are entered either over *powers*—the labor contract—or over *things*—the barter and trade contract. With regard to the first type of contract, one party either altogether alienates his right to enter a contract over the application of his powers with anyone besides the *one* privileged [person], [i.e., the right] to work for anyone else. Or he alienates it only insofar as the other party to the contract can make use of his labor himself. [In other words,] he binds himself, whenever he has spare time to work for someone else, to first enquire of the other party whether *he* does not need him. In this context, there can also be stipulations made in advance [and] forever regarding the wage for his labor so that the worker is obliged to this or that amount of labor for a certain price, even if he could receive more from someone else. It is always presupposed here that the one party has not already given up, through the initial contract of privilege, the right to dispose of the use of his powers at all. For, in that case—of which we will speak further below—no other contract could take place.—With regard to the *trade contract*, the right to market one's products or manufactures to anyone but to the only privileged [person] can either be alienated altogether or only in the case that the privileged [person] wants to buy them. Consequently, the privileged either has the *exclusive purchase* [right],[15] like several cantonal cities of Helvetia over their peasants, or the *right of first refusal*,[16] like many German landowners over their subjects. Especially in the last case, something can be determined regarding the price of the goods so that the seller is obliged to yield them to the privileged [person] for a certain amount of money, even though he could receive more for it elsewhere. Or, conversely, it can [315] be agreed that one party must either buy *all* his goods, or those which the privileged [person] has, or only *certain* goods exclusively from the privileged [person], or that this party must buy them from the privileged for a certain price, although he could get them cheaper elsewhere. Consequently, the privileged [person] either has an *exclusive trade* [right][17] or an *advance trade* [right].[18] The cruelest and most spiteful modification of this type of contract is that where the suffering party is obliged to take a determined amount of a certain good and to pay a determined price for it, as the government in several countries does with salt and as Frederick II coerced every Jew for a while to take a determined amount of porcelain upon his marriage.

The second type of rights that could be alienated through our contracts with privileged [persons] were the rights over *things*, [i.e.,] the right to property in the broadest sense of the word. Commonly, one only calls the *continuous* possession of a thing the property. However, since only *exclusive* possession is the distinctive characteristic of property, the immediate enjoyment of a thing that is only enjoyed once and is consumed through the enjoyment is also true property. For, while somebody enjoys it, everyone else is excluded.

Now, this right to property can be alienated, just like the right of contracts, *entirely* or *partly*. It can be alienated entirely. The most immediate property, which grounds all other property of a human being, is that

---

15. *Alleinkauf*

16. *Vorkauf*

17. *Alleinhandel*

18. *Vorhandel*

of his powers. Whoever enjoys the free exercise of those, already has an immediate property in them, and he cannot fail to obtain before long property external to him through the exercise of them. The complete alienation of the right to property can therefore not be imagined other than in *such a way* that the free exercise of our powers is alienated, that the right to freely dispose of their application is transferred to someone else, and that thereby they [the powers] have become *his* property. According to the letter of the law, this was the case for all slaves among the ancient peoples and it is the case for all peasants belonging to the landed estate among us. If the master wanted, or wants, to refrain from his strict right, then it is an act of benevolence on his part, but he is not constitutionally bound to it.—Even so, this alienation only takes place under *one* condition: the master must assure a livelihood to the slave who cedes the direction of his powers to him. That is not benevolence. The subject has the complete right to demand it from him. Every human being must live: that is an inalienable human right. It is not valid [316] to say, "if I do not feed my slave, he dies off. I lose him and the damage is mine. Prudence will surely drive me to sustain him." This is not about your damage but about his rights, not about your prudence but about your indispensable duty. Your slave is a human being. The owner of an animal may let it perish, if it does not bring in the costs of its [own] maintenance, or slaughter it; not so the owner of a human being's powers. This livelihood is owed to him [the slave]. It is his property, which he has in his master's property, and as often as he eats, that which he eats is his immediate property. Thus, even the complete alienation of property is not possible, since, in fact, no human right in itself can be alienated but [it can admit] only particular modifications of it. It is clear that the person who alienated the free direction of his powers has relinquished all property except for this property [the livelihood].

The right to property, too, can be alienated only partly. The property in *powers* can be alienated in part so that a certain portion of it belongs to the privileged [person], regardless of whether we need them ourselves or not—as is the case with *measured* labor services§—or so

---

§For the few, who do not know this! The serf (*glebae adscriptus*[19]) has *unmeasured* labor services. He must work as much as the master demands. As a general rule, he demands six days of feudal service on his field and errands on the seventh, or hauls to the city. The free farmer, in whose soil the master has only a part of the property rights, has *measured* services. He performs a determinate number of labor services.

19. (A tenant) belonging to the land

that the excess thereof, which we do not need ourselves, belongs to him conditionally or without conditions—as is the case with restrictions on the right to enter labor contracts, which we have spoken of above.—The property in certain things can be alienated so that we may not acquire them in any way. Among these belongs the exclusive right to hunt, fish, keep pigeons, and the like, [as well as] the ordinance in some regions that the oak tree which grows on the peasant's land does not belong to the peasant but to the master, pasture and cattle track regulations, etc.

That all these rights as well can be repealed unilaterally by the disadvantaged party cannot be doubted anymore after the above argument. At this point, we only have the question about compensation in the case of a unilateral repeal. In the case of the first kind of restriction of our right to enter contracts, where the right is repealed entirely, [317] no complaint by the privileged can in general (we will get to speak about the particular [complaints] soon) be imagined. Only that, in the hope of the continuation of our contract, he missed out on entering the contracts that are useful and advantageous for him. But this [complaint] can be answered briefly like this: we, obliged by the contract with him, have likewise missed out on entering the contracts that are useful and advantageous to *us*. Until now, we have entered none. Now we cancel [the contract] with him [and] henceforth he knows what he has to expect of us. He should henceforth use his time as well as he can. We will likewise seek to use ours. We did not take advantage of him. We placed ourselves on equal footing with him.—Yet, his complaints get more precise. Regarding the exclusive labor contracts as well as the entirely or partially alienated disposition of our powers, he will complain that he will no longer get his labor done if we rescind the contract. Thus, he either has to work more than one individual can handle, or he cannot or does not want to work himself. The first supposition, as it is written here, would, properly translated, mean as much: he has more needs than can be satisfied with the powers of one individual, and, to satisfy them, he demands to use the power of others, who ought to break off as much of their own needs as they use power for the satisfaction of his. Whether such a complaint is to be rejected should not require any further examination. But he invokes a more valid reason in order to justify the greater abundance of his needs. Although he does not have more powers than the other directly, he still has the *product of multiple powers*, which perhaps has been passed on to him through a long series of ancestors. He has more property, the use of which requires the powers of many.—To be sure, this property is his and must remain his. [But] if he requires foreign powers to use it, he must see to it under what conditions he can get hold of them. A free barter trade arises over parts of his property and the powers of those whom he hires to labor on the whole. In this trade, every party seeks to gain as much as he can. He may make use of whoever offers him the cheapest conditions. If, in his hour of need, he overstrains his superiority over the oppressed, he may [have to] bear the cost, [as] the oppressed will cancel the sale as soon as the burdensome hardship has passed. If he offers him modest conditions, he will have the advantage that his contracts last longer.—"But, in that case, if everyone estimates [the value of] his labor as high as he can, he will no longer be able to put his property to use as extensively as before. The property's value will depreciate considerably."—That may perhaps [318] happen, but what's that to us? We have pinched not a hairbreadth off his estate. We have taken not a coin from his pile of cash. We were not allowed to do that. But to repeal a contract with him that appears disadvantageous to us we were allowed, and that's what we did. If his inheritance is thereby diminished, it must have been augmented through our powers before and our powers are not even his inheritance. And why is it necessary in the first place that, for the man who has a thousand farms, each one of the thousand brings in as much as one single farm [brings in] for the man who has one? Almost in all monarchical states, one complains about the unequal distribution of wealth, about the immense possessions of a few next to the host of human beings who have nothing. And this occurrence astonishes you in view of the present constitution of these states? And you cannot find the solution to this difficult problem of effecting a more equal distribution of property without interfering with property rights? When the currency multiplies—it multiplies through the dominating obsession of most states to enrich themselves by means of commerce and factories at the expense of all others; through the swindling trade of our age, which is steadily approaching its collapse and threatening everyone who even remotely has a stake in it with the complete destruction of their wealth; through the unlimited credit, which increases the printed money of Europe more than tenfold—when, I say, the currency multiplies thus out of proportion, it increasingly loses its value compared to the things themselves. The occupant of the products, the landowner, continually increases the price of the things that we need to have, and thereby his estates continually appreciate in value compared to the value of cash. But do his expenses increase as well? At best, the merchant, who provides him with the needs of luxury, knows how to be compensated; less so the craftsman, who does the indispensable labor for him and who is driven into a corner by both. But the peasant? He is still either a part of the estate or he does labor services without payment or for a disproportionately meager pay. His sons and daughters still serve as forced servants for the master in exchange for a scrap of money that, even centuries ago, bore no proportion to their services. He has nothing and will never have *anything* but the miserable subsistence wage for the present day. If the land owner knew how to restrict his luxury, he would already be—or if the present trade system suffers an upheaval, as it surely will, he would certainly become—the exclusive owner of all wealth in the nation and [319] no human being besides him would have anything. If you want to prevent this, do what you are responsible for doing anyhow: liberate the trade of the natural inheritance of human beings, of their powers. You will witness the peculiar spectacle *that the revenue from landed property, and all property, will be in inverse proportion to the size thereof.* Absent violent agrarian laws, which are always unjust, the ground will on its own gradually be distributed among several, and your problem will be solved. He who has eyes to see, see. I continue onwards on my path.

If the privileged [person] does not have the valid excuse of inherited property, he must work regardless of whether he wants to or not. We do not owe it to him to feed him. But he *cannot* work, he says. Trusting that we would continue to feed him with our labor, he neglected to cultivate and to form his own powers. He has not learned anything so that he could feed himself. And now it is too late, now his powers are too weakened by long idleness and, as it were, too rusty to still allow him to learn something useful. Admittedly, we are to blame for this because of our imprudent contract. If we had not led him on to believe since youth that we would feed him without his help, he would indeed have had to learn something. We are therefore obliged, and that as a matter of law, to compensate him, i.e., to feed him until he has learned to feed himself. But how should we feed him? Should we continue to go without the necessities so that he can live in abundance? Or is it enough if we provide him with the essentials? And thus we stand before a question, whose thorough answer belongs among the requirements of our age.

One has seen melancholic sentiments and heard bitter complaints among us about the supposed misery of so many who suddenly sank from the greatest abundance to a much more mediocre condition. One has heard them be lamented by *those* who never had it as good in their happiest days as they [have it] in their most unlucky, and who may have considered enviable the tiny leftovers of their luck. The enormous lavishness that has hitherto ruled at the king's table[20] has been restricted somewhat, and people who never had nor will have a table like that restricted [table] felt sorry for the king. A queen had a shortage of dresses for a little while,[21] and those [people] who would have been very happy [320] if they were allowed to share *these* shortages lamented her misery. Although our age lacks in many praiseworthy qualities, at least good-heartedness does not appear to be among them!—Do these complaints perhaps inevitably presuppose a system in which a given class of mortals simply has who-knows-what right to satisfy all the needs that the extravagant power of imagination can possibly invent? In which a second must have not quite as much as this [one], and a third not quite as much as the second, etc., until one finally descends to a class that must dispense with the most essential things in order to be able to deliver the most inessential to the higher mortals? Or does one only assume this legal ground in practice and argue thus: because *one* family has hitherto consumed the essentials of millions of families, it must necessarily continue to consume them? It is a remarkable inconsistency in our manner of thinking that we are so sensitive to the misery of a queen, who for once has no fresh linens, while we find the deprivation of another mother very natural, a mother who, dressed in rags herself, also bore healthy children for the fatherland, which she sees walking around her naked while the milk that the youngest demands with exhausted whimpering dries up in her breast due to the lack of food. "Such people are used to it, they do not know any better," says the rich hedonist in a stifling voice while he sips his delicious wine. But that is not true. One never gets used to the hunger, to unnatural foods, to the dwindling of all powers and all courage, to nakedness in harsh seasons. Herr R. found it naive that he who does not work should not eat. He should allow us to find it no less naive that he who works should eat nothing or what is most inedible.

The reason for this inconsistency can be found easily. Our age as a whole is much more sensitive toward the requirements of opinion than

---

20. An allusion to Louis XVI, 1752–93, king of France, who was executed in January 1793.

21. An allusion to Marie Antoinette, 1755–93, queen of France, and her imprisonment in the tower of the Temple in Marais.

toward those of nature. Pretty much all of those judges [of our age] have the essentials and have had it since youth. They directed everything that they could break off from the essentials to the inessentials, to the needs of luxury. It is the universal lot not to be able to satisfy all these needs to the extent that each desires. You have a modern household appliance, but you still lack a picture gallery. Maybe you get one, then you will only lack a chamber of antiquities. That queen only lacked the precious [321] necklace,[22] but you can be sure she suffered no less for it than your fashionable wife when she lacked a dress in the latest color.—But [it is] not enough that we cannot always satisfy the growing desires as they grow. Oftentimes, we are even compelled to regress, to chip away at needs that we are already used to seeing satisfied, that we already reckon among the essentials. This is suffering that we know from experience. Everyone, who feels it, is our fellow brother in tribulation, [and] we sympathize ardently with him. Through its magic art, our imagination quickly puts us in his shoes: that unlucky king had a number of his dishes withdrawn, so the wealthy cathedral canon imagined *himself* without his fine wine or without his favorite terrine, and the petit burgess or the affluent farmer's wife [imagined themselves] without their café au lait. Every member of the more or less genteel world [imagined himself] without satisfaction of those needs that he had acquired last. And how should everyone not have felt ardent compassion for him?—We assess and distinguish the *inessential* and *essential* only *according to the habit of possessing it* because we ourselves have experienced how many things have become indispensable through habit that were not before. We have no idea of the true difference between the two according to [their] *nature*. Or if we had obtained a concept of it through contemplation, we would still not have an idea animated by the imagination and set in motion by our sensation, because we have never stood on this outermost border ourselves and have always carefully averted our eyes against the sight of others on it. "That is unnatural, that's not how you hunger," we say with that tenant farmer in Diderot,[23] because *we* have never hungered like this. We think that one should become accustomed to enduring food shortage, or cold, or nakedness, or exhausting labor, as we have

---

22. This is an allusion to the Affair of the Diamond Necklace, 1785–86, a scandal in which Queen Marie Antoinette was accused of defrauding diamond jewelers in an elaborate confidence scheme.

23. Denis Diderot, 1713–84.

accustomed ourselves without much effort to going without a more lavish table of the grands, or their more splendid clothes, or their persistent, blissful idleness. We do not know or do not feel that these things are different not merely in *degree*, but in *nature*. We forget that many of the things we deny ourselves, we deny with a kind of voluntariness and that perhaps we could have them for a time if we wanted to expose ourselves to the subsequent deprivation of the essentials. [322] But in the case of their deprivation not *a* trace of free will remains, and they are forced to go without everything they go without. At other times, we rely that much on the difference between voluntary and coerced sacrifice when we consider the affairs of the privileged. Why then do we forget it here when we discuss the affairs of the oppressed?

It is not habit that decides what is *inherently* inessential and *inherently* essential, but nature. Everyone who works must have nourishment healthy for the human body in the quantity necessary for rejuvenating his powers, sound clothes appropriate to the climate, and sturdy, sound lodging: that is a basic principle.

Beyond these limits, however, on the field of things that nature does not declare to be essential, habit decides. And here suffering increases approximately to the degree that accustomed needs are not satisfied. I say *approximately* for two reasons: [First,] a great many of our needs are merely and exclusively needs of our imagination. We only need them because we believe to need them. They do not provide us with any pleasure once we have them. Their need only announces itself through the unpleasant sensation of going without them. Things of this kind have the distinctive mark that we have them only for the sake of others. Under this kind may be included everything that belongs to splendor which is mere splendor; everything that belongs to fashion insofar as it is marked neither by beauty, nor by comfort, nor by anything of that sort, but only by the fact of being fashion. In pursuing these needs, we can have no other aim but other people; not our taste, for these things are not characterized by beauty, but only to make known our obedience to the general forms and our affluence. Since these things are only esteemed for the sake of other people, these other people can absolve us completely from the obligation to have them. Until now, they have handed over the cost of it to us. If they withdraw the cost now, it is understood that they no longer expect the continuation of this kind of effort from us. Our circumstances are now known to the world. It is known to the world that our income no longer suffices to continue this effort with honor. Do we nevertheless persist, i.e., do we demand to shine through our dishonor? Such a demand is so foolish, the suffering over the denial of the [needs] is so nonsensical, that it deserves no mercy at all, and reasonable human beings cannot let this be brought to a reckoning. By denying these needs, no harm is caused to the person who, known to the world, satisfied them at other's expense, [323] and in the record of this relationship these needs are to be deducted from the sum.—Second, insofar as the satisfaction of needs really causes a coarse or fine sensible enjoyment, a titillation of the nerves or a lighter movement of the imagination, it can still not be denied that there is a great variation in degree and therefore in the degree of the need developed through habit. There is a vague outermost boundary to the irritability of human nature. Beyond it, enjoyment becomes very weak and unnoticeable. There is little doubt that the luxury of our century has reached this boundary and has crossed it here and there. The deprivation of what lies on this boundary, even more of what lies beyond it, cannot nearly cause the unpleasant sensation stirred by unsatisfied desires still within the boundaries of the greater irritability. This, too, is to be taken into account in the record of the proper relationship between denial and suffering.

[Once we have] deducted what must be deducted, a sum of the suffering of the privileged remains, however, that must arise from the limitations on the familiar luxury as a result of the repeal of the contract by us; suffering that we are, however, to blame for completely, due to our good-natured promise to continuously supply them with the needs of unlimited luxury. We are bound to remove these sufferings insofar as justice *allows* it, on the one hand, and *demands* it, on the other.

Insofar as justice allows it on the one hand—everyone must have the essentials, as we determined above. That is an inalienable human right. Insofar as their contract with us deprived any one of us of the possibility to have it [the human right], it [the contract] was in itself legally invalid and must be repealed without any compensation. As long as there remains only *one* [individual] who cannot acquire this [human right] through his labor because of them, their luxury must be limited with no mercy. I say "to acquire it through his labor" because he is only entitled to his essentials under the condition of the purposive application of his powers. It is not required at all that the privileged [person] should feed all idlers. We apply [the statement,] "who does not work, should not eat," with no less strictness to the common citizen than to the privileged—if the latter could work.

Insofar as justice demands it on the other hand—the privileged person appeals to the force of habit not to work and to consume much. [He says] his legal ground is the same as ours. His actual misery, the source of all his sufferings that we opened, must be closed by us as well. Just as he gradually got used to doing nothing and to wastefulness, [324] he must also gradually wean himself. From the hour of the repeal of our contract, he must form his powers, as far as he is still able, and use them as well as he can. The suffering that this application of power may cause him cannot be brought into account at all because it is suffering that nature imposed on us for benevolent ends and of which we have no right to free him. No human being on earth has the right to leave his powers unused and to live through foreign powers. He must estimate approximately how much time it will take him so that the use of his powers procures him the essentials. Until then, we have to provide for his livelihood. But, in exchange, we also have the right to supervise whether he really improves his skills so as to acquire the latter [livelihood] himself in time, since we no longer want to feed him.—From the hour of the repeal of our contract, he must gradually learn to withhold the satisfaction of ever more needs from himself. In the beginning, after the deduction of the [needs] calculated above, we will give him what is left of his previous earnings, then less, then gradually still less, until his needs have come approximately into balance with ours. And in this way he will have [no cause] to complain about injustice or undue harshness. If, additionally, he should become good and wise through these efforts, he will thank us one day for having turned him from a wasteful idler into a frugal worker and from a useless burden to earth into a useful member of the human society.

Chapter Five

On the Aristocracy in Particular, in Relation to the Right of Constitutional Change

[324] "All ancient peoples had their aristocracy," the statesmen say, who are at once held to be great historians. And they silently lead us to conclude from this that the aristocracy is as old as civil society and that there must be one in every well-ordered state. It is curious that precisely these men, [325] for whom the necessity of an aristocracy in every state is self-evident, get lost in conjectures that are supported by nothing but more conjectures whenever they engage ad nauseam in explaining the origin of today's aristocracy.

I do not speak of the *personal* aristocracy—of the fame or the advantages that a great man acquires for himself through his *own* deeds. I speak, as is required, of the *hereditary aristocracy*, of the fame or the possible advantages that he *passes on to his descendants* through the memory of his deeds.

Regarding this hereditary aristocracy, I distinguish between the aristocracy *of opinion* and the aristocracy *of right*. This distinction appears to me [to be] the guide that must lead us out of the blind alleys of conjecture onto an even, straight course. The neglect of this distinction was without doubt the reason for all errors that rule among us regarding this object.

There is some truth behind the claim about the aristocracy among the ancient peoples, but also some falsehood. Usually, they all had an aristocracy of opinion. They did not, setting aside a few short, temporary cases that were brought about through violent oppression and not through the state constitution, have an aristocracy of right.

The aristocracy of opinion necessarily emerges where human tribes live in continuous association and acquaintance. There is almost *no* object to which it [the aristocracy of opinion] cannot adhere. There is an aristocracy of scholars. Great scholars, indeed, rarely leave behind children. We may not believe in seeing the descendants of these great men in a *Leibniz*,[1] a *Newton*,[2] a *Kant*. But who can see a *Luther* unfamiliar to him without assuming a descendant of that great German man in him and directing closer attention to him? There is an aristocracy of merchants. And upon the mention of certain names that are immortalized in the history of trade, we would more often believe we see the descendants of the men who immortalized them, if the prefixed "Graf" or "Freiherr" or "von"[3] did not forbid this thought,* or perhaps if even the worthy name did not appear most dissimilar, [i.e.,] perhaps if the man had not [326] transformed himself into a mountain or into a valley or into a corner. There is an aristocracy of virtuous deeds. Everyone who lends a certain fame to his name passes the fame of this name on to his house along *with* the name.

Where human beings live in a state, a similar civil aristocracy must emerge very soon in order at least to maintain the state. A name that appears frequently in the history of our state, that has frequently attracted our attention in the narratives of that history, with the peculiar owner of which we have shared compassion and anguish or fear as well as the honor of accomplished grand deeds—is an old acquaintance to us. We see someone who carries it [the name], and all the ancient images attach themselves to our imagination *with* this name. At once, we survey the stranger's ancestry before he can tell us about it. We know who his father, his grandfather, his collateral relatives were and what they did. Everything passes before our soul. Our attention is thereby drawn to the owner of the noteworthy name and our interest stirred. We observe him

---

*The famous merchant is still eager for the honor of being an unknown aristocrat! This debasement of their illustrious names ought to be and remain far from dignified German scholars!

1. Gottfried Wilhelm Freiherr von Leibniz, 1646–1716.

2. Isaac Newton, 1643–1727.

3. *Graf* and *Freiherr* are German titles of (lower) nobility, which generally correspond to "count" and "baron" in English. *Von* indicates the particular place or estate from which the family takes its name.

more closely from now on in order to continue our comparison between him and his great ancestors. The word "nobilis" whereby the Romans designated someone—per their manner of thinking—noble, expresses this fittingly. They called him someone very recognizable, of whom one knows quite a few [things], whom one will observe more closely and will know even better soon. Nothing is more natural than for this attention to turn soon into respect and trust toward the man with the famous name, and that one presupposes the talent of his great ancestors or relatives in him, as long as he does not formally find us guilty of our error. If an undertaking were to occur that was the special, unique enterprise of some great man in our history and we would assign it to him if he were among us now, where will the memory of him direct itself rather than to one of his descendants? And since we cannot assign it to him, to whom will we rather assign it than to his name? It was a Scipio[4] who brought Carthage close to its destruction. From no one but a Scipio[5] does one expect with more certainty the complete obliteration of this state.

Such an aristocracy of opinion existed among the ancient peoples. It existed among the [327] *Greeks*, however, less noticeably, because the prevailing practice among them, that the son did not carry the name of the father but one of his own and that the names of houses were not common, did not support that deception of the imagination that clings to mere words. One first had to inquire about the ancestry of a young Greek, or he had to declare it himself. And the impression on which the young Greek relied for his appearance in the great world lost much through this pause to collect the news or through this necessary self-declaration. Even so, the appearance of a Cimon[6] or a Conon[7] certainly renewed the memory of the Battle of Marathon.[8]—Nowhere, at least in the free [part of] Greece, do I find an aristocracy *of right*, i.e., exclusive

---

4. Publius Cornelius Scipio Africanus Major, c. 235–c. 184 BC, won the battle of Zama against Hannibal in 202 BC, and led to the end the Second Punic War.

5. Publius Cornelius Scipio Aemilianus Africanus, c. 182–129 BC) was the adopted son of the older son of Scipio Africanus Major. In 146 BC, he conquered and destroyed the city of Carthage and erected the Roman province of Africa.

6. Cimon, c.507–446 BC, son of Miltiades.

7. Conon, d. 392 BC, son of Timotheus.

8. In this famous battle of 490 BC, the Greeks were victorious over the Persians under the leadership of the Athenians commander Miltiades, c. 550–489 BC.

rights of certain families, except perhaps the royal house of Sparta itself, the Heraclides. However, seeing that this government was more of a hereditary obligation than a hereditary privilege, since Lycurgus's[9] legislation was most restrictive, standing under the strict superintendence of the merciless ephors, the distinction of this family can be traced back to very different basic principles than the inheritance of personal privileges by birth. It [the distinction] was founded on the hereditary property of Laconia and, accordingly, its aristocracy was more comparable to our liege aristocracy—of which we will speak more below—than to our lineage aristocracy.[10] According to the system prevailing in Greece in Hercules's time, kingdoms are bequeathed to children and children's children and divided among them, [so] Hercules was entitled to several lands of the Peloponnese. His later descendants finally succeeded after multiple attempts to assert this hereditary right through the violence of arms. Two brothers[11] settled in Sparta and viewed Laconia as their inheritance, thus, their family privilege. In Rome, this aristocracy of opinion, this nobility,[12] had wider leeway and was integrated into a kind of system, in part due to the family names introduced among them. The division of Rome's citizens into patricians, knights, and plebeians appears to point to another [kind of nobility] than merely an aristocracy of opinion, but we will treat of this below. This nobility was founded on the administration of the first three state offices—the consulate, the praetorship, and the aediles, which were called curule dignities. The more men who had held these honors a family could count among its ancestors [328], the nobler it was. The images of their entitled ancestors were mounted in the most inner parts of their houses and presented to the corpse at their funerals. It is very natural that, for the sake of this opinion, the people eminently favored the old houses in its elections. But the latter were so far from having an *exclusive prerogative* to this honor that precisely this people took the pleasure from time to time to elevate a new, still unknown house. The founders of new houses were not in the least

---

9. Lycurgus, the legendary founder of the Spartan state and military constitution.

10. *Lehnsadel, Geschlechtsadel*

11. Eurysthenes and Procles, according to tradition.

12. Fichte uses a Roman Latin term here, *nobilitas*, which referred to the "noble" social status of the family of someone who held high political office, in particular, the office of the consul.

ashamed of the obscurity of their origin. Instead, they even took pride in publicly recalling that they had risen up themselves, through their own strength, not supported by any fame of [their] ancestors. It shows a laughable ignorance to equate *this* nobility with *our* aristocracy and *these* founders of new houses (*novi homines*) with *our* new aristocracy. If, with us, attendance at certain state services would be ennobling, if, for instance, the descendants of a state minister, a general, [or] a prelate would necessarily be aristocrats by virtue of their birth and without all further formalities, then a comparison would be valid.

Indeed, from the division of the Roman citizens into patricians, knights, and plebeians, one could assume a different [kind of] aristocracy than that of mere opinion. But such a conclusion would confuse the essential and the accidental, right and violent arrogation, time and place. It was Romulus who laid the foundation for this division and who thereby wanted to designate temporary honors and relationships in the state, but in no way hereditary prerogatives of certain families—of which he could have had no concept. He selected the *fathers* and their subsequent multiplication, the conscripts, according to [their] age, which made them dispensable in war [and] likewise more fit for counsel and the internal government of the state. They were determined to stay in the city during the incessant wars that he led and to preside over the state administration. Do we believe that this insatiable warrior and capricious regent intended to let their young and strong sons inherit the paternal prerogative not to drag them to war? Or that he wanted to narrow his choice of future senators—as they would exit through death—to these sons and [that he] did not reserve for himself the freedom to choose the eldest and wisest from the entire citizenry in the future, as hitherto, regardless of whether they had been knights or plebeians before? Most likely, one son of his first senators became a knight, the other plebeian, however it seemed most convenient to the king.—[329] He selected the *knights*, determined to serve on horseback, according to wealth. They had to be wealthy in order to sustain a horse. Whoever had nothing but physical strength—which was certainly no disgrace among this still developing people—was determined to serve on foot and was called *plebeian*. I wish it were possible to track down the origin of this word. Unless I am very mistaken, it originally meant a soldier on foot, without a hint of a contemptible connotation. It cannot be substantiated according to what basic principles these relationships between citizens were ordered under subsequent governments. It *is* likely that the son of a knight most often became a knight in turn because the required wealth from his father's inheritance could be supposed with certainty. But—setting aside the senators who had already acquired a certain superiority through Romulus's violent death, if this was not perhaps a later invention out of plebeian jealousy—it *is not* likely that every son of a senator became a senator in turn and [not likely] that no son of a knight or of a plebeian could become one. *Wise* counsellors are always in need, and wisdom is not always inherited by birth. This remark could not be lost on a Numa.[13]

This simple constitution became by far more complex under Servius Tullius[14] through the introduction of the census. An aristocracy of wealth emerged that was important enough during the period of the Republic and, in terms of external distinctions, finally produced the *lex Roscia theatralis*.[15] The aristocracy, however, was not founded immediately on birth, but on the riches inherited by birth. The descendants of a citizen of the first class sank below the *Aerarii*[16] whenever they had lost or wasted their inheritance and lost their seat in the theater alongside their wealth.

Under the despotic government of the young Tarquinius,[17] and even more under the disorder precipitated by the revolution and maintained by the cunning efforts of the expelled Tarquinians, the *patricians*, descendants of the old senators, seized immense prerogatives. And the people—sucked dry by the tyrants' oppression, by the expenses of incessant military campaigns, by its own inefficiency, and by the [330] harshness of its creditors—had to allow it. Not as citizens but as dependent debtors, they elevated those families exclusively to all state honors, which the families desired, and the expense of which the families alone could be

---

13. Numa Pompilius, 715–672 BC, was, according to tradition, the second king of Rome.

14. Servius Tullius, 578–538 BC, was, according to tradition, the sixth king of Rome.

15. The *lex Roscia theatralis* of 67 BC, named for the tribune Lucius Roscius Otho, its sponsor, awarded knights the right to reserved seats in the theater.

16. A particular social class under the Roman Republic. They were citizens but lacked many political rights and were subject to an arbitrary tax determined by the censor. This class included those who were inhabitants of a conquered town, had a certain degraded profession (e.g., performing arts), were convicted of certain crimes, or had committed some kind of dishonorable act in their private life. They were excluded from the thirty tribes and thus could not vote, become magistrates, or join the army.

17. Tarquinius Superbus, 534–510 BC, was, according to tradition, the seventh and last king of Rome. He is supposed to have died in 495 BC.

equal to through their wealth. At *this* point in time, there existed in Rome a true hereditary aristocracy of right. Its prerogatives, however, were not founded on the state constitution but on accident and violent oppression. They were unrightful rights.—Desperation restored to the neglected classes those powers that tolerable misery had wrenched from them. In the long war with the patricians, they gained back all the civil rights they had in common with them, and henceforth the difference between patricians, knights, and plebeians was a mere name. Everyone could become everything in the state without restrictions. The exclusive aristocracy of the patricians disappeared, and that nobility took its place. From the time that trade and wealth entered the republic, the knights appear to have focused above all on increasing their riches, to have contented themselves with the aristocracy of wealth, and to have left the administration of expensive state offices to others. We find their houses less [often] among the great houses of the republic. The plebeians, however, did not allow the patricians any advantages. We find just as many noble houses among the former as among the latter, and at the same rank.

The barbaric nations that became known to the Romans had no aristocracy but that of opinion and could have no other. And when Roman writers discern a nobility among them, they certainly use this word in the meaning of *their* language. But this will soon emerge in examining the question, what kind of aristocracy our European aristocracy actually is, and—in order to make a judgment on this—whence it arose? For it is not without benefit to dive into history with our aristocracy and its defenders in order to show them that even there what they are searching for cannot be found.

The most and mightiest peoples of today's Europe stem from the *Germanic* people that roamed about the woods free and lawlessly like the North American savages. They first formed into stable states in the *Frankish* Empire. The most eminent empires of Europe originate from this [Empire]: the German Empire, France, the Italian states. The remaining empires not [331] of immediate Germanic origin were alternately ruled, cautioned, formed, and basically created by this [Frankish Empire], or by the branches that sprung forth from it, especially the most important, the German Empire. The spirit of the Frankish order is to be found in the forests of Germany. The foundation of the modern European institutions is to be found in this empire.—There were two estates among the Germanic people: freemen and servants. Among the former, there was an aristocracy of opinion; there was none of right. There could not have been one. What should the aristocracy's prerogatives have been among these peoples? To their *fellow citizens?* Among people who lived in the greatest independence, who knew no stable, enduring society but family relations, and who followed almost no orders but for the duration of a short, temporary single enterprise? Or to the *landed estate?* Among people who did not love the cultivation of fields and resided in a different place every year? Whoever distinguished himself through strength and bravery, through robbery and victory, on *him* all eyes were set. He became subject of conversation. He became famous and noble, according to the expression of the Romans. His people remembered his deeds [and] honored his memory upon seeing his son or grandson, [and] it had the great advantage for them that they [the sons] would be similar to their ancestor. Driven by these good prejudices and by the memory of these deeds, his offspring often did become [like him]. "They select their kings according to nobility; their leaders according to their personal bravery," Tacitus said.[18]† Who were those kings and who were those leaders, and how did they differ from one another?—Without doubt, the former led the whole roaming hordes, guided their direction, determined their locations, and assigned them fields and meadows. Whoever wanted to obey, obeyed. Whoever did not, broke away from the horde with his family and wandered alone or sought to unite with another horde. Such a leader of the horde must have had considerable esteem. And among a people that places value on nothing but martial bravery, what could this have been based on except on the memory of his ancestors' deeds, which he brings back to their memory through his own [deeds], known to the entire people that participated in the election? If the entire horde went to war, precisely this king led them. But usually that was not the case. Individual parties made separate expeditions [332] as audacity and sudden ideas advised them.‡ The purpose of these [expeditions] was loot. Here one person thought up a bold endeavor, there another. Everyone

---

†*De moribus Germanorum*, chapter 7.[19]

‡Tacitus, *De moribus Germanorum*, chapter 14.[20]

18. Publius Cornelius Tacitus, 55–117 AD, Roman historian and author of *De moribus Germanorum*, or *Germania*, in English.

19. Tacitus, *Germania*, 7.1.

20. Tacitus, *Germania*, 14.2.

shared his design and recruited companions, as many and as good as he could. Each party elected one of the best-known, bravest men as their leader. Each went their way. Could the king have led all these individual parties, [as] oftentimes several went off to steal and loot in different directions at the same time? They came back, went on other expeditions in other company, and maybe elected someone else as their leader, but always bold, brave men.—Those are the leaders that Tacitus is speaking of. The name of him who was often leader of this kind and accomplished his endeavors with luck and bravery, became famous among the entire people as little by little he led every single member. No bold venture was decided where one did not wish him to be the leader. He now became noble himself, in the same manner in which the king became noble once. And if the latter died, he—or someone educated under his supervision, a son walking in his footsteps—could easily be elected king. Thus, there is not the slightest trace of a hereditary aristocracy of right yet.

This is how it was in Tacitus's time, when the individual peoples of Germany were still associated closely, when each formed more of a body, and every single member of the body still had the possibility of becoming known for the deeds of the bravest among them and for the deeds of their ancestors. Later, these peoples broke apart due to the general turmoil among them, the pressure from the east, and the expansion of their dwelling places toward south and west. After mingling with each other, new [peoples] emerged, who, in turn, mingled incessantly to form new [peoples], the names of which cannot be found in any of the older historians, [consequently] even this aristocracy of opinion had to mostly disappear. Someone who was still among his people today, who still knew its deeds and its fathers' deeds, as well as its greatest and most famous men, may have been subjected to a nation tomorrow of whose heroes he knew just as little as they of his. This is how it was for those peoples [333] who, less oppressed, remained in Germany, as, for example, the Saxons, the Frisians, etc. But most certainly this is how it was for the peoples that moved into the Roman Empire, for the Burgundians, Vandals, Franks, Allemans. Regarding the latter two, one can tell by the name that the first [the Franks] coalesced from various free men, the second [the Allemans] from all kinds of Germanic peoples.

One kind of connection still remained among certain members of these peoples that were generally dissolving and mingling. [This connection] became the foundation of all connections that would one day unite them again. Examining this is therefore most important.

Tacitus reports§ that, among the Germans, "young men who are not already surrounded by other young men thanks to the glory of their ancestors affiliate themselves with a seasoned warrior who is long since distinguished by his own deeds, and no one is ashamed of this brotherhood in arms. If a skirmish took place, it would be a disgrace for such a leader to be surpassed by his brothers in arms in bravery, a disgrace for his brothers in arms not to achieve their leader's bravery, but[, even worse, it would be] a lifelong stigma to make it out of a battle alive in which he [the leader] was killed. To shield him, to defend him, to deposit their own heroic deeds into his account, is their first and holiest oath." Such a hero was the rallying point for his brothers in arms, everything revolved around him. Wherever he went, they accompanied him. Wherever he stayed, they stayed. Those were the only remaining fixed points among peoples in constant flux. And they had to pull the other dispersed elements towards themselves. The uncertain peoples, scattered about without a shepherd, attached themselves wherever they saw such an association. And the bigger the horde was and the braver the men among them, the more numerously they attached themselves. Everything was swept along in their maelstrom, and thus these crowds, growing like a snowball with every step, invaded the provinces of the occidental empire and conquered it.

[334] The conqueror split the loot among his faithful brothers in arms, as he owed it to them. "A large brotherhood in arms can only be maintained through war," Tacitus said.** "They expect their warhorse and their bloody and victorious spear from the generosity of their leader. And feasts, where not delicacy but abundance rule, are their pay. This expense is financed with the loot from the war." The more pleasant climate, the cultivated lands, [and] the manifold indulgences that the luxury of the conquered people had offered them, invited them to enjoy in peace what was there and to abdicate the roaming lifestyle of their unfriendly woods. They developed a taste for agriculture and for its associated permanent dwelling. Fields now also became loot for them, and the conqueror satisfied them [his brothers in arms] with fields. In the process, he emulated the politics of the woods and, in order not to

---

§*De moribus Germanorum*, chapters 13 and 14.

**In the cited passage.[21]

21. Tacitus, *Germania*, 14.2.

let them acquire a taste for idleness, he did not grant them the fields as permanent possessions but merely to be enjoyed for the time of his discretion.

Here you see the origin of the *feudal system*. We suspected that this [system] is connected with the origin of our contemporary aristocracy. [However,] we forgot to raise the question *whether the aristocracy is the source of the feudal system or the feudal system the source of the aristocracy*, since its answer alone could give us the right perspective.

The conqueror's brother in arms obtained lands from him as a reward. Was he perhaps obliged by the enjoyment of the land to accompany him in war? Not at all. He was already obliged to it long before by his oath. He depended on him through his *person*, not through his *land*. If he [the conqueror] had never given him land, never been able to give it to him, he [the brother in arms] would nevertheless have remained obliged to accompany him in all his endeavors, according to and on the strength of his oath. It may be that the gift became disadvantageous for the creator through the enjoyment of the quiet lifestyle and through the comfort of the bestowed possession, and that the vassal refused to accompany his lord into the battlefield now that he possessed something from him. Whereas before, when he possessed nothing, he would have done it without thought. The next thing that the lord could do was indeed to take his fief from him. But this was no adequate punishment. It was no punishment at all. [335] Even absent this breach of duty, he had the perfect right to take back his lands.

These vassals of the conqueror were, however, in possession of the nobility of opinion. It was natural that the eyes of the remaining free men were directed at people who had initially fought by the side of the victorious conqueror, who had distinguished themselves before their eyes through this or that brave deed, who were in the company of their prince daily, who ate at his table. It was equally natural that the people also paid a part of the respect due to the fathers to their sons, if they did not make themselves unworthy of it through their own cowardice. But I see no *aristocracy of right* here yet. Or did it perhaps consist in their exclusive entitlement to their lord's fiefs?

Obviously, only the companions and brothers in arms of the conqueror could lay claim to a share of the booty and, in particular, the lands as a part of the loot. The others demanded nothing but a dwelling in the conquered lands. But what was it that actually afforded them this privilege? Was it perhaps their birth? Or was it anything other than their brotherhood in arms with the king? Every other free man was actually excluded from possessing a fief. However, [this was] not because he was *nothing more than a free man,* but because he was *no brother in arms of the king.* This brotherhood in arms was the source of the right. To demonstrate the existence back then of an exclusive privilege of certain families, it would have to be shown that not every free man but only a few among them had the right *to join the company of a hero.* Where could such an exclusive right have arisen? *In the woods,* where—according to the emphatic words of Tacitus—only those who did not have enough ancestry to gather a circle of young men around themselves joined the company of a stronger warrior? *Or after the emergence of the monarchy?* And, in the latter case, *who* actually had the exclusive privilege? Perhaps those who already belonged in the company of the monarch? Or perhaps their children?

Montesquieu assumes the existence of an exclusive aristocracy of birth before the conquest, however, without engaging the distinction between nobility of opinion and aristocracy of right. He offers two arguments for its [the aristocracy of birth's] existence. [336] Since he is of the same opinion as we are regarding the origin of the feudal system, he must thus assume, according to the conclusion above, that *only the supposed aristocracy was entitled to join the company of a hero who was about to set off in conquest.* And *this* is really what his arguments must prove.

Louis the Pious[22] had freed a certain Hebon, who was born a slave, and had elevated him to the archbishopric of Reims. The biographer of this king, Thegan,[23] rebukes Hebon for his ungratefulness and addresses him like this: "What kind of thanks have you given him? He freed you. He did not ennoble you, which is impossible after manumission."†† From this, Montesquieu wants to prove that a civil distinction between a mere free man and a noble man already existed back then. But what does this passage say? We do not want to explain, like l'Abbe Du Bos, [337] whose explanation Montesquieu rightly criticizes.[24] The biographer says

---

††*Spirit of the Laws,* book 30, chapter 25.—Fecit te liberum, non nobilem, quod impossible est post libertatem.

22. Louis the Pious, 778–840, was the Frankish king and Roman emperor from 814 to 840.

23. Thegan of Trier, before 800–c. 850, was a clergyman in the Rhineland. He outlines the life of Louis the Pious until 835 in *Gesta Hludowici imperatoris.*

24. Jean-Baptiste Dubos, 1670–1742. Montesquieu is referring to his *Histoire critique de l'etablissment de la monarchie françoise dans les Gaules,* 1734.

that it is impossible to grant nobility to a freedman. In what regard is it impossible, physically or morally? Or politically? Based on natural causes or due to the imperial constitution? Thegan is either saying something nonsensical or he did not want to say the latter. If the possession of the fief was the only sign of aristocracy, if the brotherhood in arms with the king was the only way to attain a fief—as Montesquieu must admit, provided that he is consistent—then the bishop was already excluded from the feudal nobility per se. Even though the bishops, at least those of Germanic descent, did personally go to war in these times, no man ordained in the church could be dedicated to a king as earnestly and to the death as the brothers in arms were. One obviously excludes the other. Therefore, Thegan should have said, "it is impossible to grant nobility *to a bishop*" but not "it is impossible to grant nobility *to a freedman*." Therefore, Thegan is not talking about a political, but about a physical and moral impossibility, and [he] is referring to the nobility of opinion. That Hebon was born a slave was already known. He had only become so much more famous through the negotiation of his manumission and through the high office to which the king had raised him. [Yet] after such a brash announcement, the king could perhaps not command public opinion and demand that everyone should believe Hebon was born from an ancient free tribe. Maybe Hebon had been scorned for the sake of his inferior birth, and this had embittered his mood and stirred his hatred against the king, who, according to Hebon's opinion, had exposed him by raising him to this high position. As it were, Thegan tries to exculpate the king from Hebon's [charges]. Thus, all that this passage could prove would be that in this age someone born in slavery was not regarded as highly as someone born free, a remark that surely fits every age without qualification. One ought not reproach this explanation for presupposing a philosophical distinction in Thegan, which cannot be expected from him! If in Thegan's time, there was no other aristocracy but that of opinion—which is taken as demonstrated—Thegan did not *have* to distinguish anything, and his words could have had no other meaning *for his contemporaries* than the indicated [meaning]. Montesquieu, on the contrary,—in order to attribute *the* meaning to the author's words that *he* associates with them—[338] must presuppose that Thegan already had a concept of a hereditary aristocracy of right [and] that such an aristocracy therefore already existed in his time. In short, for the purpose of his explanation, he must presuppose as already demonstrated what he wants to demonstrate with his explanation.

Charlemagne[25] decreed in his edict of partition that his sons' vassals should not possess a fief elsewhere than in the realm of their [respective] lords‡‡ but should keep their allodium§§ regardless in whose part it was located. However, he permitted every free man whose lord had died or who previously had no lord to choose *whomever* he wanted as a lord in *whoever's* part he wanted. In a similar treatise of partition, which was entered by Guntram,[27] Childebert,[28] and Brunhilda[29] in Andelys in the year 587 and which resembles Charlemagne's edict almost in all parts, the same regulation regarding vassals occurs, but none regarding free men. Montesquieu concludes from this that the free men only acquired for themselves the right to possess a fief or—which in my opinion means the same—to offer themselves to accompany a king or another great man between the rule of Guntram and [the rule of] Charlemagne. But I do not see [339] how this follows, unless one presupposes it in advance. I shall presuppose the opposite, and we shall see whether this difference between the edicts of partition cannot also be explained naturally.—If, since the beginning of monarchy, i.e., before and in the time of Guntram, the free man had the right to give himself to a lord of his choosing, it would have been entirely superfluous to include a provision regarding it in the edict of partition of Andelys. No new right should or could be introduced. Whether a free man gave himself to Guntram or to Childebert, he became a vassal and was subject to his orders. And since the

---

‡‡Montesquieu in the cited work, book 31, chapter 25.[26]—From this edict it follows also, among other things, that in the times of Charlemagne the feudal constitution still prevailed in its old guise. Even before that [edict] took power, his sons had their vassals, but they did not yet have fiefs to grant. Therefore, their vassals were bound to their person not through the possession of some fief, but merely through their personal oath.

§§Those properties, which a free man possessed not as a fief but as property, were called *allodium*. Back then, all lands were one of the two: fief or allodium.

25. Charlemagne, 742–814, was the Frankish king and West Roman emperor from 768 to 814 and united much of western Europe.

26. Montesquieu, *Spirit of the Laws*, 31.24.

27. Guntram was king of the Burgundian part of the Frankish empire (Kingdom of Orleans) from 561 to 593.

28. Childebert II was the titular king of the Austrasian part of the Frankish empire from 575 to 596.

29. Brunhilda, 543–613, was the wife of Sigebert I, who was assassinated in 575. She became the advisor of her son Childebert II, and as guardian of her grandson was the actual ruler of Austrasia. She was executed by her political opponents in 613.

fief was granted only under the condition of company in arms, which, however, bound the vassal to the person of his lord, he could not be the vassal of another [lord] nor possess a fief from him. This much follows from the nature of things without any further arrangements.—However, these free men, who became vassals now, possessed allodia. Since these were under no circumstances conferred, they could not be confiscated under any circumstances either. They remained the owner's untouched. If a freeman, who possessed an allodium in Guntram's territory, offered himself to Childebert for a fief, he could henceforth not—according to the nature of things—possess a fief in Guntram's territory. Yet, his allodium had to remain his.—Now both entered war. By virtue of his allodium, he was obliged to provide military service under one of Guntram's counts; by virtue of his feudal oath, he was obliged to serve immediately under Childebert. He could not divide himself. The fief took precedence because it bound his person immediately to the person of his lord. But how should Guntram be satisfied? He was not allowed to intervene in the property right of the allodium and perhaps to transfer it to someone else, who would have rendered him the associated military services. Manifold disputes must have arisen between the kings over this. Most likely [340] the ancestors of Charlemagne sought to resolve these disputes either through an unlawful interference with the property right of the allodium or through an equally unlawful [interference] in the right of free men to choose as their liege lord whomever they want. They either confiscated the allodia located in their territory of those men who had given themselves to another regent as their lord, as if they were fiefs, or they barred all occupants of allodia in their territory from choosing a lord other than themselves. Cautioned by the experience of previous ages, Charlemagne found it necessary to prohibit *expressly and with precise words* what was already prohibited *by the nature of things* and what his ancestors could not possibly have prohibited without this prior experience. Moreover, a new exit had now been found to avoid the collision of feudal and allodial duties. It had been permitted by express ordinance, which one finds cited in Montesquieu, to let someone else perform the services associated with the allodia.[30]

Thus, this situation proves nothing *in favor*, but the words of this edict prove everything *against* Montesquieu and topple his system, beyond salvaging, to the ground.—Whoever has lost his lord through death is here called *free*, just like he who never had one. But what was

---

30. Montesquieu, *Spirit of the Laws*, 31. 25.

the vassal before his lord died? Was he *free* then? In this relationship, the law calls him vassal. Therefore, the free man is called free not only in *contrast to the slave*, but also in *contrast to the vassal*. And according to the original constitution, really no one was less free than the vassal, as we have seen above with Tacitus. How does one thus want to find a hereditary aristocracy where the vassal lost his quality as vassal even for his own person through the death of his lord and returned to the common class of free man? How could one believe that something higher than a free man existed *there*, where the noblest must always look forward to becoming one? Was he perhaps relieved of his nobility through the death of his lord? After such a decisive proof, one should, I think, not waste *another word* defending this system.

[341] I do not renounce my admiration for the great man on whose shoulders I stood, if, supported by him, I believe I see further than *he* saw. It is rather a warning than a titillating sight to see one of the greatest men in the realm of literature—greatest precisely because of his immeasurable knowledge and his admirable acumen—get carried away in the defense of preconceived ideas from which these qualities should protect him.

We have not yet found a hereditary aristocracy. We have not even found *personal prerogatives* for the king's immediate brothers in arms, besides that which necessarily follows from the brotherhood in arms, a share of the loot.—The conquerors made laws, and it was to be expected that their companions in arms and at the table would be benefitted eminently. Whoever killed a free man or a freedman paid 200 shillings according to the contract with the dependents of the dead. Whoever killed a loyalist of the king paid 600 shillings.*** This, indeed, was a privilege. However, if it should serve as evidence for a hereditary aris-

---

***Solidus.*[31] No one will think of our shillings here. It was a coin, the value of which does not need to be determined. Entirely in the spirit of their erstwhile constitution (see Tacitus, chapter 21),[32] a murder was viewed not as violation of the state, but merely of the family in the absence of the lord, or, if he was a slave, of the owner. The latter two had the right of retaliation. This [right] was bought by the above sum determined by the law. Later on, the murderer also paid a third of this fine under the name *Fredum* (peace) to the law court that mediated the affair.[33]

31. A gold coin in late imperial Rome.

32. *Germania*, 21.1.

33. The German word for "peace" is *Frieden*, which is ostensibly derived from the Latin *fredum*.

tocracy of right, it would have to be shown once again that certain free families were excluded from the feature to which it was attached: *from the company of the king*. But the exact opposite has been shown. Therefore, it was merely a personal privilege that ceased to apply to the family with the death of the vassal, and that he even lost in his own person if his lord died sooner than he did and he could not find a means to be admitted among the company of his successor.—[Imagine] one man was the vassal of Charlemagne and whoever would have killed him would have paid 600 shillings. Charlemagne dies, and he does *not want* to *nor can* become the vassal of Louis the Pious, and, according to Charles's edict above, he is now called *a free man*. He is [342] killed. According to the law above, how much does his murderer have to pay?—Besides this, they [the vassals] had such few advantages in a court of law that every nobleman, who accused a slave and challenged him to a duel by law, was obliged to battle him on foot and only in his shirt with his [the slave's] weapon, a staff.††† It is to be expected that the son of one of the king's fighters, maybe educated in weapon exercises under his supervision, gladly took over his father's obligations, and that the king was more willing to transfer them easily to him rather than someone else. He thereby entered into the rights that his father had possessed, but *not* by virtue of his birth, rather, by virtue of his *own* dedication to the king. In the case of selection, however, the grateful memory of the ancestors' merits must have persuaded the kings to prefer the descendants of known and famous men over unknown and unfamiliar families. But no *law* obliged them to do so. Therefore, those complaints about the setback of old houses and the preference for unknown or foreign families that were already raised under some of the *Merovingians* and became louder and more severe under Louis the Pious and Charles the Bald[35] were not founded on a violation of the imperial constitution, which the already

---

†††See Montesquieu, book 28, chapter 24, where he cites his source.—"Villain" is written in Beaumanoir's text and that can mean nothing else than *slave*.[34] Every free man was obliged to perform military service. Even if he was no vassal, he was therefore trained in the craft of weapons. Only the slave was excluded from the former and the latter. This is not the place to derive this meaning of the word from the language.

34. Montesquieu is referring to the *Coutumes de Beauvaisis*, chs. 6 and 64, by Philipe de Beaumanoir, c.1250–96.

35. Louis the Pious, 778–840, son of Charlemagne; Charles the Bald, 823–77, West Frankish king from 843 to 877 and Roman emperor from 875 to 877.

mighty and independent vassals would certainly not have tolerated anyways. [Instead] they [the complaints] were founded on a neglect of the grateful memories, wherever they were not founded merely on the jealousy and the presumption of the nobles.

Meanwhile, the spirit of the people had increasingly educated itself [away] from the belligerent desire to plunder, towards the peaceful enjoyment of what they have. The fiefs were granted for a *lifetime*. Finally they became *hereditary*, and the entire system was practically inverted. Before, the brotherhood in arms [343] with the king was the foundation of the fiefdom and the personal prerogatives. [But], with the first [vassal] who *inherited* his father's fief, the fiefdom became the foundation of the brotherhood in arms with the king and its associated personal prerogatives. Before, the military services gave *the warrior* the right to demand *the fief*. Now, the fief gave *the king* the right to demand *military services*. The inheritor of the fief inherited at the same time the obligations attached to it and its associated prerogatives only *by virtue of these obligations*. Only now was there a kind of aristocracy that *inherited rights*—the two exclusive hallmarks of our modern aristocracy. And only in *this* manner, and only under *these* conditions, could any people, no matter how barbaric, come up with the idea to bequeath something that can only be *adopted voluntarily* according to its nature, but in no way *transferred*, [i.e.,] obligations and rights. They bound them to something that can actually be inherited: *the ground*. Whoever did not want it [the ground] was free from the obligation and relinquished the prerogatives. Everyone remained free to do that, [since] the law of contract remained unviolated. Whoever *did* assume it, also assumed the attached obligations, not through a tacit but a formal contract—through *the feudal oath*, which had superseded the oath of dedication that was common in the woods. Associated with these obligations were personal prerogatives that he did not inherit with the feudal ground but first acquired through the adoption of the attached obligation—i.e., that he did not acquire by *inheritance* but by *contract*.

This is the first *cause of the emergence* of our hereditary aristocracy of right, but it is by far not the hereditary aristocracy *itself* yet. It was still not *birth* that bestowed the aristocracy. It bestowed the fief, and only the *fief* bestowed the aristocracy. If an immediate imperial vassal had multiple sons and only *one* of them inherited the fief, then only this *one* inherited the aristocracy as well. Usually, such a son gave parts of his fief to his brothers as subfiefs, and thereby they became *his* nobles, as he was the nobleman of the king.—But we will get to talk about this soon.

Our contemporary hereditary aristocracy supposes that it inherits prerogatives not indirectly through something that can be bequeathed, i.e., estates, but directly through birth, and not by virtue of particular, assumed obligations, but free from all obligations. In order to track down the emergence of this aristocracy, one must descend into an equally dark yet more corrupt age, where the ancient barbarism prevails without its ancient consequences, and where they continued to build on the aftermath of a system that had long been destroyed in its very foundations.

[344] In all countries of the former Frankish monarchy, those original fiefs were divided infinitely into further, subordinated fiefs. Each one was like a tree that sprouted branches and the branches, in turn, sprouted twigs and the twigs their leaves. Every vassal got himself his subvassals and every subvassal, in turn, his [sub-subvassals], each with a view to resisting his immediate feudal lord and being able to make himself independent of the lord by means of his subvassals' might. No one suspected beforehand what each was to find out shortly, [namely,] that his vassals would soon turn that power, which he had taught them to turn against *his* feudal lord, against *theirs*. The greatest feudal lord, the empire, lost its strengths first. It was followed gradually by the immediate fiefs, according to their respective size. And so it went, the enfeeblement continued to the distant and further distant [fiefs]. The empire was divided into as many states as there were large fiefs, then those were divided into as many states as there were subfiefs, and so forth. The free occupant of his allodium, who was no one's lord and no one's servant and who had hitherto been under the protection of the empire, lost his protection as the empire lost its strength. If he was not mighty enough to protect himself, and if his allodium was not extensive enough for him to obtain his own vassals by dividing it, he had to attach himself to a mighty party and subsume his allodium into one of the mightier imperial fiefs, affirming it as a subfief of the latter. In this manner, all allodia gradually became fiefs and the empire lost its last possessions, after it had already lost its first, the fiefs, by bequeathing them. In the upheavals and wars of previous times, many free men had lost their freedom. Whoever had preserved his freedom and had no manor to buy the half-freedom that was still permitted, certainly lost it now. From now on there were only *slaves* or *vassals*. There were no more *free men*.

Ever since laws and courts of law had been introduced, the vassals held jurisdiction in their feudal dominions. They granted prerogatives to their vassals before their [court of law], similar to those they had before the imperial court of law—it was called their *court*‡‡‡[36]—and their vassals, in turn, [granted prerogatives] to theirs, if they had any. The [345] empire had its noblemen and every smaller feudal dominion theirs.§§§ The counts, judges of free men concerning their allodia, had long lost the jurisdiction that they had exercised *as such*. There were no more allodia. They themselves had acquired their countship by inheritance and probably possessed the largest part of it as a fief. All courts of law were feudal courts, and all vassals that belonged to them were ennobled before them. Therefore, there were only noblemen and slaves. No third estate existed back then.

This quite distant aristocracy still rested on the possession of a fief. The vassals were named after their fiefs. There were no family names.**** Those descendants of vassals who could not obtain a fief

---

‡‡‡*La cour, palatium*, hence *comes palatinus*—a holder of immediate imperial jurisdiction, where the imperial vassals were judged, in contrast to a count, who in the name of the empire judged the free men concerning their allodia.

§§§Hence the *Pairs, pares*, for immediate imperial vassals and imperial nobles. Those were equals among each other. They were at the same level. The distant and further distant aristocracy in the feudal domination and subfiefs were not equal to them.

****Hopefully, no one who knows just a little bit of the history of the Germanic nations will deny this. The names of the Merovingians, the Carolingians, the Capetians have only been invented later by historians for an easier overview. Merovech[37] (presumably, Clovis[38] did not know his ancestors beyond that), Charles, [and] Capet were personal names and Louis XVI was right not to want to be called Capet.[39] If he should not be called King of France anymore, he would have no name at all except his given name.[40] No king or ruling prince has another [name]: King, Duke, Prince are designations of dignity, but not names.

36. In German, as in English, *Gerichtshof* (court of law) and *königlicher Hof* (royal court) are etymologically related, because the former has its historic origin as an institution within the latter. However, Fichte generally refers to courts of law by the shorter German word *Gericht*, and so the insertion here serves to point out the etymological connection in German, while in English it may appear redundant.

37. Merowech was the legendary founder of the Merovingians, originally petty kings of the Salian Franks. The first historically authenticated Merovingian was Chlodio, c. 430.

38. Clovis I, 466–511, was the Frankish conqueror of Gallia and founder of the Frankish kingdom who ruled from 481 to 511.

39. Hugo Capet was count of Paris and duke of Francia, French king from 987 to 996, and founder of the House of Capet. The main line of the Capetians ruled France until 1328.

40. After his arrest, Louis XVI was called "citoyen Capet" by his opponents, because he belonged to a House of Bourbon, which was a branch line of the Capetians.

fell back into darkness. There was nothing by which one could have identified them. It is impossible to say what became of them—*ignotis perierunt mortibus.*[41]—There was still no aristocracy by birth alone, when something small, a painted board, brought it about.

The great vassals trained the children of their vassals in weapon exercises at their courts. These courts gradually became more lustrous and gallant. The spirit of knighthood emerged and with it the tournaments. Covered from tip to toe in iron, the fighting knight wanted to distinguish himself somehow and did it, after quite a few other attempts, with [346] a picture on his shield. Made famous by deeds of boldness and strength, this picture obtained something ceremonious for his descendants. The family's rallying point was found, and whoever did not inherit anything from his father inherited at least the picture that had been painted on his shield, and oftentimes he was also named after him. The names of our old German families either stem from their erstwhile fiefs—and, in that case, one will usually be able to point out villages or castles of the same name—or from their coat of arms, and then the similarity is visible. The important scientific discipline that deals with coats of arms calls such a coat of arms a "canting arms."—Back then, the name was derived from the coat of arms. Among the newly ennobled families, it is the other way around. Usually the coat of arms is derived from the name.

Meanwhile, a main factor in warfare had also changed. Previously, only free men went into the battlefield. Now the number of those had diminished considerably—they had become nobles through the subjugation of all those who could not become noble. The number of feuds, however, [had] increased greatly as a result of the fact that every vassal, as petty as he can be, waged war. The mightiest vassal could not have offered resistance to his enemies if he led only his noble vassals into battle. How much less [resistance], then, could the owner of a small village [offer], who had his wars too? Peasants in bondage now performed military services. The mightiest vassals expected to be able to use the military-trained descendants of their vassals, on whom they could not confer a fief, as leader of those bondsmen in their feuds. And, arguably for the sake of their utility, they granted them prerogatives as their true vassals at their courts and before their courts of law. This became a habit and now even those on whom *no one* had explicitly conferred these prerogatives arrogated them to themselves as something self-evident. No

---

41. Horace, *Satires*, 1.3: "deaths unknown to fame."

one could or wanted to examine this [claim] and in this way the bizarre opinion arose that one could obtain privileges[42] *ahead* of other human beings and *over* other human beings immediately by birth.

I have shown in the previous chapter that this is inherently impossible because it goes against natural, inalienable human rights. In the present [chapter, I have shown] that this was not maintained in any of the old states and in none of the modern [states] either for a fairly long time and that this prejudice was not founded on the state constitution but on ignorance, abuse, and arrogation. [347] But let us now go through all the demands of the nobility individually, one after the other!

In the first place, they lay claim to our opinion: they want to be seen as gentler. The nobility of the ancient peoples likewise imposed opinions. In this, the modern [nobility] is entirely similar, yet it differs very noticeably in the manner. "I am of nobility," says the modern nobleman, which was something altogether different than when a Roman called himself a Brutus,[43] a Scipio, an Appius, or Cimon [called himself] son of Miltiades![44] *Certain* deeds by *certain* men then passed before the soul of the people to which he disclosed himself, and became tied to the man who renewed the memory of his name or his father's name. But what do *we* think upon hearing the indeterminate, complex term *"nobility"*? At least, it is nothing clear. Even if the modern nobleman tells us his name—I am Herr von X*** or Herr von Y*** or Herr von Z***—neither he nor we are thereby much assisted. In general, we are much less invested in our national history than the ancient peoples, because we are deterred as much as possible from taking an interest in public affairs. And whatever we do know stirs our concern to a far lesser degree, because it is usually so undeserving of [our concern]. Now, if we had been educated very precisely on the deeds of the progenitors of house X*** or house Y***, what would we know? Perhaps, that one of them fought in a tournament of Emperor Frederick II.[45] Another participated in a crusade. In modern times, a third was a minister, as all [nobles] tend to be ministers. A fourth [was] a general, as all tend to be generals. A

---

42. *Vorrechte*

43. Lucius Iunius Brutus was, according to tradition, the leader of the uprising that expelled the last king of Rome, leading to the founding of the Republic in 510 BC.

44. Miltiades, Athenian commander around 500 BC.

45. Frederick II of the Hohenstaufen was the German king from 1194 to 1250 and Roman emperor from 1215 to 1250.

fifth, as an ambassador, entered an exchange agreement over a couple of villages or honored a displaced region. A sixth feigned to be upright in this or that meeting. Indeed, but how did he feign to be upright? Can one not learn of the individual traits of his valor, nothing particular about the circumstances? All these questions! Enough. He feigned to be upright; it's written in this or that chronicle. Presently, I would not know any country where mentioning certain names awakens strong associations, except perhaps the Prussian states. I hear a Keith,[46] a Schwerin,[47] a Winterfeldt[48] mentioned. [348] Then the deeds of Frederick's heroes of the same name perhaps come into my mind, and I become eager to know whether this stranger perhaps descends from them and whether he follows in their footsteps. But in the soul of the friend of humanity a wistful sentiment soon attaches even to these memories, when one remembers *for what* these feats were accomplished. Otherwise the heroes of our history hardly have a physiognomy. This history only has one form for the upright, the faithful, and the skillful, according to which it casts them all. If we have seen *one*, we have seen them *all*. Does the fault lie with our heroes, or with our historians?

A little bit always with the heroes, and in recent times almost entirely. Among us, everything has a certain rule and our states are clockworks, where everything moves according to how it was once set. The arbitrary will, the individual character has almost no room at all. It is not supposed to have any. It is superfluous, it is detrimental, and a good father or teacher carefully seeks to keep his pupil, whom he prepares for business, away from this disadvantageous commodity. Every head is carefully cast in the conventional form of its age. The pupil asks, "why is this or that like so? It could also be different. Why is it not different?" "Be still," replies a sophisticated teacher, "it is thus, and must be thus, because it is thus." And by repeating this, he will persuade his pupil and the latter will henceforth refrain from his uncomfortable questions. Among the ancients, not only particular persons had character. There were even quite strongly marked family characters. Usually one knew rather specifically what to expect from a man with a certain name. If the patricians wanted a sturdy, immovable dam against popular unrest, they

---

46. James Keith, 1696–1758.

47. Kurd Christoph Graf von Schwerin, 1684–1757.

48. Hans Karl von Winterfeldt, 1707–57.

resorted to an Appier:[49] those were inborn enemies of popular power. If the Romans wanted to have an oppressor of freedom eliminated, they wrote their man, "can you still sleep, Brutus?" and this important name, *Brutus*, conveyed more than the longest speech. It was the hereditary office of the Brutuses to destroy the usurpers. When Augustus[50] ruled, there were no more [Brutuses], otherwise he [Augustus] would not have ruled long.—Didn't you want to tell me, what particular family characteristics the Herr von X*** or Y*** or Z*** has—and what I may especially expect—when someone mentions one to me?

[349] Finally, the main difference between the aristocracy of opinion among the ancients and us, which completely spoils our case: the ancient [aristocracy] was granted, ours is taken. In the former case the opinion was established voluntarily, now it is dictated. The ancient aristocracy is not visibly distinguished by anything. The Roman nobleman bore his three names just as the meanest citizen bore his. The portraits of ancestors were a private affair. They remained locked away in the innermost parts of their houses and only left them once after the death of the occupant. At this point, the portraits did not promise the people similar deeds, but merely sought to invite the people to compare the recently deceased, after an accomplished career, with his ancestors. They did not lay claim to any greater expressions of respect or to special titles in society and were more obliging the more noble they were and the more they wished to raise the nobility of their stock to new dignities. How very differently our noblemen act. They distinguish themselves from us based on their name. Merely for the sake of this name, they demand—from real dignitaries—primacy and distinguished expressions of respect. And they do this with as little claim to public opinion as the former had, and they believe in replacing the scarce reasons for regarding them highly with shameless demands. But opinions can never be dictated, and they take revenge on all who treat them against their

---

49. Appius Claudius was a common name among the aristocratic Claudius family in the Roman Republic. The name began with Appius Claudius Sabinus Regillensis, 505–480 BC, who was consul in 495 BC and clashed with the plebeians over debt relief and war with the Sabines.

50. Gaius Julius Caesar Ocatvianus Augustus, 63 BC–14 AD, ruled the entire Roman Empire from 30 BC to 14 AD. Here, Fichte is alluding to both Marcus Iunius Brutus, 85–42 BC, who was a leader in the conspiracy against Caesar in 44 BC, and Lucius Iunius Brutus, who, according to tradition, expelled the Tarquinia dynasty in 510 BC.

nature. In times when they resembled our aristocracy, the patricians were chased with the bitter hatred and mockery of the other classes, but as soon as they were put back in their place and another aristocracy, the aristocracy of mere opinion, replaced them, we no longer find that the aristocracy was mocked or hated among the Romans. But what is the fate of our aristocracy? Ever since *it*—and the monuments to the manner of thinking of the ages—have been in place, it has always been an object of fear, of hatred, and of the bitter remarks of the other estates. Even the monarchs have always sought to degrade and weaken that [institution] which was, in fact, their only support and presented for our eyes a natural stepladder up to their unnatural elevation. And, in our age, it has come so far that the nobleman who is nothing further than that can only be tolerated in the circle of the eminent civil estate—of scholars, merchants, and artists—through exaggerated humility.

Herr Rehberg, a worthy defender of such a thing, is indeed also of the opinion that the descendants of eminent men must be honored *as a matter of law*. "It sticks"—the nobility of his subject appears not to [350] have ennobled his language—"it sticks to highborn persons," he says,††††"that they have always belonged among the eminent [persons] of the country. He may be able to disgrace this dignity through his vices just as he honors it through his virtue. But he cannot destroy it unless he takes it so far that the administrator of the law breaks his coat of arms *as a matter of law* and annihilates his title." I should like [to know], Is this *dignity*, if it was one, now destroyed? After the administrator of the law has broken the coat of arms,‡‡‡‡ is *the* man no longer his father who was his father before, and this man's father no longer the same? Did his ancestors now cease to belong among the eminent [persons] of the country? Have the things they have done become undone? This court lady reasoned more correctly than Herr R.: "God the father cannot take my birth from me." Or does the man perhaps want to say something different than what he actually said, and a little vagueness merely slipped through? As much as follows from his other vagueness—that may indeed be the case—"An established nobleman, whose ancestors have belonged among the first of the country for many centuries, holds a very respectable dignity, even if his person should not be respectable," he said

††††Page 64.

‡‡‡‡A proper administrator of the law, who breaks seals by his own hand.

before.[51] "No monarch in the world" (on earth?), he says further below, "can make the person he ennobles equal to an established nobleman. He cannot mandate that human beings [must] respect this one, who just climbed upwards himself, as much as the other, in whom they honor the entire ancient stock."[52] He therefore appears to be speaking of that *dignity* which popular opinion bestows. According to his own diction, this [opinion] cannot be issued through any command, but it can be taken away through a legal decision. We cannot be mandated to honor someone, but we can be ordered to stop honoring someone. Certainly, a very thorough philosophy! But, we want to translate him entirely as best as we can. This dignity, so it seems, should indeed not depend on free opinion. It should be valid by law. Only this law, which makes it valid, should not be the monarch's dictum but should be founded on the necessary institution that is civil society itself. "The latter does not consist of individual human beings, who were born equal to each other, *like young cattle*" [351]—he expresses himself with characteristic decency—"*in a herd, perfectly similar to the old [cattle] when it is born, becoming identical to them as it grows up.* [Instead,] it consists of tribes."[53] If this holds, then we must still honor the established nobleman, whose coat of arms Rehberg's administrator has broken, because he remains in the same tribe. But this is all fabrication and clumsy sophistry. We never honor anyone *as a matter of law*. High esteem can never be mandated, neither through the constitution itself, nor through a single dictum of a monarch. It is given voluntarily and, indeed, it falls easily on the descendant of a deserving man, if he does not make himself unworthy of it through his own contemptible behavior. If he does that, he is despised, even without his nobility being repealed by a legal decision. Such a formal legal decision could at most have *the* effect that the offense of the punished would become universally known as legally proven. But the simple demonstration of the facts with evidence would affect the popular opinion in the same way. If a despot relieves an established nobleman who had boldly and manly resisted an unjust demand of the former of his nobility, we would not therefore honor him *less*, we would honor him *more*. *This* [is how] little the nobility depends on legal decisions and legal origin in the popular opinion.

---

51. Rehberg, *Untersuchungen*, 1:63.

52. Rehberg, *Untersuchungen*, 1:64.

53. Rehberg, *Untersuchungen*, 1:65.

It is neither an enjoyment nor an honor to declaim against an author whom nature has denied the talents to be who he would like to be—a dazzling sophist—and who, in terms of thought and expression, belongs to the last class of authors that walks just ahead of the scribblers. And, certainly, I would have spared myself this thankless labor, if precisely the same author did not appear to have worn down a few good-natured readers by means of his sharp tone to place him in the first class of Germany's authors. As a consolation for our readers, we promise herewith to carefully watch out not to cross paths with him again in the remainder of this writing. But—one may still object—even if we cannot be legally bound to honor the descendants of great men in our hearts, because this is an internal disposition that is not in our power, it may nevertheless be possible to imagine an obligation to grant them certain external signs of reverence, [352] which are indeed in our power, [i.e.,] an obligation, the observance of which can be judged by someone else. [However,] if we asked what purpose should be served by such external demonstrations of respect—of which one could never know whether they spring forth from inner reverence or not—it can hardly be expected that our noblemen will say, "so that we can at least maintain the sweet illusion that you honor us, even though you may despise us in your hearts." It is therefore not possible to imagine any other purpose for these external demonstrations of respect but that others, who may be willing to honor the nobleman merely for the sake of his aristocracy, are not disturbed by us in their good will. Although we do not want to honor them, we should not instigate others, who otherwise may want to honor them, with our behavior as well. Rather, through our reverential behavior, we should inspire in others that deep awe for them which we cannot grant them ourselves. This depends either on the answer to this question of prudence—"Is it useful, that certain estates in the state are honored above all, and, in particular, that these estates are designated by birth?"—the answer to which does not belong in the present book, since it deals only with right, but not with usefulness. Or it is a question of fairness: "Since the merit of great ancestors does not bestow a well-founded legal claim to our respect on their ancestors, is it not at least in accordance with fairness that we make it easier for them to have the possibility of being respected, as much as it is up to us?" And this question is indeed related to our project and, in fact, opens up the transition to the [following] examination for us: What follows from the aristocracy of opinion for our behavior toward noblemen?

"I am of the aristocracy" usually means this much to begin with: my ancestors have lived affluently for a large number of generations. I myself have been accustomed to this affluence since youth and I have therefore gained a kind of entitlement to live more comfortably than the rest of you, who are not used to it. It only "means" it, I said, because there are provinces, which I do not want to name here, in which the noble origin rather implies the opposite, a youth spent in base pursuits, in filth and deprivation. Or, "I am of the aristocracy" means this much: my ancestors lived with a certain esteem among their fellow citizens. In my childhood and youth, I was honored for their [my ancestor's] sake. I am used to being honored and I now want to make myself honorable through my own deeds. But in those provinces, where the fathers built a small estate in the darkness with their own hands, it does not mean that either. However, where it means both, what could follow from it? [353] That we must honor the man for the sake of his fathers' reputation and affluence and place him in affluence at our expense? Simply, no. Thus, it only [follows] that he has a greater demand than us to achieve the affluence and the fame that he is used to enjoying, that he may exert all his forces to swing himself up above his fellow citizens. Thus, his birth could at most be a license[54] for his ambition, supported by his own talents and forces. But, I should like to know, who would not be granted this license, simply for these talents and this unique predominance of force, even in the absence of [noble] birth? Let him make the best use he can of popular opinion in order to gain an edge that his personal force does not grant him. We will rightly seek to weaken this predominance. We are engaged in an open feud, and everyone makes use of his weapons. Whoever has been overcome must bear his misfortune. When two men with the same talents and the same force, one coming from a famous house and the other of unknown descent, vie for the same dignity in the state, can the former demand that the latter make way for him? May he say to him, "you require an elevated position less than me, [as I] have to struggle with the fame of great ancestors. For you, a lower [position] is high enough"? What if the latter replies, "you rest on your ancestors' laurels. The people's veneration will not evade you. I am honored only for the sake of myself. I have to avenge the lack of fame of my entire house, I have to work for all my unaccomplished ancestors as well." Do we want to agree with him less? But I believe neither one of the two is right. Everyone may do as much as he can. Chance or superiority of force will decide the victory.

---

54. *Freibrief*

"I am of the aristocracy" can also mean: my ancestors lived with a publicity that compelled them to adhere strictly to the basic principles of righteousness and of honor. They could not commit any bad deeds in their elevated position without drawing the eyes of the world on them [and] being discovered and punished. Since they were not [discovered and punished], it is to be assumed that they committed nothing dishonorable. These basic principles, passed down from father to son in a long succession, becoming, as it were the family's inheritance, have finally been passed on to me. Honorable, irreproachable behavior can more certainly be expected from me than from people who were educated according to basic principles that we do not know. And thus we come to the aristocracy's characteristic love for honor (*point d'honneur*).

That sense of honor which the aristocracy considers to be its exclusive inheritance [354] is a relic of times and morals that are not ours. As much as it may have been effective once and of good use, it is now neither of the two. It is a stranger in our world that does not know how to fit into its spot and how to claim its place. All newborn peoples who carry the disposition for the state of nature over into their first constitution place virtue entirely in courage and strength. This is how it was among the most ancient Greeks, this is how it was among the Germanic peoples, and this is how it will be once the savages of North America will establish states. The attitude that is achieved by this disposition is indeed adequate in these simple state edifices: contempt for lies, deceit, and sycophancy, protection of the defenseless, magnanimity vis-à-vis the weaker. Educated, raised to manhood, and grayed under danger—which, ultimately, he always conquered—the rough warrior's courage was unwavering, and he scorned taking the crooked way anywhere, since he was certain to make it to his destination through all dangers on the shorter, straighter [path]. As a people raises itself from this condition to the enjoyment of peace and its arts, its needs multiply as do the temptations to which they are exposed. More ways to excel ahead of others open up. Mere courage no longer suffices for everything. Now prudence, flexibility, complaisance, and persevering silent patience are also required. Indeed, in the beginning the rough warrior will fall in line with this new order of things with difficulty: prudence will look like deceit to him, flexibility like meanness, complaisance like sycophancy. But gradually he will come to a better realization. Who will vouch for him that his less prepared son or grandson will not be dragged across the narrow borderline and descend into the vices which his rough ancestor already shunned and fled in the related virtues? The foundation on which this sense of honor was founded is now torn away. What was once a dignified, solid edifice is now a castle in the clouds.—"He who says, 'I did not do it,' perfectly satisfies him who feels insulted," was the most sublime basic principle of your father.—Yes, he [who says "I did not do it"] did give in to the manner of thinking of the times, [but provided] a horrible satisfaction if he did it after all. He debased himself so deep below him [the father] that he lied out of fear of him. He was dishonored by his own sentiment, which lifelong practice had sharpened. Before the world and posterity, he was branded deeper than your brand marks go when the lie was discovered. And could such a basic principle [355] still be applicable today, when we forgive each other easily for having embellished the truth and alleviated its harshness? When we do not merely forgive each other, but even pride ourselves on it? This is the true distinction between the sense of honor of the former aristocracy and that of the greater part of our contemporary [aristocracy]: the former did not want to *do* anything ignoble, the latter does not want to *hear* that it did it. The former was proud, the latter is too vain to be proud. Ever since courts and courtiers, court intrigues and court aristocracy have existed, how many families, do you think, are still left who can demonstrate for us that none of their ancestors have gained [but] a part of their house's luster, which they like to flaunt, through baser arts, through flattery and sycophancy, and lies, and robbery of the defenseless? We know, indeed, that you are still ready to skewer anyone who says an ignoble word. But stick to your age, an age when we no longer infer the delicacy of your moral sense from the delicacy of your ear, as certainly as we perhaps had done in the time of your ancestors. It is true, [you] branch of a noble tribe, the honorable basic principles of the honest knights of old could indeed have run down to you. But it is equally possible that you have inherited the basic principles of courtly art. We can know neither. Look, we do not want to presuppose the latter, [so] do not ask us to assume the former. Go, and act, and we will then judge you according to yourself.

Yet, not too long ago there were tribes in some provinces where the former [the honorable basic principles] could be presupposed with great likelihood and maybe they still exist—the aristocracy of war of Frederick II. He did not hold court, and in his states no actual—i.e., no corrupt—court had been [held] before him. His aristocracy of war drew from his remotest provinces, and he won his noteworthy battles because of it. With the entire inheritance of his father, a sword and an unblemished name, the youth went into the field and soon absorbed the national pride that inspired this army. He grew up in the turmoil of battle. He was used to sharing daily with his comrades in arms whatever the day yielded. [Thus] his passion could not sink into the possession of riches. Battling dangers daily, he learned that there was none through which the sword did not cleave a way. Courage made everything available to him. He easily went without the other arts that he could do without. And, like a miracle, the heyday of older times was repeated in our age. However, such an aristocracy is useful where courage and a sense of honor (for the generation of which, this courage is enough) mean everything—in war. Here, and as [356] long as war is still necessary, everyone who belongs to this aristocracy, may boldly demand precedence. But he may not step over the boundary into a foreign area.

[Let us] finally conclude this examination into the aristocracy of opinion. The prejudice in favor of the grandson of great ancestors is a good of fortune. Everybody may use as much as fortune offers him as well as he can, just as he uses every other good of fortune—e.g., wit, a pleasing form, bodily force—as [well as] it is possible for him. It is a voluntary gift of the people just as the latter are voluntary gifts of nature. It does not bestow any legal rights on him, not even the continuation of this prejudice, which he cannot enforce.

Since this aristocracy is not property,[55] and by its nature can never be, any state moved by prudential ulterior motives to wish its disappearance has the perfect right not indeed to annul this kind of aristocracy itself— this is physically impossible, [since] opinion cannot be mandated—but to annul the possible external distinctions on which this opinion has hitherto relied. Wherever popular opinion is still decided in favor of the aristocracy, such an abrogation will take effect only slowly. Wherever it takes effect quickly, the opinion must already have begun to disappear. These kinds of orders are most effective when they are least needed, and least [effective] when they are most needed. There are more expedient means to influence [popular] opinion than orders, and, in our case, we can almost leave this concern entirely to the aristocracy itself. Moreover, I do not comprehend how the state could prohibit any one of its citizens from giving himself a certain name, or how it could prohibit his fellow citizens from calling him by this name, if they are used to it and want to do so voluntarily. I do not understand how this could be compatible with natural freedom. However, I do believe I understand how it [the state] could either permit the hitherto inferior estates no longer to make use of certain designations for the hitherto superior [estates] or permit everyone

---

55. *Eigentum*

who fancies it to adopt the same designations henceforth. Whether Herr von X***, or the Knight, or the Baron, or Graf von Y*** continues to write his name as he has done hitherto or whether he adds a number of additional names to his existing name, [all this] appears to me to be very irrelevant. But who may object to the state when it permits and advises all its citizens to henceforth call the Herr von X*** and the Graf von Y*** merely Herr X*** or Herr Y*** and when it promises [357] to protect them from the ostensible nobleman in their exercise of this permission? Or also, who will prevent it [the state] from ennobling all its citizens, from the highest to the lowest [rank], and from perhaps allowing the poor shepherd boy to call himself Baron or Graf of as many counties as he thinks right? The distinction will disappear on its own once it is no longer [an honor], and everyone will name himself as short as possible once the length of his title is no longer helpful. A well-known aristocratic free state where the houses that were able to govern were partly aristocratic and partly not aristocratic suddenly ennobled all these houses. This was another way of abrogating the aristocracy. A distinction that no longer distinguishes is as good as abrogated.

The descent from great, deserving men arouses in the people an advantageous prejudice for his offspring: this is what we called the aristocracy of opinion. This aristocracy *itself* cannot be demanded, i.e., through legal process, because, according to its nature, opinion cannot be mandated, and, by the same token, no legally valid entitlements to actual prerogatives *follow* from it, because what does not reside in the cause cannot reside in the effect. An aristocracy that raises claims of this kind is therefore to be simply dismissed, together with its claims. In order to understand this more clearly in all particular cases, let us now go individually through the prerogatives that our [aristocracy] demands. Admittedly, in modern times and in several states, for reasons not relevant here, the aristocracy had to share with the middle class several prerogatives that it had hitherto held exclusively. Even so, it [the aristocracy] continues to assume even in those states that such a case, when it occurs, is merely an exception to the rule but by no means the rule itself. It views it as a kind of violent infringement on their prerogatives by the bourgeois. Therefore, on the whole, we are not doing any injustice to the aristocracy when we also count the following rights among those it claims to hold exclusively. If its claims are not always satisfied, the fault is probably not with the aristocracy itself. Among these belongs above all its alleged prerogative to own the knight's estates. Admittedly, the origin of such a prerogative can be easily shown. The knight's estates are originally fiefs. The possession of them tied them to the company of the lord in arms, to which aristocracy was attached. Thus, it is natural that all who possessed one were not already aristocratic but became ennobled through the possession of it—as is apparent from our considerations above. It is, however, absurd—if anything was ever absurd—that this prerogative still persists, because these knight's estates are [now] inherited and even sold to strangers from other families and [358] no military services immediately depend on them anymore. The aristocracy insists that this possession of the knight's estates is a prerogative that must be asserted to maintain it and that following its loss this estate will become impoverished and perish. It [the aristocracy] must therefore gain something considerable through this prerogative, as can be plausibly demonstrated as well.—To be fair, we will skip over [the situation] where a son does not want to alienate his knight's estate inherited from his father. Maybe he wants to maintain it as a son, as a common occupant, but not as a nobleman. Everyone has the right to claim his property in whatever manner he wants.—But [imagine] a knight's estate is offered for sale. The latter's yield is estimated precisely. Whoever can pay for it, will possess it. Why should only the nobleman who can pay for it have the right to buy it, but not likewise the bourgeois who wants to pay the same? "Possession of property is the most secure and advantageous way to store one's money, and this advantage should be granted exclusively to the aristocracy for the maintenance of its luster." Is that so? According to this, one and the same thaler should earn more in the hands of a nobleman than in the hands of a bourgeois? Thus, it should also have a higher value in the hands of the former than in the hands of the latter? One thousand thalers, when a nobleman possesses them, correspond to the price of a certain piece of land, [yet] precisely those thousand thalers, when a citizen possesses them, do not correspond to the price of this piece [of land]. I do not want to examine here what follows from this for the stimulation of the acquisitive drive,[56] when precisely the most acquisitive social class is prohibited from investing its money securely. And this is obviously the case in states where all free estates are knight's estates that can only be possessed by aristocracy. [I also] do not [want] to examine what will follow from this for the distribution of wealth and the security of property in the families, when the bourgeois is compelled to let his capital circulate in the increasingly risky trade or to lend it with almost as much risk and for disproportionate interest. But I cannot refrain from admiring

---

56. *Erwerbungstriebe*

the profound politics of our modern times to which was reserved the invention of a secret by which the universal currency of things is given an additional, particular value derived from the person of the occupant and by which a sum increases or decreases only by passing from one hand into the other. This rebuke tolerates only one exception, in which the aristocracy [359] solely and exclusively obtains loans from regional banks[57] for acquiring knight's estates, usually at very low interest. The purchase of estates is thereby made considerably easier for him, and he must indeed soon become the sole occupant of the estate. These loan banks, however, are funded by the aristocracy. The funds belong to the aristocracy. Like every owner, the aristocracy must be free to lend out its property to whomever it wants and under whatever conditions it wants, and no one else may persuade it in this matter. The corporate spirit[58] and crude egoism indeed prevail in these measures, but one cannot say that they are downright unjust. Nevertheless, even in those states, the bourgeois must be free to purchase knight's estates if he can match the aristocracy's credit with the [same] amount in cash. The categorical prohibition of this purchase is unlawful everywhere.

However, other prerogatives are attached to the possession of the knight's estate. The aristocracy is jealous of these, and it does not readily want to let them fall into the hands of the bourgeois. Well, let us examine precisely these prerogatives themselves in order to find out on what right the landowner, be he of the aristocracy or not, can base his claim to them [the prerogatives]. In the first place, we find rights to the *estates* of peasants: measured and unmeasured labor services, pasture and cattle track rights, and the like. We do not want to examine the *real* origin of these rights. Assuming we discovered the unlawfulness of the latter, still nothing could be concluded from it, because it might likely be impossible to find the true descendants of the first oppressors and the first oppressed, and to order the latter to the man he has to stick to. The *legal origin* of these rights can be shown easily. The fields are either partially or not at all the property of the peasant. And the peasant pays off the interest on the lord's capital, which rests on his field like an iron trunk, §§§§ or on the entire estate not *in cash*, but through

---

§§§§For the few who do not know this, capital that rests on the land and must be paid a certain percentage in interest by the occupant of the land, but may never be paid off, is called an "iron trunk."

57. *Landschaftskasse*
58. *Zunftgeist*

services or through *advantages* that he grants the lord on his owned or borrowed ground. Even if these prerogatives did originally not come into being in this manner, everything is soon made the same through the sale of knight's and peasant's estates. It is natural that the peasant pays as much less for his acre[59] of peasant's estate as the encumbrances resting on it, converted into money as interest, would generate in capital. And [it is natural] that the occupant of a knight's estate pays much more for an acre of knight's estate as the corresponding services [360] of that peasant amount to as capital. Consequently, [it is also natural] that the knight paid the capital, resting on his estate, for the peasant and rightfully demands the payment of interests. Thus, nothing needs to be borne in mind against the lawfulness of this demand *itself*. Indeed, it was a grave interference with property rights when, a few years ago, the peasants of a certain state wanted to divest themselves of these services in a violent manner and without the slightest compensation. [It was] an interference that originated from their own ignorance and from the ignorance of a part of the aristocracy that was not informed about the legal foundation of its own entitlements. That [interference] would have been redressed more expediently and more humanely through thorough and comprehensible instruction than through ridiculous dragonnades[60]*****

*****"The peasants, armed with scythe and pitchfork, almost fought off the courageous attack, but Lieutenant N. *avenged the honor of the Saxon's weapons*," tells a pompous historian of this glorious campaign.[61]

59. *Hufe*, an old German unit of measurement for agricultural estates. The unit was not standardized throughout Germany and the size of the *Hufe* varied greatly by region, depending on the yield capacity of the ground. While the typical *Hufe* seems to have been roughly 30 acres, it could range from 14 acres up to 60 or even 120 acres, where aided by many farmhands and technological advances.

60. French policy of intimidation of Huguenot families, French Protestants, instituted by King Louis XIV for the purpose of either driving out the Huguenot families or pressuring them into converting to Catholicism. "Dragoons," mounted infantry, were stationed near Protestant families and given implicit permission to abuse them and steal from them. The policy was successful in driving out a huge number of Protestants, to the detriment of the French economy, as those individuals took many important skills with them.

61. Friederich Ernst von Liebenroth, *Fragmente aus meinem Tagebuch, insbesondere die sächsischen Bauernunruhen betreffend* [Excerpts from my diary, especially concerning the Saxon peasant unrest], (Dresden: Richter, 1791), 276–77. Both Fichte and von Liebenroth are referring to the Saxon Peasant Revolt of 1790, an armed conflict between the aristocracy and the peasants.

and dishonoring punishments in the construction of fortresses.[62] Much should be borne in mind, however, against *the manner* of paying off this interest. I do not want to talk about the general harmfulness of *pastoral rights*. After all the objections against them that have been wasted fruitlessly for quite some time, one is not easily tempted to waste even more. I want to talk about neither the waste of time and effort, nor the moral abasement that result from the *constitution of serfdom* for the entire state. Precisely the same hands that, as serfs on the lords' fields, work as little as possible because they work begrudgingly, would work as much as possible on their own field. A third of the serfs, hired for a cheap wage, would work more than those unwilling workers altogether. The state would have gained two-thirds of the workers. [361] The estates would be worked better and used more efficiently. The sentiment of servitude that profoundly depraves the peasant, the mutual lawsuits between him and his lord, and the displeasure with his status would disappear, and he would soon be a better human being, and his lord likewise. [But] I want to attack the foundation directly and ask: Where does the right of your iron trunks stem from? I see that they redound to the great advantage of those who possess something, especially to the advantage of the aristocracy that invented them. But I am not asking about your *advantage* here, I am asking about your *right*. Your capital must not be plundered. That is self-evident. We also cannot justifiably compel you to accept it paid back by us in cash. You are, as it were, co-owners of our estate, and we cannot coerce you to sell your share of it to us, if it is not for sale by you. So be it! But who says that this *one* estate must necessarily be indivisible and *one* estate? If your co-ownership and the particular manner in which you use it no longer pleases us, why should we not have the right to give your share back to you? If I possess two acres of land and only paid for half of their value because the second half has to remain as your iron capital, is not half of two acres *one*? I paid for *one* and the second is yours. I keep mine; you take yours back. Who could object to this procedure? It is most inconvenient for you to take it back? Perhaps! If it can be convenient for me to keep it, we shall make a new contract over the provision for interest that is not only advantageous for you, but also for me. If we agree, it may be. These are the basic legal principles from which manifold means arise to abrogate the oppressive system of

---

62. *Festungsbaustrafe*: a type of sentence in some states, including Prussia, where felons were used as laborers in the construction of fortresses.

servitude without injustice and without interference in property rights. If only the state were serious about it, if only its objections were not merely evasions, if only it did not secretly prefer the advantage of the few advantaged to the right and the advantage of all.

If we apply precisely this basic principle to the peasant who does not own his estate but merely borrows it for use from his lord, it is immediately apparent that he has the perfect right to return the estate, if the compulsory labor services resting on it appear unjust or oppressive to him. If the estate owner nevertheless wants him to keep it, they may haggle with one another until they agree.

[362] "But no," says the conventional law, "the peasant, who does not share any property in the ground, belongs to the ground himself. He himself is the property of the lord. He may not move away from the estate as he wishes. The estate owner's right pertains to *his person*." And this is a grave opposition to the right of humanity itself. It is slavery in the true meaning of the word. Every human being can have rights to things, but no one [can have] an immutable right to the personhood of another human being. This is the inalienable property of each individual, as has been sufficiently shown in this pamphlet. As long as the serf wants to stay, he may stay. As soon as he wants to go, the lord must let him go by virtue of his right. He may not say: "I paid for the right to the personhood of my serfs when I purchased the estate." Nobody could have sold such a right to him, because no one had it. If he did pay something for it, he was defrauded and he may approach the seller. Thus, no state [should] extol its culture where this inhumane right is still valid and where *anyone* still has the right to tell another [person]: "*you are mine!*"†††††

Among the prerogatives that the aristocracy wants to hold exclusively and that it must every now and then behold with deep repugnance

---

†††††Two neighboring states made a contract over the mutual extradition of renegade soldiers. In the border provinces of both states, servitude—[i.e.,] property right in the person of a peasant—was established. For a long time, every now and then a wretch fled across the border in order to escape the inhumanity of his lord and was free whenever he reached it. The estate owners mutually rushed to extend the contract to include the extradition of peasants. Among other consequences, a serf escaped because of a few stolen grapes and was extradited, and he died shortly after an arbitrary caning. And this happened in the last half of the previous decade in that state which considers itself the most enlightened in Germany.

in the hands of a bourgeois, belong all high offices in the administration of the state and in the [battle]field. Such a demand is obviously unjust. No office in the state—as long as it is a genuine office and not merely an empty trapping, as long as it [exists] for the needs of the state and was not invented solely for the needs of the occupant—is merely a privilege. It is a heavy burden, which the state places on the shoulders of one of its citizens. The more important the office is, the more obvious becomes the right of the state to watch over the allocation of it. The rarer the talents required for the administration of it are united [in one person], [363] the more extensive the circle must be from which it [the state] chooses. Or, if it does not exercise the right of choice directly but through representatives, it has the perfect right to demand that they be limited by nothing but the number of citizens. "But," one could say, "is it not permissible to determine a narrower circle of select men from which the most important state offices will be filled?" And I reply: "Not only is this allowed to happen, but it will also have very beneficial consequences for the facilitation of the selection and for the speedy allocation of the vacant position." But how then should the selection into this circle itself be determined? Certainly not by birth, if the aim is the true advantage of the state. For, given the same spiritual development,[63] which in modern times and most states is obviously the case with aristocracy and the better civil estate,[64] why should it follow that the talented and good human beings descend only from certain houses and [that] the offspring of all other families must be knuckleheads and base human beings in comparison? At least to my knowledge, no defender of the aristocracy has yet committed the insolence of claiming this. Thus, the admission into the circle of select citizens destined for the most important state offices could be founded on nothing other than on skill and loyalty, proven through prior smaller services to the state. And, once again, we would stand before our first maxim in the allocation of offices. Every higher dignity would have to be earned through the loyal and faithful administration of lower [offices]. No state has relinquished this right to choose the ablest for the administration of its public offices and to select this person from the entire multitude of its citizens according to its best conviction, and [no state] could have relinquished [this right] without

---

63. *Geistesbildung*
64. *Bürgerstande*

contradicting its [own] end and abrogating itself. But what does a caste do which arrogates to itself the exclusive ability to be chosen for these offices? We want to assume [that] this caste chooses the worthiest that can be found among them according to its best conviction. It follows neither that this is the worthiest among all citizens of the state in general nor that he appears [to be] the worthiest in this caste to the other citizens. If this caste alone constituted the sum of the citizens overall, then its procedure would be lawful. By means of this procedure they conduct themselves as [if they were] the entire sum, [and] therefore as the state. What are the remaining citizens then? Apparently, a separate state, subjugated by the latter and arbitrarily ruled. Such a prerogative not only turns the aristocracy into a state within the state, which has a separate interest from the other citizens, [364] it also destroys entirely the remaining social classes among the ranks of the citizens of the state, abrogates their civil rights, and transforms them into arbitrarily ruled slaves, insofar as those state offices that cannot be filled from among their midst are related to them. And what is unlawful if this is not?

We are not committing an injustice against the aristocracy. It is the direct content of its demand that it wants selections only from its midst, that it wants to constitute[65] the *eligible* citizens [body]. That it also wants to vote itself, that it also wants to constitute the *voting* members, follows straight from the previous demand, once it has been satisfied. Who votes for the highest state services? Who fills the vacant positions? Princes who know their own people are rare. It is indeed impossible, improper, and even harmful for them to go into the details of the different branches of the state administration and to know and watch the subordinate members of the administrative state bodies closely. They must leave the selection to the higher [ranking] members of these bodies, who are more capable of judging the aptitude of their subordinates. Once these higher [ranking] members are *all* of the aristocracy and inspired by the corporate spirit of their estate, they will, [they] *must*, as a consequence of their basic principles, remove everyone who is a bourgeois from every position as long as there is still a nobleman who covets it. The aristocracy is its own judge in this matter. And as the number of noblemen who require the revenues from state offices increases, the circle of aristocratic positions extends as far as the aristocracy wills. For example, in some states, the aristocracy has lately usurped postmaster

---

65. *hergeben*

positions and Protestant clerical positions that had previously been left to the bourgeois. What is the aristocracy's boundary in this matter? None other than its needs. What is its law? None other than its good will. Where positions remain that are given to the bourgeois, there the latter has solely to thank this good will. If they [the positions] were more profitable or more honorable, they would not come down to him. I claim nothing new here, and nothing that could not be proven through daily experience. [Imagine] in the department of government, or justice, or finance a position of a councilor becomes vacant. At least nine out of ten times it is filled with a nobleman. And how should it be possible that among the three- or four-times larger number of civil secretaries who have worked half their lives in this profession, a [person] equally suitable for the councilor's position is found much more rarely than among the much smaller number of aristocratic secretaries who only work in [this profession] for a short time? [365] Surely the positions are not filled in accordance with the greater skill? In fact, consistent noblemen do not even feign this. [Rather] they claim that they *must* be filled according to birth. Precisely on this point I do not agree with them. I claim that every office in the state must be filled according to superior merit. One may not object that, once elevated to the higher state service, the bourgeois will let himself be ruled by the same corporate spirit and try to elevate [other] bourgeois only because he is bourgeois, to the exclusion of the worthy nobleman. I do not know whether he will [or will] not do it. I do not want to vouch for it. But where else does this separation between the two classes, this partiality on both sides originate but from your preceding demands, with which I have to deal here? If noblemen and bourgeois had never existed, if nothing other than citizens of the state had ever existed, neither the nobleman nor the bourgeois could favor his kind, because *everyone* would be his kind.

This is a direct injustice against the state. I want to demonstrate another indirect [injustice] that arises from this institution only briefly. Whoever devotes himself to a branch of the public business is driven to exert his powers in the same place far too little by the usually meagre salary that is handed to the busy and to the idle in equal measure. A stronger incentive must be set in motion. From the position that he has achieved, everyone must behold a higher [position] before him as the price for the worthy claim to his present [position]. But what does the citizen who has climbed as high as he can climb according to the constitution see before him that is even higher? If he is not driven by the mightier incentives of altruistic virtue and love of the fatherland, for which any bourgeois has as little sense as any nobleman, the state will lose in addition to the remaining power of the aristocrats—who in any case are certain of their advancement by virtue of their birth—also the same portion of the powers of those bourgeois, which they need not necessarily expend in claiming.

In no profession is this as obvious as in military service. Where an aristocracy exists that can demonstrate the inheritance of the somewhat raw yet forceful mindset of the old knighthood in its family, it is in fact, in belligerent states, exclusively entitled to the occupation of officers' positions! Even where the aristocracy has deprived its spirit of the old strength through court life, a fleeting acquaintance with the sciences or even through trade—giving it a flexibility that makes the aristocracy equal to the middle class—even there, it still claims the [366] superior office. But this office requires less thought to be able to turn about right and left or present one's rifle, or, if it should ever get serious, to murder or be murdered. Maybe the bourgeois will yield this advantage voluntarily and without envy in exchange for more important affairs, for which he prepares himself through a more arduous education. However, to admit the bourgeois into this estate but to cut off his hope of climbing to the higher levels, as is happening in several states, is most absurd according to the very constitution of this estate. Was it possible for the most inventive jester to identify a deeper debasement of the middle class than to persuade it that it has been put on a level with the aristocracy in regard to the holiest [attribute] that the latter believes to have, while [in fact] it has been placed next to it for the continual contemplation of its own lowliness? Than to oblige the bourgeois captain, from an estate where subordination is the highest principle, to command the aristocratic cadet or lieutenant and to vouch for his behavior, while both of them know perfectly well that after the passage of a few years the nobleman will be the colonel or the general of the bourgeois captain? In an estate that requires sacrifices that only honor can pay, what demand does the bourgeois who has reached his highest destination still feel in order to make these sacrifices?

"But the aristocracy must be helped up," one repeats. And thus we find it [the aristocracy] precisely in those positions claimed exclusively by it, and the occupation of these positions presupposes a proof of ancestry. If, why, and how far it must be helped up—a few words to conclude! Since we have seen that one may not help it [the aristocracy] by means of the exclusive occupation of those positions that require overwhelming talents, let us now examine only what [means] still remains to help it. First, we encounter the *positions of the cathedral canon*, of which a certain number can always only be occupied by the aristocracy. Specifically, I am speaking only of Protestant endowments here. The necessary [observations] about the Catholic [positions], the occupants of which are true men of the cloth, will appear in the following chapter. One cannot say that particular talents are required for the administration of these positions. Therefore, the aristocracy's exclusive occupation thereof cannot be contested on these grounds, as, for example, the exclusive occupation of higher state services. But perhaps on other [grounds].

When we go back into the history of the establishment of most bishoprics—and, in the Protestant part of Germany, of all [bishoprics]—we find that their only final end was the livelihood of those men who cared for the instruction and culture of the people, [367] a final end that evidently intends the best for the state. We do not have to examine here where the goods for these endowments came from. For the most part, they came either from the loot of the conqueror, who had violently interfered with property rights or, where no stable state and no certain inheritance law had existed yet, they had no owner at all. If they did not come from the estates of the aristocracy, which was not even a distinct popular body then—and provided that all looting does not belong to it by law—and if it is not to be feared that the previous rightful owners may come forward (not their ancestors since they could not inherit prior to the introduction of inheritance law)—then they [the goods] were gifted to the state itself as a donation for the state's benefit. Consequently, they became the rightful property of the *state*, i.e., of the entire citizenry.—Profound darkness descended over the peoples. And the church, which is something entirely different than the state and which confounded its darkening existence with the enlightening existence of the teachers of the people, usurped the state's property. The Reformation, which—in the true sense of the word, the meaning of which we will explain in what follows—destroyed the *church*, restored the property to its first and rightful occupant, the state. Without doubt the state had the right to dispose of its property. If it had either become superfluous for the attainment of its original final end or the state had more immediate final ends, for the advancement of which it wanted to use [its property], it was without doubt authorized to do so. But how, then, did a single caste come into the exclusive possession of that which was the rightful property of all citizens of the state? Were the excluded citizens of the state consulted in disposing of the property? Did they voluntarily surrender their share to that caste? Did they have no more urgent concern than to enrich that caste? In no way. Once again, the aristocracy acted as if it alone were the state, as if no one besides itself existed anymore. That such a procedure is unlawful and invalid, and that the excluded citizens have the never-expiring right to demand the restoration of the whole to common deliberation—indeed no doubt is possible about this [matter] after what has hitherto been said in this writing.

And, I should like to know, are those goods really that expendable to the entire state? Is the state in such serious dilemma regarding the application of these goods that, in order to be divested of them, it must loan them to that caste as an empty embellishment?[66] Does the state have no more urgent need at all [368] than cultivating the reputation of having a rich aristocracy? Have they [the goods] only become this expendable for the promotion of the original intention? As long as there still are in these states either direct teachers of the people, who languish under oppressive shortages; or actual scholars, who are rewarded meagerly or not at all for their services on behalf of the sciences and thereby indirectly on behalf of the people's enlightenment; or as long as important undertakings for the enhancement of human knowledge must still be omitted due to lack of support—how can the aristocracy be insolent enough to desire these goods for the assertion of its estate? This is the true purpose[67] of the revenues of the bishoprics: first the proportional pay of the teachers of the people. If some of the revenue is left, reward for the scholars and promotion of the sciences. And the possibility of this application, it seems, still persists.

The second class of prerogatives that the aristocracy possesses exclusively are the *courtly offices*. These [offices] are founded either in order to satisfy opinion alone and are as such very appropriately filled with creatures of opinion, or they serve the actual, and not just the imagined, needs of the prince. They are his company and his friends. Or, finally, precisely because they are the latter, they believe they indirectly have a very large influence on the administration of the state. In regard to the

---

66. *Zierrat* refers to decoration or embellishment, but Fichte is also playing on words here, as *Rate* refers to interest rate.

67. *Bestimmung*

first, no individual citizen—be he of the aristocracy who feel its worth, or not—will perhaps envy the man who demeans himself as merely the embellishment of a radiant court, and who debases himself as something an artificially contrived speaking machine would probably be better at. But the citizens altogether, if they should rise up enough to be able to go without this spectacle and to overcome false shame in front of other states, are without doubt entitled to ask why they should still maintain this expensive splendor through considerable sacrifices? Without doubt, they are entitled to abrogate not only the aristocracy's exclusive prerogative to accompany these positions but even the positions themselves.

Regarding the second intention for their institution [of courtly offices], the prince, just like everyone else, most certainly has the right to choose from among the entire human society whomever he wants as his friends and his company. If his choice falls on men who per chance are of the aristocracy, or even if he has such a peculiar taste that a certain line of ancestors is the exclusive condition for attaining his company, [369] no one must persuade him, just like he must not persuade anyone about whom he should choose as a friend. He may acquire his friends how anyone acquires friends, or he may buy his company or his flatterers with his private wealth or with the salary that the state grants him for his personal needs, as many and whichever he wants or can—this is not the concern of the state, nor of any citizen of the state. But just as the bourgeois has little right to complain when the prince wants to choose nothing but noblemen as his company, the aristocracy likewise has little right to oppose him or to make it a state-wide complaint[68] when he also admits bourgeois, or only bourgeois, into his company. The prince's will is free in this matter and the prohibition on restricting him is valid for both parties. It is to be admired that the aristocracy did not turn the position of the court jester, which in a certain age was important enough at most courts, into an exclusively aristocratic position. Or did the aristocracy perhaps find it easier to provide the positions of a court marshal or chamberlain than that [of the jester], and did it require a wider circle than that of the limited noblemen to find the necessary talents? In any case, it does not bring the aristocracy honor that it could not fill out the recreation hours of the sovereign,[69] tired from the tribulations of government, well enough to make such a recourse unnecessary.

---

68. *Landesbeschwerde*

69. *Landesvater*

Finally, the aristocracy demands the exclusive company of the prince, because—allegedly—it is important for the country that the latter is surrounded by people of good basic principles. If this were right, the exact opposite of what the aristocracy wants to argue would have to be the conclusion. Then the company of the prince would belong among the most important state services, which, according to the basic principles above, are to be filled with the greatest and best men from the entire mass of citizens and not merely from the aristocracy. But I admit in advance what must soon come to light anyway, [namely,] that no prince on whose basic principles and good will much depends and who must, like a child, be protected from evil persuasions, is particularly pleasing to me. *The law* must rule through the prince and it must rule *him* most strictly. He must not be able to do anything that the law does not will. And he must have to do everything that it wills. He may, if God wills, love the law in his heart or he may indignantly gnaw at the fence that holds and guides him. The prince, as prince, is a machine animated by the law that has no life absent it [the law]. Insofar as he is a private person, *he* or society may look after his moral character [but] the state only looks after the character of the law. The prince does not have company; only the private man does.

Thus, absolutely no lawful means remain for us to help up the aristocracy. [370] But why should it be helped up in the first place? The aristocracy, as aristocracy, i.e., as the present popular body designated by birth, does not have to claim *legal entitlements* at all, because even its existence depends on the free will of the state. Why does the state need to entertain its demands for very long? If the aristocracy becomes burdensome through this, the state itself can abrogate it and is thus rid of all its demands. For what is not, cannot make demands either. Once the aristocracy is abrogated, no other privileged popular body can claim *legal entitlements* from the state in its place, since it must exist before it can make demands and it cannot exist without the privilege from the state. Thus, the question is actually not *about right*. It is a question *about prudence* and it is to be phrased like this: *Is it useful for the state that there should be one or more classes that, because of their reputation and their wealth, are always skilled and ready for important businesses and enterprises for the state? And in what manner and by what means are such classes designated, brought forth, and maintained most expediently?* The answer to these [questions] does not belong into the present book.

Chapter Six

On the Church, in Relation to the Right of Constitutional Change

[370] Diversity and variability is the nature of the bodily world; sameness and invariability the nature of the spiritual [world]. Leibniz claimed and proved through close inspection that no two tree leaves are identical, and he could have added boldly that even one and the same [leaf] is not identical to itself two seconds later.[1] This very Leibniz rightly asserted the universal validity of this claim and of all his [371] metaphysical claims for all right-thinking heads. Among all possible opinions regarding the same object, only *one* can, according to the judgment of all of us, be the true one. And whoever believes to have found it claims that, since the beginning of spirits and as long as they will exist, everyone who understands him and grasps the reasons for his claim must necessarily agree with him. One can err in diverse ways, [but] the truth is only *one*. It has been the same since eternity and will also remain the same into eternity. Again, only one [thing] is *right* or *true in practice*. And this [practical] truth, the most important for every free spirit, is hardly hidden, [so] that human beings agree much more easily both on its necessary universal validity in general and on the particular clauses that they derive than [they do] on theoretical truths. The recognition of this truth, to which they can hardly close their eyes, engenders certain hopes, anticipations, [and] demands in them, of which not the slightest trace manifests itself in the world of appearances and the validity of which they can demonstrate neither to themselves nor to others, as

---

1. Gottfried Wilhelm Leibniz, *Nouveau essais sur l'entendement humain* [New Essays on Human Understanding] (Amsterdam, 1765), 2:27, §3.

perhaps [they could] the accuracy of a mathematical theorem. Even so, they presuppose as certain that all rational spirits must agree with them about this, too. And this generates the—probably universal, albeit not always clearly thought—idea of an invisible church, the agreement of all rational beings on the same faith. But such an invisible church itself is only imagined, and that to which all other articles of faith adhere is itself only an article of faith.

Since the truth means infinitely much to everyone who has this faith, yet he can never—neither through experience, nor through argument—demonstrate it with complete certainty, he grasps at everything to strengthen his faith. Divested of internal arguments, he searches for external ones. "If my faith is true, all rational spirits must have the same faith," is the sentence he begins with. And since he may not justifiably hope to find anything more than he already has to prove the premise, he at least seeks to educate himself about the conclusion. He concludes backwards: "if all rational spirits have the same faith as I have, it must surely be the true [faith]." And he seeks to investigate, as far as his sphere of influence possibly reaches, *whether* they do have it. However, since he is actually concerned not with instruction but with confirmation, since he is not looking for lessons but for proofs, since he is already in agreement with himself about the truth and only wants to be confirmed in it, he does not hear anything but the wished-for [372] "yes, I believe the same." And wherever he does not hear it, he labors to convince the other through persuasion, only with the intention of finally obtaining the desired confirmation of faith. In general, it is an inborn tendency of human beings to produce unanimity of thought in all kinds of objects. [This tendency] is founded on that necessary uniformity of everything spiritual, the idea of which lies deeply in the human being. Yet one decides much more easily in the theoretical [realm] either to remain divided and to let the matter rest or even to accept the other's convictions in place of one's own prior [beliefs], than [one does] in the practical [realm]. Here, one is not as easily dismissed or converted. Here, one rarely wants to be lectured but almost always [wants to] lecture. Thus, there is a tendency in the human being to transform that invisible and merely conceptual universal church into a visible one, as far as it is up to him; to actually represent this idea in the material world; to not only believe that the other has the same faith as *he* does but, insofar as it is at all possible, to know it as well; to tie his belief system at least at *one* point to something that he knows.—This is the reason for the church union.

The visible church is a true society² that is based on a contract. In the *invisible* church, no one knows anything about the others. One's faith develops from the soul of each individual, independent of everything that is external to it. Agreement, if it exists, emerges by itself without anybody having the goal to bring it about. No one could know whether it exists except a spirit in whose knowledge the manner of representation of all spirits is combined. [In turn,] the *visible* church presupposes the agreement and its consequence, the strengthening of faith, as an end. Everyone who tells the other what he believes, wants to hear from the other that he believes the same. The first principle of the church contract is the sentence "*tell me what you believe; I will tell you what I believe.*" However, since, as has already been noted, the purpose of the union is not at all to gather different opinions, to instruct oneself through the comparison of them, and to form one's own [opinion] accordingly, but to confirm and strengthen one's opinion through the agreement of the other's opinion with one's own, this principle is, in fact, not sufficient for the foundation of a church. It must not only be determined *that* the other should say what he believes but also *what* he should say he believes. The church contract therefore presupposes the groundwork of a legal confession of faith, and its basic principle now reads "*we all want to unanimously believe the same and confess this our faith to each other.*"

[373] One may perhaps find an internal inconsistency in this contractual formulation. We should not remain silent but *confess* our faith loudly. Our silence would lead the members of the church to suspect that we either do not believe anything at all or that we believe something different than *they* [believe] and [that we] disturb them in their faith. We should say *sincerely* what we believe and not merely feign our faith. If the church assumed its members' confessions were merely pretense, only a work of the lips and not originating from any inner convictions, its end would be negated once again. A confession of faith deemed false and insincere cannot strengthen us in our faith. Even so, we ought to swear a *particular, already predetermined* confession of faith with this complete conviction. But if we are simply not convinced of the truth of the latter, nor able to convince ourselves of it, what should we do then? No church takes this case into account. Every consistent church, i.e., every [church] that is a real [church], must absolutely deny the possibility of this case, and all churches that have proceeded consistently have indeed denied it. The first premise without which no church contract is possible

---

2. See footnote 29 on page 86 on "society."

at all is this: that the confession of faith underlying the church contract contains without doubt the only and pure truth at which everyone who is searching for the truth must necessarily arrive; that it is the only true faith. The second [premise] that directly follows from the first: that it is in the power of every human being to bring forth this conviction in himself, if only he wants it; that unbelief is always founded either on a lack of attentive heeding of the evidence or on willful stubbornness, and that faith depends on our free will. A *duty to believe*[3] therefore exist in all church systems. Yet, nothing can be a duty that is not in our power. No church has ever denied that. Both principles can be found in any Catholic textbook that one may open. We will have opportunity further below to say a few words about the inconsistent proceedings of the Protestant congregations, in that they want to be distinct churches and want to have church rights—in this and many other points.

Against the claim that the church is founded on a contract, some readers may raise the objection—supported by facts, whether true or invented, I do not know—that it is actually of monarchic origin and therefore not founded on a contract between the members but on the superior force of a lord. But even if it were true that the [374] consciences did not originally surrender but were subjugated, a band of isolated slaves who all serve the same lord would thereby admittedly have come into being, but they would not know of their common servitude [and so would be] nevermore a society. The same faith would have emerged in the hearts of all, but [there would be] nevermore a mutual, uniform confession of faith. At least two [slaves] must make a start to admit their mutual subservience and invite the others, whom they perhaps suspected of the same subservience, to confess. Otherwise millions of human beings would never have formed a church.—It is indeed physically, although certainly not morally, possible that an earthly state comes into being through subjugation. A superior conqueror can subjugate slaves and place them in a union and in [a relationship of] mutual influence on one another through his orders. The bodies[4] of the subordinates and their subservience to the commands of their lord indeed appear in the material world. That a spiritual state should come into being in this manner is, however, as physically impossible as it is morally impossible. The latter

---

3. *Glaubenspflicht*

4. *Leiber*: Fichte differentiates between *Leib* and *Körper* here. *Leib* refers to the animate, or lived-in body, while *Körper* means merely the physical object.

only subjugates the consciences and not the bodies,[5] and the subservience of the spirits does not come into view unless it reveals itself voluntarily. The church, moreover, struggles with a far greater difficulty than the one indicated above, [i.e.,] that its confession of faith is predetermined, of which it relieved itself in such an easy fashion.—The accomplishment of its end is based on the *truthfulness* of its members. If it cannot assure itself of this truthfulness, if it can give no credit to the members' confession of faith, the mutual strengthening of faith does not take place. Instead, the tempers[6] are only angered further and bewildered. It would be better for them to have believed in silence that everyone else thinks precisely as they [do] than to be plunged ever deeper into doubt by daily confessions they cannot trust.

There is no external tribunal as such for lies. The tribunal is internal, in each individual conscience. Whoever lies has to be ashamed of himself. He must despise himself.—In case we cannot convince ourselves of the truth or falsehood of an alleged fact by means of experience, we must leave it, in civil life, to the conscience of each [individual] whether he wants to speak truthfully or lie to us; we must leave him to the punishment that he does, or does not, inflict on himself by speaking falsehoods. Such an internal punishment, which, however, always remains doubtful and never comes to light, cannot satisfy any society that is built on truth and stands and falls with it.

[375] Through the almost unanimous faith of all human beings, this inner tribunal has already been alienated[7] to a being external to us, to the universal moral judge, to God. That a god exists and that he punishes lies is perhaps the unanimous belief of all churches. Thus every [church] can expect the punishment of its insincere members by God. But the punishment by God is remote. It merely waits for the sinner in the next life. The end of the church, however, is intended for the present [life]. When these punishments are doled out, they will indeed see who told them the truth or who merely feigned belief. But then they no longer need the strengthening of their faith, for which they entered the church association. If the unbeliever is completely and resolutely unbelieving, he believes in no god at all, no future life, and no punishment of his

---

5. *Körper*

6. *Gemüter*

7. *veräussert*

falseness. Thus, he does not fear the threat of God's punishment and hence will not worry about making a false confession if he has ulterior reasons to do it. Or, if maybe he was not entirely an unbeliever, he maybe hopes to settle with God in a different manner and to evade the discovery of his falseness and the punishment through some means. This imposes on the church the task of preponing the punishment and, since it cannot move God for its [own] sake to punish earlier than he would otherwise have punished, to take up the office of judge itself. In this way, the inner judgeship of conscience is once again alienated, namely, to a judge who can pass judgment on the spot, to the visible church.

This new alienation of the inner judgeship, this judgment in the place of God, is the fundamental law of every consistent church. Without it, the church can simply not prevail. Whatever it looses, must be loosed in heaven, too, and whatever it binds, must be bound in heaven, too.[8] Absent this judgeship the church vainly demands authority over the souls of human beings, [an authority] which it cannot claim through any [other] means. It vainly threatens with punishments, which it admits it cannot adjudicate. It still leaves human beings dependent on themselves in their faith, which, nevertheless, it demanded to dictate. It nullifies[9] its own concept and stands in inner contradiction with itself.

Since it wants to judge the purity of heart of human beings, whose interior it cannot probe—as well as dole out punishments and rewards to them accordingly—a new task emerges for the church, namely, this: to contrive its confession of faith in such a manner that it becomes apparent in external effects whether [376] one is convinced of its truth or not; to give itself such a constitution that it can judge the obedience and the devotion of its members based on certain and unsuspicious attributes. To be sure not to err, it [the church] will make these attributes as obvious to the eye as possible. This takes place in two different ways: through harsh oppression of their [the members'] understanding and through strict commandments that are placed on their will.—The more fantastical, absurd, and contrary to sound reason the teachings of a [given] church are, the more firmly convinced it can be of the devotion of such members who listen to all this earnestly and with a straight face, [who] repeat it eagerly, [who] memorize it in their head with difficulty and effort, and

---

8. Matthew 16:19, 18:18.

9. *aufheben*

[who] take care not to drop a single, little word to the ground. The harsher the refusals and self-denial are, the crueler the penances are that the church demands, the more firmly it can believe in the faithfulness of such members, who submit themselves to all this only in order to remain united with the church, who relinquish all earthly pleasures in order to be blessed with the church's heavenly goods. The more one has sacrificed, the more strongly our attachment must be to that for which we have sacrificed everything.—After the church placed the fruits of faith in external exercises, the observance or omission of which is visible to every eye, it thereby opened an easy view into the heart itself. It may be rather difficult to explore whether someone believes in the primacy of Saint Peter[10] or not, [but] whether someone kept the fast mandated by a successor and representative of the latter is discovered much more easily. If he did not keep [the fast], his belief in [Saint Peter's primacy], in the infallibility of all his successors, and in the indispensability of obedience to all their commandments for salvation must not be very firm and the church can assume he is an unbeliever with great certainty.

By means of this institution, necessary in itself, the church gains two additional, very substantial advantages. To begin with, if it invents those articles of faith purposefully, imposed to verify the faith, it acquires through them a rich supply of various punishments and rewards in another world, which it needs in order to mete them out to its very diverse members according to desert—to each in accordance with his belief or unbelief. Instead of simple heaven, it gets innumerable levels of salvation and an inexhaustible treasure of saintly merits to be doled out among [377] its obedient members. Besides simple hell, it gets purgatory, which is capable of endless variations in terms of agony and duration, in order to scare the unbelievers and unrepentants—each according to his need.—In the second place, the church strengthens the faith of its members by not leaving it idle but giving it plenty of work. At first sight, this appears contradictory, but it is most often confirmed by experience, and the reason for this appearance will be located soon—the more incredible the things are that one turns into articles of faith, the more easily one finds faith. One is most likely to deny that which is still rather believable, because it appears to be too natural. But [if] one sets

---

10. Jesus confers special authority on his apostle Peter, and so Peter is understood to be the first pope or to hold primary authority in the history of the Church. See Matthew 16:17–19; Luke 12:31–32; John 21:15–17.

this denied statement atop a more wondrous one, and this [statement] atop an even more wondrous one, and multiplies the fantastical step by step, the human being will get dizzy, as it were. He has no chance for sober reflection anymore. He tires, and his conversion is accomplished. It is nothing new that many a person, who did not believe in God was converted through belief in the devil, hell, [or] purgatory. And the Tertullian[11] [expression], "this is nonsensical, hence it comes from God," is excellent as proof for his man.[12] That is because the ordinary head surveys one, two, three principles with their natural causes and consequences. He is thereby invited to contemplate them and believes to be able to judge their truth or untruth based on rational grounds. You, [however,] in order to prevent him from this undertaking, set them [the principles] atop other, artificial grounds, which in turn are articles of faith themselves, and those again on others, and so on into infinity. Now he cannot survey anything anymore. He wanders around in this labyrinth without a guide, he is terrified by the enormous work he has imposed on himself, he tires over the vain search, and, out of a kind of lazy desperation, he surrenders himself blindly into the hands of his leader and is glad to have him.

Do not get me wrong. I am not saying that all founders or proselytizers of the church system have always clearly conceived the intention to subjugate the consciences of human beings through such wicked yet completely expedient means. No, guided by instinct, anxiously conscientious natures, already frightened beforehand, went by themselves down the path that afterward they took with others. They deceived themselves first, before they deceived others. One inconsistency that must not be forsaken but believed out of fear and anxiety [378] leads to countless [others]. The more astute the conscientious contemplator is, the more plentiful the haul of dreams will be that he brings back from the land of chimeras.—But for our contemporary zealots for the maintenance of their pure [and] only saving faith, who for the most part do not strive with the same honesty, I must offer a teaching that generously compensates [them] for the vexation that they could be caused by the perusal of this chapter.—If they seek to assert their faith, for example, by abandoning

---

11. Quintus Septimus Tertullian, c. 160–240.

12. Fichte is paraphrasing Tertullian, *De carne Christi*, 5:23–26: "And the Son of God died: it is credible, because it is unfitting. And he was buried and rose again: it is certain, because it is impossible."

the most fantastical principles and trying to bring it [the faith] closer to reason, they seize a means that downright opposes their end. Through this concession, they arouse the thought that there could perhaps also be things among the retained [principles] that will be given up over time, too. Yet, that is still the slightest damage. By abridging the system and divesting it of a part of its wonder, they make the verification and survey of it easier. If the prior [system], which was more difficult to verify, is in danger, how will the latter, which makes it [the verification] easier, maintain itself? Take the opposite route. Boldly substantiate every inconsistency that is utilized with another [inconsistency] that is slightly greater. It takes some time until the frightened human spirit comes to itself and sufficiently familiarizes itself with the new phantom, which initially blinds its eyes, in order to examine it up close. If it [the phantom] is in danger, you donate a new one from the inexhaustible treasure of your inconsistencies. The preceding story repeats itself, and it goes on like this until the end of time. Only do not give the human spirit a chance for cool reflection, never leave its faith unexercised, and then [you] defy the gates of hell so that they overwhelm your rule.—You obscurantists and friends of the night, do not become suspicious of this advice by surmising that it comes from an enemy. Even against you, deceit is impermissible, even though you use it against us. Inspect it [the advice] carefully, and you will find it completely right.

According to these principles, the church is the judge on earth in place of God. In God's place, it doles out the rewards and the punishments of another world to its members. In one well-known church, one has also made use of temporal punishments against unbelief and unrepentance. But this is an infelicitous measure, founded on misunderstanding and excited zeal. [The] temporal consequences of church punishments can be nothing but *atonements*[13] to which the believer submits himself with his good will and with the good will of the church, in order to escape the consequences of punishment in the next world. Whoever castigates himself for his [379] unbelief and fasts and pilgrimages wants to satisfy the church in order to be absolved from its curse for the next world. Even the person who allows himself to be burned by the holy office, can be burned on no other condition than that he is allowed to remain in the church, if not in this life, at least in the next. He bequeaths his sinful flesh to Satan to perish so that the spirit

---

13. *Abbüssung*

may become blessed on the Last Day. This is also the original meaning of corporal correction,[14] as can be clearly seen from the formality with which they are exercised. It was unhinged vengefulness that made use of corporal correction as *punishment*,[15] thereby altered the spirit of these institutions and straightforwardly works against their proper end. When these atonements become punishments—i.e., they are imposed *against his will* on someone who does not want to remain in the church under this condition, who does not want to obey it, who scorns and derides its curse or blessing, who is resolutely unbelieving—they cause exactly that which they should prevent. They cause *hypocrisy*. If I have nothing to risk but the punishment of the church in the other world, I will certainly not subject myself to its penances if I do not believe in its threats. My unbelief is uncovered, the church is purged of a bad seed, which it can now put under all the curses that it invents. However, if I have to expect punishments in this world, regardless of whether I believe or not, I will hide my unbelief as long as I can and rather subject myself to a smaller evil in order to escape the greater.—I skip here over [the fact] that it is an obvious injustice for the church to punish human beings who have renounced their submission or never promised it, over whom it therefore has no right at all; and that such conduct provokes the aversion and irreconcilable hatred of all who were treated unjustly.—The Roman Church, a model of consistency, acted inconsistently only in this matter. The prosecution of the Jews and of the confessed schismatics by the Inquisition, the execution of every unrepentant [sinner] as long as he was unrepentant, the association of temporal ban with the spiritual ban against the regents, the release of their subjects from the oath of allegiance, and the command to desert their princes were such inconsistencies and they came to cost the church dearly.

The church has laws of faith and thus *a legislative power*. This [power], however, can be very divided. The *substance* of these laws, the articles of faith, do not have to be given by the unanimous voice of the members. Either *one* member or *several* can be exclusively authorized to this. In this regard, the church can be a monarchy or also an oligarchy [380]—this point is determined by a fundamental law. According to their *form*, however, as *laws* of faith, they become binding for no individual in any other way but through voluntary adoption.—Sure enough, as has

---

14. *körperliche Züchtigungen*
15. *Strafen*

already been shown above, the church assumes original universal validity for all human beings, independent of any freedom of the arbitrary will,[16] and, as a consequence of this basic principle, it is surely entitled to curse and ban all who do not accept them [the laws of faith]. But it cannot demand that these curses should have the slightest consequence in the world of appearances, where the natural law rules, which knows of no original law of faith and entitles everyone not to let anyone else arbitrarily impose a law on him. Whoever considers the law to be arbitrary will not believe in the ordinances of the church. Whoever considers it to be originally binding will submit to it without effort.

These laws must all be equally binding. They may, for the purpose of assessing them, be divided into essential and nonessential [laws], but they must all be equally essential for the faith. Whoever does not believe in the smallest church provision—be it pertaining to a dogma, a fact, or the church discipline—must be assumed to not believe in any of them. The foundational law that contains all other [laws] is the belief in the church as the sole, infallible law-giver and judge in lieu of God, as has been shown above. No article of faith must be believed because it is worthy of belief, but because the church orders belief in it. The church demands belief in *all* [laws]. Thus, whoever dissents from the slightest [law], dissents from the church, and the belief in the other [laws]—which he cannot possibly believe based on obedience to the church, but perhaps on other grounds—cannot help him [because] it is not the demanded church faith.—Regarding this harshness and the greater harshness still to follow, I benevolently caution certain of my readers not to forget in which domain we are; not to commit the inconsistency of telling me that this may perhaps have been [a] basic principle in the past [but that] the times are much better now. I do not want to know what has been a basic principle in the past, now, [or] ever. I am not in the domain of history, but in the domain of natural law, which is a philosophical science. I am developing the concept of a *visible church*. I deduce principle after principle from this concept. I say, *if* any association[17] has ever claimed to want to be a visible church, and *if* this association was consistent, it necessarily had to assume this and that. *Whether* such an association existed [381] and *whether* it was consistent, that I do not know. I am only wrong if I argue wrongly. The church has

16. *Freiheit der Willkühr*

17. *Gesellschaft*

a *judicial office*, and it must be determined by church laws, which constitute articles of faith on this point as much as on any other [point], who ought to administer this judicial office.—The *teaching office* is not an essential office of the church. Rather, it is accidental. The teacher may not add or subtract anything. He must only recite the church doctrines as they have been defined. He explains the law and inculcates [it], and it is appropriate that this office be administered by someone who is at the same time a judge, because both [offices] presuppose the perfect knowledge of the law.—The exclusive task of the priest in a church society, as is known, does not consist in teaching. Everyone may teach. [Rather,] it consists in judging, in hearing confession, absolving, and condemning. The sacrifice of the mass itself is a judicial action, and the foundation of all other [actions]. It is, if you will, the ceremonious enfeoffment of the church with the judicial office of God, repeated before everyone's eyes and for everyone to know. If *it* [the church] shall judge, judge with supreme authority, God must not have anything left to judge. And if he shall not have anything left to judge, the church must have done enough for him. It must be absolutely pure, holy, and without sin. It must be the adorned bride that has not one stain or wrinkle, or something akin, but must be holy and inculpable. The church becomes this through the merits of the church members who have done enough for the entire church, merits that the church offers up to God during the mass and thereby buys its complete freedom from him. Only by virtue of this redemption[18] does the church have the right to judge its members itself.—Everyone who reads mass must be able to hear confession; everyone who hears confession must be able to read mass; and both are a consequence of the authority of the church to perform its judicial actions. The judgments of the church are infallible, since, by virtue of the sacrifice of the mass, it is the *sole* judge for the invisible world. They [the judgments] had to be infallible, if the church should be possible. How can an association[19] assure itself of obedience if it cannot punish disobedience? And how could the church, whose punishments affect an invisible world, punish disobedience if it was not certain that its pretensions are valid in this invisible world and that the punishments that it imposes will certainly take place there?—The Lutheran Church is inconsistent and tries to cover up its inconsistency. The Reformed

---

18. *Loskaufung*
19. *Gesellschaft*

Church[20] is frankly and honestly inconsistent. Both have laws of faith—their symbolic books. Or even if only the bible were this symbolic book, the sentence "the bible is God's word, and what it contains is true [382] *because* the bible contains it" would necessarily justify the entire church system as we have developed it here.—Whoever believes them [the laws of faith], will become blessed; whoever does not believe them, his blessedness is not hurt either. If I must trust the reputation and cannot convince myself based on reasons, I do not understand why I should prefer to trust the reputation of one church rather than the reputation of the other, since I can become blessed in both. And if I should know of yet a third [church], that professes to exclusively own the right to make blessed and that condemns everything without exception that I do not believe, I must *necessarily* subject myself to it.—I want to be become blessed, that is my final end goal. All churches assert that this is not possible through one's own reason and force, but only through faith in the church. According to their own assertion, I must therefore believe them if I want to become blessed. All three churches teach that one can become blessed in the Roman Church. If, in order to become blessed, I enter the Roman Church, so I believe all three. I will therefore become blessed according to the assertion of all three. The Roman Church teaches that one cannot become blessed in the other two [churches]. If I am in one of these two and nevertheless believe I become blessed, I do not believe *one* church. Thus, according to the assertion of *one* church, I will not become blessed.—According to the unanimous teaching of all churches, faith is not founded on rational grounds but on authority. If the different authorities ought not to be *weighed*—this could only take place on rational grounds, which are prohibited—nothing else remains to be done but *to count the votes*. If I am in the Roman Church, I become blessed through all votes. If I am in one of the others, only through two and I am condemned by one. According to the teachings of all churches, I must choose the greater authority. Thus, according to the teaching of all churches, I must enter the Roman Church if I want to become blessed.—Can this easy conclusion have escaped the Protestant teachers, who have basic church principles? I hardly think so. I think that in their hearts, they condemn everyone who does not think as they do, and that they just do not dare to say it out loud. In that case, they are consistent and for that, they deserve their praise.—The

---

20. Fichte is referring here to the continental Reformed Church.

Reformed Church does not have a judicial office. The Lutheran only appears to have one. The Lutheran priest forgives my sins, under the condition that God will forgive me for them [the sins], too. He confers life and blessedness, under the condition that God will confer them, too.—I should like to know, what peculiar thing does he do there? What does he tell me that someone else or I could not have told myself just as he told me? I wanted to know with certainty *whether* [383] God has forgiven my sins. [Yet,] *he* tells me [that] he wants to forgive them *if* God forgives them as well. Why do I require *his* forgiveness? I want forgiveness from *God*. If I were certain of the latter, I would not need his [forgiveness]; then I would tell myself. He must forgive *unconditionally*, or he must let it be entirely.—The Lutheran priest thus only gives the appearance of being able to confer blessedness. He cannot really do it. He may not even impose punishments for the sake of appearances. He can undertake nothing further against sin but forgive it. He may not keep it [the sin], but [lead it] before the entire congregation on a wild goose chase[21]. He can only promise heaven. He may not threaten anyone with hell. His mouth must always be turned into a benedictive smile. (*D'un air benin le pécheur il caresse.*[22])

The church has an *executive power*, but not in this life. Its judgments will only be executed in the future world. It already follows from the above, that the execution will, and must, agree exactly with the judgment, that not more nor less will happen than the church has determined and decreed. What is bound by the church on earth—in this life—is likewise and no differently bound in heaven—in the other world—and what the church has loosed here, must also be loosed there.[23]*

---

*Linguistic usage and context prove, at least to *me*, that the Catholic explanation of these and the foregoing words[24] (excluding the application to the pope, as Peter's successor) are the only correct [explanation] and that there could be no other, without doing the greatest violence to both. In our modern times, this passage perhaps deserves revision by a thoroughly learned yet impartial interpreter.—If it [the passage] must indeed be explained like this, if the much-feared primacy and infallibility of Peter is really found here, what could be concluded against the *true Protestant*?

21. *ins blaue Feld hin*

22. He caresses the sinner with a benign air.

23. Matthew 16:19, 18:18.

24. I.e., Matthew 16:17–19.

It follows likewise from the above why and to what extent the executor of these judgments can be no other than the members of the sole, only saving church, and, in any case, this is well known. According to the teachings of the church, Jesus, the head of church,[25] his first confessors, the twelve apostles—sitting on twelve chairs, all of the saints, who contributed from their superfluous merits to the treasury of merit that the church administers—will have the judgments executed there.[26]—[384] In this world, a consistent church cannot have any executive power, because, as shown above, it runs against its [the church's] end goal to attach physical consequences to their sentences. If the church permits atonements, which must be performed on the penitent by certain servants [of the church] whom the church can indeed appoint, the latter do not act in the name of the church during the execution, but in the name of the penitent unbeliever, who voluntarily decided on the atonement and must have instructed the selected servants to perform it on him.

This is the necessary system of the visible church, which—as is made evident by everything that has been said—can only be a single and universal [church] according to its nature. If multiple churches are spoken of, it is certain that either all of them or all but a single one proceed inconsistently. We now have to examine the relationship of this church to the human being under the natural law and under the law of the state; the relationship of the church to human beings as such and to human beings as citizen. Regardless whether they [human beings] live separated or have joined themselves into a state, the church, viewed as a separate association,[27] stands vis-à-vis the other human beings under the tribunal of natural right and vice versa; vis-à-vis its own members, it stands under the law of contract, which is itself a law based on natural right.

Every human being is by nature free and nobody has the right to impose a law on him, only he on himself. The church has no right therefore to impose its law of faith on anyone through physical coercion or to subjugate anyone under its yoke with violence. I said "through physical coercion," since natural right only commands over the world of appearances. Against moral oppression, the offended may fight with no other weapons than the same—as long as they [the weapons] could be

---

25. Ephesians 1:22–23, 4:15, 5:23; Colossians 1:18.

26. Matthew 16:28; Luke 22:29–30.

27. *Gesellschaft*

exercised differently than in the world of appearances, differently than with the consent of the other party.—You fear my objections, my necessitations, my pretexts. You dread the imagination of the horrible evil of that world with which I threaten you. Can I teach you this in another way than by expressing my thoughts through signs? Don't listen to me, [but] cover your ears in front of me. Chase me out of your four pillars and forbid me ever to come back there. Or, if I do it through writings, do not read them. To all this, you have the complete right. But once you have resorted your good will to the moral battle field with me, you have alienated your right to object to me. Now enjoy the fortunes of war. If you had been able to convince me, I would have been subjected to you. Since I have convinced you, you are subjected to me. That was our agreement: you may not complain about me.—[385] The church, if it believes itself to be able to reconcile [these actions] with its own conscience, may condemn and curse whoever does not want to subject himself. As long as these judgments of damnation remain in the domain of the invisible world, where they belong, who would be able to object? It [the church] swears in its heart, like an unlucky gambler, and this gratification can be granted to everyone. However, as soon as these curses engender interference with the other's rights in the visible world, the latter rightfully treats the church as enemy and demands compensation.

Every human being becomes free again as soon as he wants to become free, and he has the right to remove obligations again that he imposed on himself. Therefore, everyone can renounce his obedience to the church as soon as he wants. And the church has just as little right to coerce him to remain in its lap through physical means as it has the [right] to compel him to take shelter in it through the same means. The contract is repealed. He returns the heavenly treasure, which he has not touched yet, to the church unharmed and leaves it free to empty out all its bowls of wrath over him in the invisible world. And the church returns his freedom of faith. Thus, all physical punishments that the church imposes on any human being against his will are contrary not only to the church's own basic principles, but also to human rights. If he does not accept the proposed atonement for eternal damnation voluntarily, he does not believe the church, since it cannot be assumed that he has well-calculated eternal damnation as his end goal. Therefore, he is no longer the church's member, and it may no longer touch him. If it does, the church places itself vis-à-vis him in the relationship of an enemy. Every unbeliever who, upon persistent unbelief, has been executed by the Holy Inquisition has been murdered, and the Holy Apostolic

Church has gotten drunk on the streams of innocently spilled human blood. Everyone who has been persecuted, expelled, [or] robbed of his property [or] civil honor by the Protestant congregations for the sake of his unbelief, has been persecuted unlawfully. The tears of the widows and orphans, the sighs of trampled virtue, the curse of humanity weigh [heavily] on their symbolic books.

If one is allowed to leave the church, several are allowed. If the members of the first church were allowed to join together through a contract and to constitute a church, the persons [who have left the church] are also allowed to join together and form a particular church. The first [church] may not prevent this through physical means. Multiple spiritual states emerge next to each other, [386] which have to lead their wars not with corporeal weapons but with the weapons of knighthood[28] that is spiritual. They may excommunicate, condemn, [or] curse each other as much as they can. That is their right of war.—"But of multiple churches all but one will be inconsistent." That may be. And what if even the most consistent [church] is wrong in its basic principles? Everyone is allowed to reason as inconsistently as he wants or can—natural right only judges over the doing, not over the thinking.

By virtue of the contract with the church, every member has the right to watch over the purity of the confession of faith. Everyone has committed to the particular confession of faith with the church and to no other. In the name of all [members], the church has the right to watch over this purity and to impose a lawful punishment on anyone who distorts it, or to exclude him from the community if he does not subjugate himself. In that case, he breaks the social contract. Since the church has the right to exclude any member for the sake of wrong belief, there can be no questions whether it does not also have the right to relieve or even exclude a teacher for the sake of wrong teaching.

Everyone who is obedient to the church has a legal claim by virtue of the contract to acceptance and to the legally determined benediction. The church must keep its promise, or it annihilates itself.

Church and state, conceived as two different separate societies, stand to one another under the law of natural right, as individuals who live separately next to each other. That the same human beings are usually

---

28. The Catholic Church instituted military orders during the crusades, originally meant to protect Christians from persecution in the Holy Land but eventually used as a standing army in Jerusalem. The best known are the Knights Templar and the Knights Hospitaller.

members of the state and the church at the same time is not relevant as long as we can separate the two persons that each [human being] constitutes in reflection, as we must. If church and state come into conflict, natural right is their common tribunal. If both know their boundaries and respect the other's boundaries, they can never come into conflict. The church has its realm in the invisible world and is excluded from the visible; the state commands in accordance with the civil contract in the visible [world] and is excluded from the invisible.

The state cannot interfere in the realm of the church. That is physically impossible—it does not have the tools for such an interference. It can punish or reward in this world. For that it has the executive power in its hands, and the bodies[29] and goods of its citizens are in its power. It cannot bestow curses or blessings in the world to come, [because] these only happen to the person who believes in it. And the state did not demand faith in the civil contract. [387] No one promised it faith, and it did nothing to obtain it. According to the civil contract, it has to judge merely over our actions but not over our thoughts. Wherever it appears that the state undertook something similar, it is not the state. It is [rather] the church, which has disguised itself in the armor of the state, and we will continue to talk about this presently.—Smaller and larger societies within the state or, if we want, the state itself can establish institutions for the instruction of human beings or citizens in moral theory or even in that which is merely *worthy of belief* (in contrast to that which is *known*), or in general for spiritual enlightenment. But that does not yet a render a church. While the church is built on *believing*, these institutions [are built] on *searching*. The church *has* the truth, the latter are *seeking* it. The church demands *faithful acceptance*, the latter try to *convince* when they can, and refrain when they cannot. They inquire of nobody's conscience whether he is convinced or not but leave it to everyone himself. The church blesses or condemns, [whereas] these institutions cede it to everyone [to be] what he wants to or can be. The church shows the infallible path to heaven, these institutions try to bring everyone so far that he can find it on its own. Only where a confession of faith and religious duties exist as well as the infallible promise of blessedness once one accepts the confession of faith, there is a church. However, where a confession of faith exists, even if it consists merely in the short sentence "what is written in the Bible is true *because* it is written in the Bible," there exist religious duties and a church, and an only saving church, and, without

---

29. *Leiber*; see footnote 4 in this chapter.

exception, everything that we deduced from the concept of a church above. It certainly exists, as long as the members of the church can follow three to four conclusions. Since these institutions do not presuppose a *found* but a *to-be-found truth*, it follows from this alone, what is understood from the above anyway, [namely,] that even the state cannot claim the possession of them [and] that it therefore has no oversight over the presentations of the teachers in these institutions.[30] They must be working in the direction of the *common sense*[31] (of the original, not according to the systems of opinion of the people). That is their only judge, and he will, without the assistance of the executive power, render a judgment. If they [the teachers] approach the common sense, they will be heard; if they contradict it, their benches will be empty soon.

The church, however, can interfere with the boundaries of the state because its members [388] have physical powers. It interferes with the boundaries when it violates human or civil rights in its members. According to the civil contract, the state is obliged to protect these rights and, in case of violation, to urge the church to [make] amends and compensation by means of physical coercion against the tools of oppression. If the church violates those rights in citizens that they do not have by virtue of being human beings or citizens but as members of the church—if it denies them the contracted reward [or] assails them with underserved punishments—the state does not have to take care of it. These encroachments take place in another world, in which the state cannot protect nor promised to protect. It must, however, protect against encroachments in the visible world. If[, for example,] the church compels a member of the state through means of coercion to recognize its sovereignty [or] if it inflicts physical punishments on anyone who does not voluntarily submit to atonement or renounces his obedience altogether, that person has the most well-founded legal entitlement to the state's assistance. If the church goes as far as to associate obedience to the state with disobedience toward its commandments, it directly interferes with the rights of the state and declares war on it. In all these cases, the state not only has a right to treat the church with hostility, but it is indeed bound to it per the civil contract.

We have conceived a certain mutual alliance[32] of church and state through which the state amicably lends the church its might in this

---

30. Allusion to the Prussian Religious Edict of 1788. See page 21, footnote 15.

31. *Gemeinsinn*

32. *Bund*

[world] and the church [lends] the state its power in the future world. The spiritual duties[33] thereby become civil [duties]; the civil duties become spiritual exercises. One believed to have accomplished a political miracle by establishing this happy union. I believe that we have united irreconcilable things and thereby weakened the force of both.—It has already been noted above that the church contradicts itself and acts against its own end of securing the sincerity of its members when it imposes earthly punishments on unbelief. Thus, I have to add no [more] words in order to prove that the church is weakened by this peculiar alliance. The state loses no less. Its rule is not as uncertain as the church's [rule] over the conscience. It commands actions that manifest themselves in the visible world, and its laws must be contrived in such a way that it can safely rely on obedience to them. It must not be possible to transgress any law unpunished. The state must be able certainly to rely on the success of every action that it commands, as one [389] can rely on each cogwheel gearing into another in a well-ordered machine.—Those declamations that the state cannot always monitor—[as it] cannot observe everything—are trivial and superficial. The state must not command any actions the performance of which it cannot monitor. None of its orders must be without effect, or they will gradually all be [without effect]. A state that borrows the crutch of religion shows us nothing more than that it is lame. Whoever implores us to obey its orders for the sake of God and of our blessedness, admits that he does not himself have the force to coerce us into obedience, otherwise he would do it without calling God to his aid.—Finally, how can such mediation by religion help? How, if we believe neither in God nor in another world nor in the rewards and punishments of the latter? The state either has other means to coerce us into obedience or not. If it has them, it does not require religious inducements. It does something superfluous if it employs them and turns itself into the tool of the church without recompense.[34] If, in the battle against our inclinations, *we* want to employ these inducements *ourselves* in order to make mandatory behavior less arduous, we may do that. But it is not the *state's* concern.—If it has no such means, it cannot assure itself of our obedience through the use of religion either, if we are resolute unbelievers. Since it lends its arm to the church, we will be careful not to disclose our unbelief. Thus, the state commands randomly.[35] If we are orthodox, we will obey. If we are not,

---

33. *Glaubenpflicht*
34. *Vergeltung*
35. *Ins blaue Feld hin*

we will indeed let it be. But the state only wanted to try. One disobedience more or less does not matter to it. What a state!—It befits them
well, however, to order our payment for the life to come when they take
everything from us in this [life], or to threaten us with hell when we do
not want to submit to their unjust acts of violence. What do they believe
while they are so frankly and honestly unjust? Either [they do not believe]
in heaven and hell or they perhaps expect to settle the matter with God
over their person. Now, what if we are as clever as they are?—Nowhere
does this show itself more conspicuously than in Protestant states. One
and the same physical person can indeed be the prince and bishop, but
the tasks of the prince are different from the tasks of the bishop, and
neither one may bribe the other. One cannot be both at the same time
in one and the same action.—Now, the Protestant princes have been
told that they are bishops at the same time, and, eager as they are, they
want to [390] fulfill their episcopal duties as well. The purity of faith lies
close to their heart, and, at least according to their limited insight, this
faith is being falsified. They grope around in just anger, grab what they
can get their hands on, and strike with it. It was the scepter. But is that
what the scepter is for? It should be the crozier. If they are bishops, they
may curse, condemn, [or] expel the unbeliever from heaven and imprison
him in hell. They may erect stakes on which everyone can be burnt who
wants to be burnt to become blessed. But they may not use the might
of the state against him [the unbeliever]. Otherwise he [will] beseech the
state for protection.—The state? Alas, in whose hands have we fallen! It
is the state who beats us down in the name of God.† "But the Protestant
bishops do not have the right to condemn."—Is that so? I should like
to know, What is *a bishop*? I thought [he was] an infallible judge in the

---

†"But if the princes were really serious about caring for the future blessedness of their
subjects after their fashion, shouldn't one at least honor their good intentions?"—
Maybe, but their understanding and their sense of justice, certainly not. Everyone has
the right to seek, to test, [and] to choose the means toward his blessedness himself,
and he rightly tolerates no foreign hand on this, his proper ground.—And *why* do the
princes actually want so eagerly to have their subjects blessed? Does this usually occur
merely out of pure love for their subjects, or perhaps sometimes out of self-love? Why
is it that most often it is precisely the Louis XIVths and the likes of them who care
so thoroughly for the blessedness *of others*? Such princes know to make use of every
[aspect of] their subjects. They have already estimated the mortal bodies, limb by limb,
so highly that no great profit can be made with them anymore.—"But," their councilor
of conscience tells them, "don't your subjects have an immortal soul as well?" and,
following this welcome reminder, they quickly devise a plan still to use them in the
eternal life and to trade their souls even to the dear God as expensively as possible.

name of the church. And what is a church? I thought [it was] the sole and last judge in the invisible world. If it is true that the Protestant bishops do not have the right to condemn, then they are not bishops and their churches are not churches.—In general, the Protestant congregations are either extremely inconsistent or they do not even pass themselves off as churches. They are educational institutions, as we described above. There is no third [possibility]. One must either throw oneself into the lap of the only saving Roman Church [391] or one must become a resolute *free spirit*.‡ What, then, do they want, those who chain us again to the symbolic books in our age, when there will not easily be many who come to the same predetermined conclusions by means of their own inquiries? What do they actually want? As soon as we allow to have any principle imposed on us, agreed prior to all examinations, we must either relinquish all sound logic or accept the crudest, harshest Catholicism. I do know that [only] very few Protestant zealots of the symbolic books accept this, but I [also] know who those are, who do accept it, and who show it to us thoroughly enough in their writings. I know which party has so eagerly

---

‡On the rectification [*Nachricht*] and vindication of a very honorable word! *Free* has surely always referred to the *form* and not the *matter*? Thus, to be a free spirit does not depend on what one believes but *on what grounds* one believes it. Whoever believes *the authorities*, be his confession of faith as short as it may, is a *believer*. Whoever believes *only his own reason* is a *free spirit*. If someone believes in Muhammad's donkey[36] or in the immaculate conception of the Virgin Mary or in the divinity of Apis[37] because he believes he convinced himself of the truth of these sentences through his own thought, he is a free spirit. And even if someone believes nothing further than that a god exists because he finds nothing else in the Bible, which, following the assertion of the church, he considers to be God's word, he is a believer.—The Reformers were the most avowed free spirits, and it seemed to many dignified men that Protestantism is actually nothing other than freethinking [*Freigeisterei*], i.e., that the Protestant must deny everything whereof he cannot convince himself. Since I wish them to be consistent, I would like it to be that way.—But then there should be no Lutheranism, no Reformed religion, no deism, naturalism, and so forth. Catholicism and Protestantism are exactly opposite concepts: the former a positive, the latter a negative.

36. Ya'fūr was a donkey used by the prophet Muhammad, which, according to tradition, was a descendant of the donkey ridden by Jesus into Jerusalem and had the power of speech.

37. A god in the Ancient Egyptian pantheon, a sacred bull worshipped as the son of Hathor who served as a kind of intermediary between humans and the more important gods.

encouraged this affair first, and the entire public knows it. Aren't perhaps those Protestant zealots the tools of those heads who are far superior to us in consistency and shrewdness? I know nothing about Jesuits and Jesuit machinations except that they ponder a large obscurantist system. And everyone who has eyes to see and a head to string together two sentences can know what the only means is to implement this system.

State and church are therefore separate from each other. There is a natural boundary between the two that neither must transgress. If the church arrogates a power to itself in the visible world, this runs counter to the [392] particular spirit of the church and it is ostensibly unjust. The state has neither obligation nor, in fact, authority to ask our opinions regarding the invisible world. However, *the* question still emerges whether *prudence* could in certain cases advise this and in how far the state is authorized to follow its advice in this [matter]. We want to treat this question, too, in order to safeguard our remarks against all possible misunderstandings.

A church can impose obligations on its members that contradict their obligations as citizens. What should a state do if this becomes known to it through reliable statements?—If the state has to judge actions only, but not opinions, it is not obliged in this case until this church opinion has become the deed of any one citizen. Then the state has to punish the deed.—"But a prudent state [should] rather preempt the deed than punish it afterwards; it [should] rather prevent the deed than avenge it." Perhaps, but how can it know whether this opinion among its citizens will really pass over into action? The church has imposed the obligation on them, and the citizen has adopted it, [though] the state does not know whether faithfully or insincerely. Should the state assume that he is honest toward the church and that he will act according to his basic principles? So it seems. But this very man has [also] adopted the opposite obligation toward the state. Following this basic principle, the state would have to assume that he also adopted this obligation in an honest manner and will act according to it, too, and then the church obligation and the civil [obligation] would cancel each other out in his soul. The church cannot enforce the demanded action through external means. The state, however, can and therefore has to rely on its superiority.—"But the force of religious opinions on the souls of human beings is [well] known. The greater the sacrifices are that it demands, the more easily it is obeyed. Oftentimes one obeys it precisely because one is heading for danger or cruel death in its service."—I could reply to this that state and society have to fight these reveries with those weapons that have been given to us especially against them, [i.e.,] with cold, sound reason; that the state only has to make additional and more expedient arrangements for the enlightenment and spiritual culture of its citizens; and that it will always safeguard itself better against religious wrath in this manner. But, now, if it [the state] does not understand this? May it make use of its rights!

[393] The state cannot compel any human being to enter into the civil contract with it. Likewise, no human being can compel the state to admit him, even if the state has no well-grounded reason for the refusal or does not want to give him one. Both parties are equally free and the union[38] is contracted voluntarily. If the state fears ill consequences from certain opinions, it can exclude all [persons] known to be devoted to them from becoming citizens. Upon entering the civil contract, it can demand from everyone the assurance that he will not adopt these opinions.—Everyone has the right to leave the state as soon as he wishes. The state may not hold him. Therefore, the state likewise has the right to exclude everyone it wants, as soon as it wants, even without citing any reason, so long as it does not hurt his human rights, property, and freedom to reside wherever he wants in space, as has been shown in the third chapter above.[39] The state may make use of this right against those of its citizens of whom it learns—after they are already in the civil contract—that they harbor opinions that appear dangerous to it.—I do not contradict here what I said above. I grant the state a *negative* oversight over the system of opinions, but I say that the *positive* [oversight] betrays its weakness and imprudence. The state may determine what one may *not* believe in order to be compatible with civil right, but to determine *what* one must believe in order to be compatible with it contends against the state's end and is illogical. I see why a wise state cannot tolerate any consistent Jesuits, but I do not see why it should not tolerate the atheist. The former considers injustice a duty, which puts the state in danger. The latter recognizes, as one usually believes, no duty at all, which does not harm the state, since it enforces the services due to it through physical force, regardless of whether one likes to perform them or not.

From this flow the rights of a state in transformation vis-a-vis the church system. The state may eliminate church doctrines that were not

---

38. *Bund*
39. See pp. 264–66, 278–82, 291. See pp. 74–76, 88–93, 101.

previously excluded from civil right because they are contrary to the state's new basic principles. The state may demand the assurance from all those who desire civil right that they have sworn off these opinions and that they solemnly adopt the new obligations that contradict those doctrines. It may exclude all those who do not want to give this assurance from its community and from the enjoyment of all civil rights. But, further, it has no right over them. Their property and their personal freedom must remain unviolated. Only if they openly or secretly wage war against the state does the state obtain [394] a right over their personal freedom, not as citizens, but as human beings, not by virtue of the civil contract, but by virtue of natural right, not the right to punish them, but the right to wage war against them. The state is placed in an instance of self-defense against them.

Yet, the main source of all mistakes between state and church is when the latter possesses goods in the visible world. And only a thorough examination of the origin and the rights of church property can solve all remaining difficulties.

The church, viewed merely as such, only has forces and rights in the invisible world, none in the visible. There, a wide unlimited field is open to the conquests of its faith. Here, the church cannot acquire any possessions through this faith—its only instrument—since in this world—let it be said with the permission of several teachers of natural right!—acquisition takes a little bit more than the will and the faith that something is ours. A member of the church can acquire[40] [something], however, not *as* a member of the church by virtue of his faith, but as a member of the material world by virtue of his physical tools. The church, as church, cannot occupy [something]. Thus, whatever it possesses, it possesses through contract, and, in particular, not through a labor contract—the church cannot work—but through an exchange contract. The church exchanges heavenly goods, which it possesses in abundance, for earthly [goods], which it does not disdain.—The church has officers, who do not live off faith alone, but who require earthly food and earthly drink for their subsistence as well. It is in the nature of every society that the members sustain those who spend their time and force in the service of the society. Accordingly, the members of the church society are without doubt bound to support their officers, too. This can take place through *mandatory* contributions determined by the

---

40. *occupiren*

law, which must—in this matter as well as for all other objects—be a law of faith necessary for blessedness and must not be transgressed without the inevitable punishment of eternal damnation. Whoever makes the contributions therefore makes them to become blessed. He exchanges that which he gives for heaven.—Or it takes places through *voluntary* contributions. If the donation is really made to the church, insofar as it is a church, and not perhaps to a person that happens to be a member or officer of the church in order to do him a favor, it [the donation] presupposes faith in the church and hence the hope to become blessed through the grace of the church.—Finally, if the surrender of earthly goods to the church occurs directly for the atonement of sins against the church or indirectly to purchase the greater blessedness of heaven, the exchange is obvious.

[395] An important consequence flows from this kind of origin of church property. No contract is fulfilled until it has been introduced in the world of appearances, until *both* parties have rendered what they promised to render, as was discussed above. A contract for the exchange of earthly goods for heavenly goods will, at least in this life, never pass over into the world of appearances. The occupant of earthly goods indeed performs his part, but the occupant of heavenly goods does not [perform] his. It is only through faith that the former acquires a possession for which he surrenders not merely the hope of transferring his temporal goods to the church, but the actual possession of these goods. Who knows whether he really has faith in the church? Who knows whether he will always keep it or whether he will still lose it before his end? Who knows whether the church has the will to keep its word? If it has the will now, whether it will never change it? Who knows whether a real contract exists between the two parties or not? No one but the all-knowing. One party, or both, can withdraw its will at any moment. Therefore, the mutual will is not introduced in the world of appearances.

The occupant of earthly goods indeed performed [his part], and in exchange he received the right to *hope* that the church will perform too. He thinks his property is the property of the church. Now he loses his faith in either the good will of the church or its power to make him blessed. Henceforth, he has no compensation to hope for. His will is changed and his goods follow his will. They had always remained his property. Now he takes real possession of them again.—If anyone has the right of regret in any contract, one obviously has it in an exchange contract with the church. No restitution of damages! We have not used up the heavenly goods of the church. The church may take them back. It may impose its punishments, its bans, [or] its damnation on us. It is free to do that. If we do not believe in the church at all anymore, all this will not impress us much. I am still considering merely the church, insofar as it is that, as occupant of our goods. We will see further below what follows *from this* for the restitution of damages when an officer of the church, as a person in the material world, possesses them [the goods].

My father has surrendered all his goods to the church for the salvation of his soul. He dies and, according to the civil contract, I enter into the possession of his goods, albeit under the condition to fulfill all obligations that he placed on the possession through real contracts. He entered a contract over these [goods] with the church [396] that was, however, never introduced in the world of appearances. Rather, it was founded merely on faith. If I do not believe in the church, such a contract is void for me. The church is nothing for me, and I, at least, interfere with no one's right when I demand my father's goods back.—The state may not hinder me in this. The state, *as* state, is likewise unbelieving. As state, it knows as little about the church as I do. For the state, the church is just as little a thing as it is for me. The state cannot protect the claims of a thing that does not exist according to it. I am, however, something and the state has to protect me against this no-thing.[41] It has promised me the possession of my father's goods under the condition that I do not arrogate the property of any other deceased citizen to myself. I did not do that, [and] therefore the state owes it to me to protect my possession of them according to the contract.—They were still my father's goods. They remained his until his death, because that contract, which in the world of appearances is null and void before the tribunal of natural right and before the law of the state, could not alienate them. He was indeed allowed to surrender them voluntarily, [and] I could have confirmed his will by means of my silence. Then the state would not have been resorted to. But now I do not confirm his will, and I resort to the state. I may give up my right, but the state may not [give it up] on my behalf.—"But my father believed. For him this contract was binding."—He appeared to believe. I do not know whether he really believed. I know even less whether he would still believe now if he still lived. Be that as it may. Even with my father, I do not have to deal as a member of the invisible world, but of the visible [world], and in particular of

---

41. *Unding*

the state. He has died, and, in the state, I occupy his place. If he were still alive and he regretted his surrender, he would surely have the right to take back his goods? If *he* would have it, *I* [would] have it, because I am he in the state, I represent the same physical person. [From the *state's* perspective,] he did not die; he only died for me. For the state, he changed his will in my person. If my father does not want that, he should come back into the visible world, take possession of his rights in [this world] again, and do whatever he wills with the goods that are once again his. Until then, I act in his name.—"But since he died in faith, I play it safer if I proceed according *his* faith. I may indeed risk *my* soul, but not someone else's."—Oh, if I think like that, I am not even [397] a resolute unbeliever of the church. [Rather,] I act inconsistently and foolishly if I only risk *my* soul. Either the church has an executive power in another life or it has none. I have to arrive at a firm conclusion on this matter. As long as I have not, I am indeed on the safer side if I do not touch the church property, because the church curses every robber until the Last Day, and justifiably so.—The right for restitution that the first heir has, the second heir has as well, and the third, and the fourth, and so on through all generations, because the heir does not merely inherit things, but also rights to things.

Even more follows from the basic principle above, and we have no reason to withhold any possible consequences. Supposing that the consequence will be much restricted through our following considerations and will permit no application in life, every [consequence] still makes the overview of the whole easier and becomes an exercise in contemplation.—Not only the rightful heir or the inheritor, [but] every human without exceptions has the right to appropriate goods that are merely church property. The church, as such, has neither force nor right in the visible world. [For] it is nothing for whoever does not believe in it. Whatever belongs to no one is the property of the very first who appropriates the latter rightfully in the world of appearances. I come onto a place (I leave purposely indeterminate here whether the place bears the trace of labor or not) and begin to labor on it in order to appropriate it. You come along and say to me: "move away from here, this place belongs to the church."—I know of no church, I do not acknowledge any church. Your church may prove its existence to me in the world of appearances. I know nothing of an invisible world, and the authority of your church in the latter [world] has no power over me, because I do not believe in it. You could have told me more justifiably [that] this place belongs to the man in the moon, because, although I do not know the man, I do know the moon. [But] I do not know your church nor the invisible world, in which it is supposed to be powerful. Let your man be at work in the moon, or let him come down to earth to show me his previous property in this place. I am the man on earth, and, until then, I will take his property at my own risk.

But the members of the church are at the same time persons in the corporeal world. They have, *as such*, force and rights in this world. The church, as a spiritual association,[42] cannot possess any earthly goods at all. It must delegate them to physical persons and those become, from the church's point of view with respect to itself, its vassals.[43] Before the church's tribunals, they are not the owners, but [398] merely the occupants. But what are they before the tribunal of natural right or state right? And what restrictions follow from this for the rights to church property deduced just now?

A vassal of the church possesses a good that is my property, be it either through previous possession that I have surrendered to the church myself or through inheritance from my ancestors who surrendered this possession.—I take back what is mine from wherever I find it. I adhere merely to *the good*, not *the person*. The current honest occupant who believes in the church [and] who considers the good to be the church's property and the church to be authorized to lend it to him is thereby harmed. He has calculated on the continuous possession [of it, and] he cannot live if I withdraw it from him. Do I have to compensate him?—I do not have to deal with him at all. Neither I nor my ancestors delegated the good to him, but to the church. The church lent it to him. He has been damaged by the church. He has to demand restitution of damages from *the church*. If I or my ancestors had lent the good to him for his person, he would have justified demands against me, not as a member of the church, but as a member of the corporeal world. Now he has to turn to the church. But am I perhaps obligated to the church for the restitution of damages? If I am not obligated to any of its members, insofar as they are members of the corporeal world—and I am not, because, insofar as they are [members of the corporeal world], no one has entered a contract with them—I am certainly not obligated to the church as a spiritual association. It has, as such, no rights at all in the

42. *Gesellschaft*
43. *Lehensträger*

material world and cannot impose any obligations in it. I would have to compensate the church in spiritual goods over which the deal was made, and, with regard to these, the church could exercise its full right of retribution against me. It can bereave me and all my ancestors of the blessedness that it distributes. It can allocate it [my blessedness] to the share of the member who has been damaged by my reclamation in the material world, if he agrees to be paid off like this. The church is free to do all that.—If the previous vassal of the church has, as occupant, improved my property and increased its *natural* value, he did that not as a member of the church—according to the opinion of the unbeliever, faith does not improve an earthly good—but as a member of the material world through his physical forces or through the symbol of them, his money. And [then] I owe him compensation for these improvements, because as a member of the material world he can indeed have rights over me. Did it perhaps occur with funds from the church? According to my own confessions, I know nothing of the church. The value is obvious in the material world. [399] For me, he is the owner. I must repay him. If he believes that he must give it back to the church for his person, he may do as his will.—However, if this improvement of my property consisted of a spiritual blessing, which only exists for him who believes in it—if, for example, the previous occupant placed a special fertility in my ground by force of his faith or [if he] banished weeds, voles, and locusts from it through this force, I do not replace these improvements since, according to my basic principles, I do not believe that he made them and he cannot prove it to me. Is my ground really splendidly fertile? Is it really excellently protected against those plagues? Do I know whether this is not due to a natural quality of it or, if it should actually be a supernatural blessing, whether it was intended for my person? He may withdraw his hand of blessing. He may send infertility and pests over my crop, if he can through his mere faith. He is free to do that.

If I do not have an express legal claim to a good that is occupied by a vassal of the church, then he is the owner *for me*. That he does not believe he is [the owner], that he believes it depends on the church, gives me no right, precisely because I do not believe in the church and [because] the church is nothing for me. In the visible world, I only acknowledge the tribunal of natural right. Before this [tribunal], the owner of the last form is the owner of the thing, and I must acknowledge him as such. He himself may think about this however he wants. I do not honor the rights of the church in him, but rather [I honor] his own [rights], regardless of whether he knows them or not. *I* must stay true to *my* basic principles. This right, i.e., to appropriate church property as [if it were] no one's property, only occurs when the latter has no occupant, and since this is rarely or never the case, very little follows from this for us [nonmembers]. But much follows from this for the vassal of the church. According to natural right, he is the owner who can prove a prior legal claim to it if no one is present. If he gives up the belief in the church, he becomes the real owner in every consideration. No one besides the church could object when he conducted himself as the real owner. Now he renounces his belief in the church. The church is destroyed for him and he cannot violate the rights of something that does not exist.—It is, as if a merchant trades with the man in the moon in a partnership. So long as he persists in imagining this trade partnership, he would like to charge the latter the profit correctly in his books. [400] But who besides himself would have the right to hold him accountable if he occasionally gives a slight advantage to his associate? Or if he gave this imagination up altogether, who could prevent him from absorbing the capital and the profit into his property and changing the previous company?—One could conclude that these basic principles will powerfully foster unbelief in the church, since they cast it [unbelief] in such a profitable light. But I cannot be held responsible for all the consequences of my principles. As long as they are correctly deduced from correct basic principles, I must further conclude whatever follows. If the church is right, the unbeliever does not have his temporal gain for free. He will be eternally damned for it. One must allow the people their freedom. Whoever prefers to be prosperous on this earth and condemned there rather than poor here and blessed there, must be allowed at his own risk.

The application of these principles to the state is easy. When the church is viewed as a member of the material world due to its possession of the ground, the state relates to the latter as an individual [relates] to an individual. They stand toward each other before the tribunal of natural right. The state is only a state through unanimity. If *all* its members—it goes without saying that the officers of the church and the clergymen also belong to the state—unanimously renounce their obedience to the church at one and the same time, the church is annihilated for this state. It has all the rights that every individual in the state of nature who does not believe in any church would have.

First of all, subject to the conditions cited above and based on the reasons developed above, the state receives back everything that previously belonged to it as *state property*, [i.e., as] common property of all citizens—[but] not everything located in the space inhabited by its citizens. The state is not a piece of ground. It is an association[44] of human beings. It does not consist of fields, but of persons.—If the state itself, in the name of and as the intermediary of the church, has loaned church property to its current occupant, it is not responsible for keeping the contract of a thing that no longer exists in its view and the intermediary of which it can therefore no longer be. But it is responsible for compensating the harmed occupant who experienced loss in part through the state's fault. The occupant is to be viewed as accessory after the fact, and the owed compensation follows the basic principles developed above in the fourth chapter.[45] If the state has no part in lending out this possession and the church acted directly, the damaged [person] has no legal claim to restitution [401] from the state, just as he had no [claim to restitution] from the individual before the tribunal of natural right. In some situations, this can be most harsh, oppressively unfair, but it is not downright unjust. Clemency and humanity can recommend many [things] that natural right does not absolutely command. And philosophical writings are surely allowed to sharply separate the realms of the two.

Every individual citizen receives back whatever he is demonstrably entitled to, based on any legal ground. All individuals can surrender these claims to church property to the state. Then the goods of individuals also become *the state's* property.

The rightful heir of certain church property is unknown and a law has already existed in the state beforehand that [says that] after a family has died out the state is heir to their property, a law that must be expressly made by the common will and is not self-evident. In this case, the state is the owner of all church property that was demonstrably surrendered to the church by past members of the state whose heirs cannot be found. I say "*demonstrably*" because no matter how probable it may be, a mere probability is never enough to found a legal claim. If such a law does not exist at all or if the particular proof applied in a given case cannot be demonstrated, such church property, like all church property over which neither the state nor an individual can demonstrate his ownership, is no one's property and falls to the first occupant. And without doubt that will always be the previous real occupant. He ought

---

44. *Gesellschaft*
45. See pp. 317–18, 324. See pp. 125–26, 132.

to be seen as owner, and no one can take possession of his property against his will. If this occupant, who now becomes owner, is a citizen, he also counts inheritance law among his civil rights and can therefore even bequeath this church property to his descendants, unless he entered a special contract over the property with the state.

However, since *the* case that all citizens renounce their faith in the church unanimously at the same time [and] thus [that] the entire ancien régime[46] with its remaining rights and obligations subsists is hardly to be expected; since such an abrogation of the church may only occur either in the case of a revolution or doubtlessly precipitated by one, the foregoing [discussion] is less applicable in the real world and rather a standard for assessment. And according to this standard, we still have to talk about the second, far more probable case, that the citizens' opinions regarding the church are divided. If they cannot come to an agreement, if neither party wants to concede to the other, the state is in a condition of revolution.

[402] Everyone who leaves the church has the right to demand back his property, which is now possessed by the church. Thus, there is no doubt that those members who are separated from the state that hitherto voted for the church may take back either individually or collectively—if they unite their claims and their forces—everything that they are personally entitled to. Everyone who leaves the state retains his property, as has been shown in the third chapter,[47] [and] therefore also the share that he contributed to the common property of the state. An individual citizen would not easily make use of the right to demand back the latter, because he is not powerful enough to protect himself but cannot undertake the restitution suit against the state without detaching himself from the state and thereby divesting himself of his very necessary protection. Once several stronger members have broken away from the state and trust themselves [to have] enough force to protect themselves, who may prevent them from exercising their right fully and, in particular, from taking back from the church their share of the state assets that has been loaned to the church? That ancien régime, which remains true to the church, retains its share and may leave it to the church, [but] it must not dispose of the share of the separated members.—It is clear from the above that those members who initiated the separation are responsible

---

46. *Alter Staat*

47. See pp. 278–82. See pp. 88–93.

for compensating the vassals of the church damaged by the reclamation for their share, if the old state enfeoffed the vassals with their goods *when they* [the separating individuals] *themselves still constituted part of the state*. In this case, they are responsible for the damage, at least as part of the whole, and are therefore obligated to replace their share of it.

As several members of the once church-believing state pass over to the new state that does not believe in the church, the new state's share of the church property becomes ever larger through the united, common, and personal legal entitlements. If, finally, all [members] besides perhaps the immediate officers of the church, or even a part of them, join that party, nothing remains for the [remaining] church officers that they could cede to the church, except their small share of the common state assets and whatever they have personal legal entitlement to.—That [property] over which no one can prove his ownership remains the occupant's. He may now choose to keep it as his property, acquired through appropriation, or as a fief from the church. The state has no right to take it. If the state wishes to appeal to its supremacy, it acts unjustly and declares war on humanity.

[403] If such an occupant of former church property did not enter into the civil contract with the new state, he does not have the right of inheritance. After his death, the state can appropriate his property according to the right of the first occupant, and [it can] make a deal and arrangements for this situation with its citizens in advance. And in this way all church property would gradually die and come [into] the state's [hands] in a rightful manner.

Afterword

The author threw the first booklet[1] into the public on a wing and a prayer,[2] and it appeared to him to have been drowned out in the flood of new writings on the same topic. He put the material that he had designated for the chapters of the second [booklet] together under various distractions and frustrations—more to keep his word than because he would have thought the public will dignify this writing with any attention.—After none of the other journals, as far as I know, dignified it with a nod, a noble man, who—I can confirm—does not know me [and] can neither guess who I am nor, if he could, would have the remotest interest to elevate one of my writings above its intrinsic worth, has recommended this almost forgotten writing in Schleswig's monthly journal—whose contributors I know not, and I am in correspondence with none—with a warmth that is a credit to his heart—whether it is [a credit] to his power of judgment as well, the author at least cannot say.[3] This encouraged [404] me to make myself even more deserving of this dignified man's generous judgment, in particular regarding what he says about my style of writing, and to save the two remaining important chapters for a more thorough treatment in a third booklet. The author, however, hopes that it will not be due to him if it does not leave the press within three to four months.

Some complaints about the darkness of the first booklet have reached my ears. The public is already accustomed to [the fact] that writers are always right and that the public's complaints about the obscurity of their

---

1. See page 8, footnote 4 in the introduction.

2. *Auf gutes Glück*

3. Fichte is referring to an anonymous reviewer, S., in the *Schleswigsches Journal*, August 1792, 515–513, who wrote an extremely flattering review of the book.

213

writings are met with a complaint about the cursoriness and distraction of the readers. For that reason, the author of the present [text] could not fancy repeating once again what has already been repeated so many times. He lets [the question] rest entirely, as to how much fault could lie with him. He does not want to invite the reader to compare his writing with others' writings that have been written on the same topics, based on the same basic principles. He does not want to remind him that philosophical examinations, in which one at least makes an effort to be thorough, cannot possibly be read as easily as a fashionable novel, travelogues, or even philosophical examinations that are built on the familiar system of opinions. He does not even want to ask of him the effort of reading a thin book a number of times in exchange for the saved effort of reading one thick book. He only wants to say that he will take care to write ever more comprehensibly and that the reader should take care to read ever more attentively.

Appendix One

Correspondence

We have translated the following letters, as they shed some light on the reception of the *Contribution*, as well as Fichte's own judgment of it. We have not included several other letters that discuss the *Contribution*, since they have already been translated into English in J. G. Fichte, *Early Philosophical Writings*, ed. Daniel Breazeale (Ithaca, NY: Cornell University Press, 1992). These are:

- Fichte to Kant, September 20, 1793 (364–66)

- Fichte to Stephani, mid-December 1793 (370–72)

- Fichte to Reinhold, March 1, 1794 (375–78)

- Fichte to Baggesen (draft), April or May 1795 (385–87)

The following letters appear in Johann Gottlieb Fichte, *Gesamtausgabe der Bayerischen Akademie der Wissenschaften*, Reihe 3, Band 2, *Briefwechsel 1793–1795*, ed. Hans Jacob and Reinhard Lauth (Stuttgart-Bad Cannstatt: Fromann-Holzboog, 1970). We include the letter number before each translation, as well as the page numbers in parentheses, corresponding to the *Gesamtausgabe*.

Letter #166 (11–13)

Zurich, November 13, 1793

Fichte to Karl Leonhard Reinhold in Jena[1]

Noble Sir,

Most esteemed professor,

Your dignified friend Baggesen,[2] who I recently became acquainted with in Bern, offered me such an invaluable proof of your benevolent disposition towards me that I cannot deny my heart to thank you for it with trust. [12]—A pamphlet was published, which you judged favorably [and] for the sake of this favorable judgment, you believed you had to take me for the author. I feel the honor of this conclusion, if it is drawn by a Reinhold, in its full extent, and have no reservations to tell you, albeit in confidence, that I am indeed the author of this pamphlet. Unfortunately, it is no longer a secret in Switzerland that I am [the author], thanks to the not quite prudent [yet] good intentions of a man,[3] according to whom I was not allowed to have any secrets. And, per my basic principle, I perhaps do not have to own up to everything that I have written, but must not downright deny it either, maybe even confess it to some. However, after the dissociation taking place on the whole between the Swiss and the North German scholars, it can still remain a secret in Germany for a long time, since no one there, besides the (undisclosed) publisher,[4] the tutor of Graf Castell,[5] Stephani,[6] and his pupil, and henceforth you, knows it *from me*. And I am not of the mind to write it to anyone besides maybe, in due time, Kant. And also, since none of our critics thinks the author of the *Critique of Revelation*[7]

1. Karl Leonhard Reinhold, 1758–1823, supporter of Kant's critical philosophy and author of *Briefe über die Kantische Philosophie* (Letters on the Kantian Philosophy), 1790. He preceded Fichte as extraordinary professor at the University of Jena.

2. Jens Immanuel Baggessen, 1764–1826.

3. Johann Hartmann Rahn.

4. Ferdinand Troschel in Danzig.

5. Christian Friedrich Graf von Castell-Rüdenhausen, 1772–1850.

6. Heinrich Stephani, 1761–1850.

7. *An Attempt at a Critique of All Revelation* (1792) was the first (anonymously) published work by Fichte. It was briefly mistaken by readers to be a fourth critique by Kant, a confusion that quickly made Fichte well-known.

is capable of the language of this pamphlet. I anticipate with confidence that one would use this argument, if perhaps something about the author was indicated by the publisher and I was not mistaken about our public. One should like, or rather, for the purpose of the anonymity of well-intentioned writers, one should like not to become aware of the uncertainty of this manner of conclusion! When Kant was not the author of the *Critique of Revelation*, I was accused of artificially imitating his style; now they would accuse me of artificially distorting mine. And yet I will perhaps write five or six more pamphlets on various topics in which none of the usual critics should recognize the style of writing of the previous without me having intended this in the slightest during their composition.—I would also like to remain incognito for quite a long time, in particular because I expected a bloody feud with Herr Rehberg and wanted to prevent it from becoming personal through my anonymity; especially for the sake of the A. L. Z.[8]—I appeal to you for your judgment, especially regarding Rehberg. Do you think that he has been wronged, or that, *in light of his relationship to the reading public and the importance of the examination and his strident tone*, he should have been reprimanded in a gentler manner?—Regarding this affair, I have set aside for myself [time for] due deliberation, since I intend to work some more especially in this field.

If you wanted to dignify me with the continuation of your benevolent disposition and with evidence thereof by means of a reply, you would thereby elicit my gratitude to you anew. At least this winter, I will remain in Zurich, where I got married a few weeks ago.

I did not want to tell you how much I discern and admire your pure love of truth, your warm interest for everything that is most important to humanity, which strengthens you to tireless research. You could not have thought of me as benevolently as you do, if you had not thought me capable of emotion and veneration.

With this admiration

Your most devoted

Fichte.

---

8. *Allgemeine Literatur Zeitung*, where Rehberg published many of his reviews of books on the French Revolution, and Fichte would publish several reviews, including his *Aenesidemus* review.

Letter #172 (31)

Jena, late December 1793

Gottlieb Hufeland to Fichte in Zurich (fragments)[9]

[. . .] I wish ardently that you will decide for our university. However, if you want to do so, you [should] do it rather soon, so that everything is in order before the Duke,[10] whom we have in the country now, leaves us again. Moreover, some people would soon use your deferment or your refusal as confirmation [of your culpability], for it goes without saying that such hiatuses are always preyed on. That is why they have also advanced your democratism against you, which you allegedly demonstrated in your *Contributions*. Even though our government is at the forefront among all those that promote freedom of learning and writing, one must still, in light of the current seething of the tempers that can easily get out of control and of the tense relations between the governments, dislike seeing any steps that can compromise [oneself] too loudly *or attract the accusations from foreign ministers*. However, I replied to all this that you only defend the democratic party in regard to *right* and entirely in the abstract, that these questions would be talked about little in the lectures, which would above all constitute your employment, and that you have enough moderation, prudence, and coolness to avoid unnecessary and inappropriate comments. [. . .]

Letter #174 (35–37)

Jena, January 12, 1794

Karl Leonhard Reinhold to Fichte in Zurich

A severe bout of an old illness of over a year and a half has robbed me for several weeks of every free exercise of the time that I could extract from my daily business, and therefore also until now of the pleasure of reciprocating your written visit,[11] which surprised me most pleasantly. I

---

9. The beginning and end of the letter are missing, yet other correspondence of both Fichte and Hufeland provides some context. Fichte had been offered a professorship at the University of Jena, and Hufeland sought to motivate Fichte to accept the position.

10. Karl August, 1757–1828, Duke of Sachsen-Weimar-Eisenach, 1775–1828.

11. Fichte's letter from November 13, 1793.

ought, then, to thank my *Baggesen*—and as I see from his last letter[12] also your Baggesen—to whom I owe so many of the purest and most benevolent pleasures of my life, also for the closer acquaintance and, as I hope confidently, friendship with you! The more often I read and think through your *Contributions*, the more earnestly I become convinced that I will hardly ever be able to repay *Baggesen* for this service with an *identical* [service]. Except [in] the *Critique of Practical Reason*,[13] I have nowhere found *this* reason *in* its influence on the mode of thinking—or rather *by means of* its influence—presented as lively, as intelligibly, [and] as thoroughly as in these *Contributions*. It has become one of my few favorite books, inseparable from me for life.

Long before your confidential confession, I never questioned for a moment that the author of these *Contributions* and the author of the *Critique of Revelation* are one and the same person. Not because I gave any credence to the widely spread rumor, at least in Jena, which mentioned the author to me before I read the book. But because I believed already in the *preface* to have unmistakably detected the particular and original [character] of the mode of thinking—and in some passages of the mode of expression—of the *Critique of Revelation*, which I had carefully studied. However, I could only adequately explain the difference in style, or rather in diction, based on the distinctness of subjects.

Wieland,[14] to whom I owe my copy of the first part (unfortunately until now I have not been able to get hold of the second [part][15]), repeatedly spoke of it with enthusiasm. [36] He said [that] the prevalent prejudices that you attack in this pamphlet are not [merely] beaten up, hacked into pieces, [and] torn to shreds, but exterminated at the root. He only regrets that he and the likes of him, as he put it, cannot form an idea of *the pure form of I*, and can only suspect what is meant by it.

I for my part am not agreed with myself whether I should or should not wish that some passages, that are only intelligible to the expert of critical philosophy, had been left out.

---

12. Baggesen's letter to Reinhold from December 20, 1793, in which he writes: "I have become most intimately acquainted with Fichte.—We have become inseparable friends (as spirits)."

13. Immanuel Kant, *Critique of Practical Reason* (Kritik der praktischen Vernunft), 1788.

14. Christoph Martin Wieland, 1733–1813, Reinhold's father-in-law.

15. The second booklet of the first part of the *Contribution* was first released in January 1794.

It is good that this booklet does not fall into too many hands, because, if misunderstood, it must bring about ever so much evil as, if properly understood, [it will bring about] good.

I am so very pleased with the tone in which you address Rehberg that I have since been embarrassed of myself for the tone in which I have addressed this certainly harmful author in an essay in the *Teutscher Merkur* in April 1793 *on the German judgment of the French Revolution.*[16] This tone now disgusts me as *untimely* and factitious moderation. However, the *note* including the one allusion to the *Sekretär,*[17] I wish with conviction to be absent from the book.

I have also detected you in your instructive reviews in the A. L. Z., without being given even the slightest hint from the editor.[18]

I would wish, however, that your rebuke of my claims about *freedom* had not preceded the advertisement of the second part of the letters,[19] in which I flattered myself with having been of some utility through the attempt to postulate the logical concept of the *will*, which has hitherto been lacking everyone, even critical philosophy. My fate in the A.L.Z. hitherto had been that not a single one of the unique concepts that I postulated was advertised or announced in the journal, while all the more were misinterpreted. I cannot say this about your observations regarding me. But since my intention in the second volume was solely to develop the concept of the law and freedom of the will, I have intentionally, with good [37] forethought, remained silent on the question of how to conceive freedom and natural necessity together, which I considered to be already answered by *Kant* and altogether foreign to my end.—With Kant, I only consider the *possibility* of freedom a postulate, or rather an article of faith of practical reason, namely, in how far the latter must be and remain *incomprehensible.* But the reality of *freedom* is to me like the *reality* of the moral law, which I can only think as a law of freedom,

---

16. Reinhold, "On the German Judgment of the French Revolution: An Open Letter to the Editor" (Über die Teutsche Beurtheilung der französischen Revoluzion. Ein Sendschreiben an den Herausgeber), in *Der Neue Teutsche Merkur*, April 1793, 387–424.

17. Reinhold is referring to the note on p. 19, where Fichte lauds a pamphlet by Ernst Brandes, *Geheimer Kanzlei-Sekretär* in Hanover.

18. G. Hufeland and C. G. Schütz.

19. Reinhold is referring to Fichte's review of the first volume of his *Briefe über die Kantische Philosophie* (*Letters on the Kantian Philosophy*) in the *Creuzer Review*. The second volume was published after Fichte's review.

as an object of *knowledge*.—The moral law is only thinkable for me insofar as it is like a law for me; a law that governs *those* satisfactions of the appetite that depend on my freedom [conceived] as a basic faculty independent of *practical reason* as well the *appetite*.—However, I have to examine this matter more closely at the next opportunity.

Through the continuation of our correspondence, you will make be ineffably happy. I embrace you in spirit with the most deliberate and deeply felt adoration and whole-hearted love.

Your

very own

Reinhold.

P.S. As I learned from a letter that has arrived from Vienna today, *Baggesen* has arrived there safe and sound.—He is obsessed with you.

Letter #213 (146–50)

Jena, June 24, 1794

Fichte to Johann Wolfgang von Goethe in Weimar

Most venerable benefactor and friend,

Already in my last letter, I merely appealed to the friendship of the noble man and great spirit. I did not think that within a few days, I would be in the position to appeal to your political reputation.

I was brought word from Weimar: "turpitudes (or rather, fooleries) are spread around there, which I [allegedly] presented in my lectures. [It is said] my situation is dangerous. A certain class has sought a formal union against me. The Duke hears you [Goethe], and what other men there are, less often than others who belong in this union. I should not be so certain regarding the consequences. In short, I could be deposed before I knew, etc. etc." They offer me advice that I would surely follow, if I were Parmenio. "[It is said that] I deny a certain anonymous pamphlet[20] that is attributed to me." Someone else may permit himself something like this; [147] I do not think it permissible for *myself*. I will not *acknowledge* an anonymous pamphlet either. Whoever wants to acknowledge his pamphlets, will do so immediately upon publication. Whoever writes anonymously, does not want to acknowledge them.

---

20. Reference to Fichte's *Contribution*.

"At least this half year I should take care not to touch on politics." I do no lecture on politics and am not appointed for it. However, *whenever its turn comes in my class*, I will lecture [on] natural right according to my conviction, *unless I am expressly and publicly prohibited from it*. But its turn will certainly not come in the first year. This half year, I act according to rules after which I will always act, and will always act as I acted this half year. I do not have a special *summer-* and special *winter-morality*.

"I should hide so that I may bring about more good." That's the morality of a Jesuit. I am there to do good, *when I can*. But I may *not* do evil under *any* condition, not even under the [condition] of future well-doing.

If I viewed myself entirely *in isolation*, I would be the last among human beings who, given my basic principles and the possible force with which I have seized them, feared anything and wanted to yield but an inch from my course. Whoever does not fear death, what under the moon should he still fear?—In general, it would be laughable, then, if I wanted to dignify these things with any serious measure.

But unfortunately, I am no longer isolated. The fate of several human beings is tied to my fate. I am not talking about my wife. She would not be [my wife] if I did not think her capable of the same basic principles. But a seventy-four-year-old elderly man, her father, is inseparably tied to her. His age necessitates rest. He cannot expose himself to the danger of being chased around to which I may expose myself. Thus, the question is, and it is necessary that this question will be answered in time: Can the prince, in whom I have confided, protect me, and does he want to? Does he want to under the following conditions?

I [will] *come to Weimar next Saturday*[21] and will introduce myself face-to-face to the people who could have something to say to me, in order to see whether they have enough courage to tell *me*, what they tell others *about me*. As soon as possible, I am having the *four lectures hitherto held publicly*,[22] [148] in which I am supposed to have said these follies and which I write down with great forethought word-for-word and read word-for-word, *printed word-for-word* unchanged.[23] It would be

---

21. June 28, 1794

22. Fichte is referring to the first four lectures of the *Kolleg de officiis eruditorum*.

23. Fichte's "The Vocation of the Scholar," 1794, translated in *Early Philosophical Writings*, 137–84.

the greatest privilege for me, if the Duke were to allow me to dedicate these to him. With complete sincerity, I could assure this prince of [my] unlimited veneration. I developed this veneration based on everything I have ever heard of him and, later, on the fact that he entrusted me with a teaching position at his university in spite of the opinion of me that has taken hold of the public, and it was infinitely heightened by the personal acquaintance with him. I would be very pleased to be able to demonstrate in front of the entire public that I can venerate a great man, even if he is a prince. And I supposed I am warranted in believing that the assurance of a veneration that pertains to the human being in him and not to the prince could not be unpleasant to this prince, who *can* place his highest worth in his humanity.—Just in case, I offer to submit the proof of the pamphlet to you or the Duke himself in advance, as well as the dedication, if requested. Even so, I admit that it would please me even more, if one thought me capable of knowing how to conduct myself in such a delicate affair without preliminary examinations.

If it is demanded, I will promise that a *certain anonymous pamphlet will not be continued.*[24] Indeed, I will even promise *not to write any anonymous pamphlets on political subjects* for a given period of time (unless self-defense perhaps makes it necessary). That I could easily promise this, yet do whatever I want afterwards, since I may hope to remain undetected, is an objection I do not expect from anyone I am supposed to confer with. I keep what I promise, even if no one but myself knows that I will keep it.

Regarding my *lectures, however,* I cannot change anything. And if they are not condoned, they will have to be *publicly* prohibited. I *shall* and *will* say whatever I *hold* to be true according to my best examinations. I may err. I tell my audience every day that I can err. But I can only concede to *rational arguments.* (At least until now, no one has even given the *appearance* of being *able* to refute what one considers to be my errors *based on principle.*) I will say it *at its place* and *its time,* i.e., whenever it [149] is its turn in the science that I teach. At the right time, my lectures will also cover *the respect for the established order,* etc., and these duties will not be inculcated with less emphasis.

Under these conditions now I demand *protection, and tranquility in Jena, at least as long as my old father-in-law* is alive. And I ask for the worthy prince's *word* on this matter.

---

24. Reference to the *Contribution.*

May I add a few considerations to substantiate the justice of my request? I took no steps to receive the offer that I received. They knew me when I was appointed. They knew what writings were attributed to me. They knew what opinion the public had of me. I wrote to an esteemed man—and the letter must still exist—"that I am rather a human being than an academic teacher and hope to continue to remain so, and that I do not have a mind to give up the duties of the former, and that, if this was the opinion, I would have to renounce the offer I received." I wrote this when certain basic principles were discussed.

I have been warned. In Switzerland, I was told by different sources that I was only appointed in order to get me in their control. I disregarded these threats. I trusted the honor of the prince, who called me. He will protect me, or, if at least for a certain time under the stated conditions he could not [protect me], he would tell me straightforwardly. In that case, this coming Tuesday, I will write my family, whom I left behind in Switzerland *not without forethought*, to remain where they are. And I [will] return to my tranquil private life after the completion of my half-year lecture.

Forgive the resolute tone with which I have spoken. I knew that I was talking to a man, and to a man with a benevolent disposition towards me. My request would be laughable, if it only pertained to me. I may not fear any danger. But my motivation[25] excuses me before my heart, and will excuse me before yours.

With warm respect

Your

most devoted

Fichte.

Letter #314 (403–6)

Osmannstädt, September (?) 1795

Fichte to Heinrich Theodor von Schön in Tapiau

I thank you for your benevolent attention, my dear; thank you for the prospect, which you offered me, of seeing you soon in these parts; thank you for all the news that your share from our fatherland.

---

25. *Beweggrund*

First of all—I can quite believe that my *Contribution* discomforts the aging and increasingly apprehensive Kant. However, the reason he furnishes for [his concern], [which is] that I do not take credit for it, is not right. Admittedly, I am no longer satisfied with most of what I said in it. Yet, not because I went *too far*, but because I *did not go far enough*. The law of nature and the law of the state must, like philosophy on the whole, still undergo an entirely different inversion. The mistakes that I find in this book are therefore of [such] a nature that no one else will easily detect them, if I had not detected them myself. For that reason, I have so far read nothing but silly, superficial prattle from those who wrote against it. I do not reveal myself because I have since come into circumstances that have the right to expect this small [act of] consideration from me. It is known the world over that I am the author. But a *public* recognition could involve my government itself in vexations, or at least provoke a prohibition to attend the academy in Jena for some native born [students]. I do not defend the pamphlet because nothing has been brought forth against it yet that would merit an answer. I will immediately acknowledge the pamphlet as soon as I will put something better in its place, and this will happen soon, I think.

"On Pure Interest in Truth" in the first part of the Horen is by me,[26] and I thank you and shake your hand in spirit for having recognized me. But what a critic, who can ascribe the *Letters on the Aesthetic Education*[27] to Dalberg!!![28] What [great] memory of Schiller, that he is capable of making at least a book out of *one* good thought! The good head of certain people must, as can also be noted from other signs, begin to become weaker. The truth is that these letters are by Schiller. Doesn't one ascribe various other [pieces] from the Horen to me? Perhaps the

---

26. *Die Horen* (The Horae), named after the Greek goddesses of time, was a journal published by Friedrich Schiller from 1795 to 1797. Fichte contributed an essay entitled "Über Belebung und Erhöhung des reinen Interesse für Wahrheit" (On the Revival and Elevation of the Pure Interest in Truth) to the first issue, published in January 1795.

27. Letters 1–9 of Schiller's *On the Aesthetic Education of Man* were published in the first issue of *Die Horen*. Schiller first developed his thoughts on aesthetics in a series of letters to Friedrich Christian von Augustenburg (known as the *Augustenburg Letters*) between 1793 and 1794. It was arguably known that Schiller was preoccupied with the topic prior to the publication of the letters.

28. Karl Theodor Anton Maria von Dalberg.

essays on the male and female form with their sequels?[29] I consider this to be an insult, and I would be ready to sue the person who expresses such an opinion. They are not by me, and, in general, nothing written in the Horen, but that essay, is by me. What is [written] by me, will always be recognizable in a way that anyone who has read something by me, will find me out.

Without doubt you have come to know something of the innovations that I am introducing in philosophy and of the manner in which the orthodox Kantians demean themselves regarding them. The matter ought to, so God will, become increasingly clearer, and certainly not pan out in their honor.

It will also have reached your ears that I have left Jena and the reason for it, which has been spread. I am writing you a few words about it. . . .

Notwithstanding everything that from time to time becomes publicly known, the students in Jena have continually led the most disgraceful life, i.e., a part of them since the majority of our [students] is very good. The reason for this is the student fraternities.[30]

[Since] morality lies close to my heart and this was soon noted, I worked through representations to persuade the members of the fraternities to give up their associations voluntarily. Two of the existing fraternities were willing, and, mediated by me, they entered into negotiations with the courts, which approved their demands and harangued them strictly. A third fraternity insisted to remain [in existence], and I, who neither has nor seeks official power, thus had nothing further to do with it. The courts had the weakness and slowness to allow this fraternity to get away with its defiance. And now certain people stir these human beings against me by means of the most nefarious lies. It was not so much the nefarious behavior of these few bad, already branded human beings, but the reprehensible indifference that prevailed regarding these matters and the utter lack of protection. I explained to the academic senate and the court—to the latter of which I must, however, do justice—that I consider it beneath the dignity of an honest man to live in a place where such things are tolerated, and moved to the countryside. Since I have

---

29. Wilhelm von Humboldt, "Über die männliche und weibliche Form" [On the Male and Female Form], *Die Horen* 3 (1795): 80–103.

30. *Studenten-Orden*

meanwhile obtained complete satisfaction, [and], moreover, since the affair got so severe over this summer that it could no longer persist and one has sincerely begun to restore order, I will return on St. Michael's Day.[31]

Grant me the pleasure of seeing you soon. Fare you well, and remain the friend

of your

Fichte.

---

31. September 29

Appendix Two

Review of Fichte's *Contribution* by Friedrich von Gentz

The following is an excerpt from Gentz's review, from the introduction, as well as Gentz's challenge to Fichte's strong individualist conception of contracts in chapter 3 of the *Contribution*. This challenge may have led Fichte to rethink this conception in his later political philosophy.

The review was published in the *Allgemeine Literatur-Zeitung* on May 7, 1794 (153–54). The full version of the review, along with several other reviews of the work, can be found in Johann Gottlieb Fichte, *Schriften zur Französischen Revolution: Mit zeitgenössischen Rezensionen* (Leipzig: Reclam, 1988), 276–95. In the following translation we include page references to this edition.

[276] One must read only a few pages of this book and understand only the first paragraphs of the introduction to notice that it could not be the product of a common head and that one would err mightily if one wanted to treat it as a common revolutionary pamphlet in any regard.

Can there be a more inviting announcement for a thinking reader than that the *French Revolution*, in fact, that any *state revolution in general*—a topic in which so ineffably many shallow heads, rhapsodic blatherers, and laughable enthusiasts have exhausted themselves—shall be examined from its foundations according to *principles*, and the highest and purest principles at that? And can something elevate the allure of this announcement as much as the conviction, which one obtains before long, that the anonymous person undertaking this examination was to no small degree familiar with the principles that he assumed? That he was deeply inducted in that most noble system of philosophy of which the modern centuries can boast?

The success be as it may, such an undertaking deserves the highest attention. And even though this reviewer must declare in advance that he cannot at all agree with the author's results (insofar as they follow from the first part), he still believes to be doing a significant service to a great part of the reading public by [offering] a somewhat more detailed account of the transition from those *principles* to those *results*.

[. . .]

[283] "If all citizens of a state have promised every individual [citizen] that they do not intend to change anything in their constitution without the other's consent, can they depart from their promise? Can they (i.e., may they rightfully), *notwithstanding their promise*, make changes without bothering about the objection of those who disapprove of the changes?" Now, common reason and, as far as the reviewer knows, every extant system of natural right would without exception have answered "No!" to this question (the hinge, on which the entire ensuing reasoning and essentially the author's entire system turns). The author answers "Yes!" and, in order to make this possible, he presents a new theory of contracts.

Hitherto one believed that under natural right a contract creates perfect rights and obligations as soon as it is entered, regardless of whether the services stipulated in it have been fulfilled or not. The author does not share this belief. The main principles of his theory of contracts are the following: 1) If the person who enters the contract with me does not in his heart have the will to keep it, I obtain no right through the contract. 2) A contract [284], the fulfillment of which lies in the future, can be revoked through a unilateral change of will before the fulfillment. 3) Even if one party has already fulfilled its obligations, the contract still does not bind the other [party]. However, the latter must pay damages to the other, if he breaks [the contract] afterwards. 4) The contract is only completed through the completion of services on both sides.

This reviewer candidly admits that neither the subtle reasons with which these principles are executed here nor the authority of Professor *Schmalz* [. . .] could convert him to this theory in the least. Because 1) every contract entered with a view to the future would be absolutely superfluous according to this [theory]. If the other's promise (mind you, which I purchased through mine) does not grant me a perfect right, what would be more nonsensical than entering contracts wherein the services are not immediately exchanged? 2) All manner of societal contracts (not merely the social [contract]), the essence of which consists precisely in their *continuation* over a certain time, would cease to exist entirely under natural right. No marriage, no collective enterprise that presupposed even just three days of being together, no manner of services that lasted longer than the present moment could take place. At least a perfect right to the other's persistence cannot be acquired through any of these contracts, even if one party made the greater sacrifices in concluding it, because the former can *rightfully* change his mind five minutes after conclusion of the contract. This is then indeed a harsh doctrine! 3) It is not foreseeable at all how a man who declares the moral law to be the highest principle can consider something to be *possible* that contradicts the moral law. For assuming one party acquired no *right* through the other's mere promise, the latter surely still contracts a *duty* and it becomes *morally* impossible for him to lie or break [the promise]. What is therefore gained by this new theory if morality should go above everything else?

[285] The very natural application which the author makes of this theory is the following: no matter how the civil contract is constituted, no matter how explicitly it is determined therein that everyone (that is to say, *several*) shall not change it without asking everyone and that no one may forsake it without having the consent of the others, everyone is still free to rightfully quit the contract as soon as he desires. . . . Now the restitution of damages should follow for that which the state has rendered to the exiting party hitherto. But what did he render to him? His property? Not at all! That is older than the social contract. His culture? The state cannot take that back from him. Thus, the civil contract also has over the other [contracts] the convenience that one may break it at one's pleasure, without worrying about compensation.

[. . .]

German–English Glossary

Note: Any deviations from the standard translations recorded in the glossary have been footnoted in the text.

abtreten	to surrender
anerkennen	to recognize
der Anspruch	claim
aufgeben	to give up
Ausspruch	expression, prouncement
die Bedingung	condition
der Begriff	concept
bestimmen (bestimmt)	to determine, to specify (determined, specified)
die Betrachtung	contemplation
die Beurteilung	assessment, judgment
der Besitz	possession
besitzen	to possess, to own
der Besitzer	occupant, owner
der Beweis	proof
beweisen	to proof, to demonstrate
bilden	to form
die Bildung	education, cultivation
die Darstellung	representation
die Denkart	manner of thinking
das Dürfen	the may
dürfen	may
das Eigentum	property, ownership
der Eigentümer	owner
die Einbildungskraft	power of imagination
der Einfall	idea
der Endzweck	final end

die Entschliessung, der Entschluss	decision
die Erfahrung	experience
der Erfahrungsgrundsatz	empirical basic principles
die Erkenntnis	knowledge
der Gegenstand	object, topic
die Gesellschaft	society, company
das Gesetz des Sollens	law of ought
die Gesinnung	dispostion
der Glaube	belief, faith
der Grund	foundation, basis, reason
der Grundsatz	basic principle
gültig	valid
handeln	to act
die Handlung	action
das Ich	the I
die Idee	idea
klug	prudent
die Klugheit	prudence
die Kraft	force
die Materie	matter
die Moralität	morality
Naturnotwendigkeit	natural necessity
die Neigung	inclination
die Phantasie	imagination
die Prüfung	test
das Recht	right
die Rechtmässigkeit	legitimacy
der Richterstuhl	tribunal
der Satz	principle
schlechthin	simply, per se
die Selbtbeobachtung	introspection
das Selbstdenken	independent thought/thinking
selbsttändig	independent
die Selbsttätigkeit	independent activity
die Sinnenwelt	material world
die Sinnlichkeit	sensuousness
die Sittlichkeit	morality
sollen	ought to, should

das Sollen	the ought
die Tat	deed
die Tatsache	fact
die Triebfeder	incentive
der Unglaube	unbelief
die Unmündigkeit	immaturity
die Untersuchung	examination
die Ursache	cause
die Urteilskraft	judgment
die Verbindlichkeit	obligation
die Verbindung	association
die Vernunft	reason
vernünftig	rational
verknüpfen (verknüpft)	to attach (attached)
das Vermögen	capacity
der Verstand	understanding
das Volk	people
die Vorstellung	idea, representation
das Wesen	being
der Wille	will
die Willkür	arbitrary will
das Wissen	knowledge, knowing
wollen	to will
zweckmässig	purposive

Index